AN INTRODUCTION TO
THE HISTORY AND RECORDS
OF THE
COURT OF WARDS & LIVERIES

BY
H. E. BELL
Fellow of New College, Oxford

CAMBRIDGE
AT THE UNIVERSITY PRESS
1953

CAMBRIDGE UNIVERSITY PRESS
Cambridge, New York, Melbourne, Madrid, Cape Town,
Singapore, São Paulo, Delhi, Tokyo, Mexico City

Cambridge University Press
The Edinburgh Building, Cambridge CB2 8RU, UK

Published in the United States of America by Cambridge University Press, New York

www.cambridge.org
Information on this title: www.cambridge.org/9780521200288

© Cambridge University Press 1953

This publication is in copyright. Subject to statutory exception
and to the provisions of relevant collective licensing agreements,
no reproduction of any part may take place without the written
permission of Cambridge University Press.

First published 1953
First paperback edition 2011

A catalogue record for this publication is available from the British Library

ISBN 978-0-521-04142-3 Hardback
ISBN 978-0-521-20028-8 Paperback

Additional resources for this publication at www.cambridge.org/9780521200288

Cambridge University Press has no responsibility for the persistence or
accuracy of URLs for external or third-party internet websites referred to in
this publication, and does not guarantee that any content on such websites is,
or will remain, accurate or appropriate.

CAMBRIDGE STUDIES
IN ENGLISH LEGAL HISTORY

Edited by

H. A. HOLLOND, M.A., LL.M.

*Emeritus Rouse Ball Professor of English Law, and
Fellow of Trinity College, Cambridge*

CONTENTS

		Page
Preface		vii
Abbreviations used in the footnotes		ix

Chapter	I	WARDSHIP AND LIVERY IN THE REIGNS OF HENRY VII AND HENRY VIII	1
	II	THE OFFICERS OF THE COURT	16
	III	THE REVENUES OF THE COURT	46
	IV	THE ADMINISTRATION OF LIVERY AND WARDSHIP	67
	V	JUDICIAL BUSINESS OF THE COURT	87
	VI	THE WELFARE OF WARDS AND IDIOTS	112
	VII	THE AGITATION AGAINST THE COURT	133
	VIII	THE FINAL DAYS OF THE COURT	150
	IX	THE SITE AND BUILDINGS OF THE COURT	167
	X	THE RECORDS OF THE COURT AFTER ITS ABOLITION	175

Appendix	I	A MEMORANDUM RELATING TO WARDSHIP IN HENRY VIII'S REIGN	187
	II	DESCRIPTION OF THE RECEIVER-GENERAL'S ACCOUNTS AND ABSTRACTS OF REVENUES IN SELECTED YEARS	190
	III	FEES PAID TO OFFICERS OF THE COURT, 1623	194

Index		206

Table A, Table B and Table C are available for download from www.cambridge.org/9780521200288

PREFACE

THIS introduction to the History and Records of the Court of Wards and Liveries originated in the work of compiling the *Guide to, and Analytical List of, Court of Wards Miscellanea*, which I completed in 1937 at the end of my temporary appointment on the Public Record Office staff. My subsequent employment—both before the war and after—as a part-time editor at the Public Record Office has enabled me to examine and list other classes of the Court's records and to obtain much of the material that I have used in this book. I therefore owe a heavy debt of gratitude to the late Mr A. E. Stamp, who as Deputy Keeper of the Records gave me the opportunity of undertaking this work, and to his successors, Sir Cyril Flower and Sir Hilary Jenkinson, who have enabled me to continue it. My debt is equally great to many of my former colleagues in the Public Record Office, and especially I must acknowledge the scholarly and kindly help of the late Mr S. C. Ratcliff, and of Mr H. C. Johnson, Mr R. B. Pugh and Mr N. J. Williams.

I am grateful to the Most Hon. the Marquess of Salisbury for his kind permission to use and quote those parts of the Calendar of his manuscripts that still remain unpublished, and to Lord Sackville for his generous agreement to my citing certain of his manuscripts. For documents in these and other private collections I have also used the printed Calendars of the Historical Manuscripts Commission.

H. E. BELL

NEW COLLEGE,
OXFORD
4 *April* 1952

ABBREVIATIONS USED IN THE FOOTNOTES

A.P.C. — *Acts of the Privy Council of England* (H.M.S.O.).

Bacon — *The Works of Francis Bacon,* ed. Spedding, Ellis and Heath, 1858-69.

B.M. — British Museum.

Bod. — Bodleian Library.

Brooke, *A.N.C.* — R. Brooke, *Ascuns nouel Cases de les ans & temps le Roy H. 8 Edw. 6 & la Roynge Mary,* edn. of 1604.

Coke, *Reports,* — *Reports of Sir Edward Coke,* edn. of 1826.

Constable. — *Prerogativa Regis, Tertia Lectura Roberti Constable,* ed. Samuel E. Thorne.

C.P.R. — *Calendar of Patent Rolls* (H.M.S.O.).

C.S.P. Dom. — *Calendar of State Papers, Domestic* (H.M.S.O.).

C.S.P. Ven. — *State Papers and Manuscripts relating to English affairs, existing in the Archives and Collections of Venice and in other Libraries of Northern Italy* (H.M.S.O.).

C.U. — Cambridge University Library.

D.N.B. — *Dictionary of National Biography.*

Dyer, *A.N.C.* — J. Dyer, *Ascuns nouel cases,* edn. of 1585.

E.H.R. — *English Historical Review.*

Foedera — T. Rymer and R. Sanderson, *Foedera,* edn. of 1727-35.

H.C.J. — *House of Commons Journal.*

H.L.J. — *House of Lords Journal.*

H.M.C. — Historical Manuscripts Commission (H.M.S.O.):

   Cowper — *Manuscripts of the Earl Cowper.*

   Downshire — *Manuscripts of the Marquess of Downshire.*

   House of Lords — *Manuscripts of the House of Lords.*

   Portland — *Manuscripts of the Duke of Portland.*

   Rutland — *Manuscripts of the Duke of Rutland.*

   Sackville — *Manuscripts of Lord Sackville at Knole.*

   Salisbury — *Calendar of the Manuscripts of the Marquess of Salisbury.*

Holdsworth. — W. S. Holdsworth, *A History of English Law.*

L. & P. — *Calendar of Letters and Papers, Foreign and Domestic, Henry VIII* (H.M.S.O.).

Ley, *Learned Treatise.* — James Ley, *A Learned Treatise Concerning Wards and Liveries,* 1642.

x ABBREVIATIONS USED IN THE FOOTNOTES

Ley, *Reports*,	James Ley, *Reports of Divers Resolutions in Law Arising upon Cases in the Court of Wards etc.*, 1659.
N.N.B.	A. Fitzherbert, *New Natura Brevium*, edn. of 1652.
P.D. 1610.	*Parliamentary Debates in 1610*, ed. S. R. Gardiner, Camden Soc.
Peck.	F. Peck, *Desiderata Curiosa*, edn. of 1779.
Powell.	T. Powell, *The Attourney's Academy*, 1623.
P.R.O.	Public Record Office:
D.L. 5	Duchy of Lancaster, Orders and Decrees.
E. 36	Exchequer, Treasury of the Receipt Miscellaneous Books.
E. 101	Exchequer, Accounts Various.
E. 163	Exchequer, King's Remembrancer Miscellanea.
E. 368	Exchequer, Lord Treasurer's Remembrancer, Memoranda Rolls.
Ind.	Index.
K.B. 9	King's Bench, Ancient Indictments.
P.C. 2	Privy Council Registers.
P.R.O. 30	Gifts and Deposits.
S.P. 1	State Papers Domestic, Henry VIII General.
S.P. 12	State Papers Domestic, Elizabeth.
S.P. 14	State Papers Domestic, James I.
S.P. 15	State Papers Domestic, Addenda Edward VI-James I.
S.P. 16	State Papers Domestic, Charles I.
S.P. 29	State Papers Domestic, Charles II.
T. 1	Treasury Board Papers.
Wards 1-16	Court of Wards and Liveries.
Wards Guide	*Guide to, and Analytical List of, Court of Wards Miscellanea.*
R.C.C.	*Report from the Committee appointed to View the Cottonian Library*, 1732.
r.g.a.	Receiver-general's account.
Staunford.	W. Staunford, *Exposicion of the kinges prerogatiue*, edn. of 1567.
Steele.	R. R. Steele, *Bibliotheca Lindesiana, a bibliography of royal proclamations.*
T.N.T.	Fabian Philipps, *Tenenda non Tollenda*, 1660.
T.R.H.S.	*Transactions of the Royal Historical Society.*
V.C.H.	*Victoria County History.*
West, *First Part.*	William West, *First Part of Symboleographie*, edn. of 1647.
West, *Second Part.*	William West, *Second Part of Symboleography*, edn. of 1641.

CHAPTER I

WARDSHIP AND LIVERY IN THE REIGNS OF HENRY VII AND HENRY VIII

THE process by which landholding became hereditary was gradual, and throughout medieval times there remained at the back of men's minds traces of the idea that, upon a tenant's death, land reverted to its lord. Perhaps notions of this kind provided the basis, and the theoretical justification if such were needed, of the peculiar conditions of succession to military fiefs. The heir to a tenant by knight service, even though he was of full age, only succeeded to his inheritance upon paying the lord a relief for it; if he was not of full age, the lord had the rents and profits of the land in the intervening period and the wardship of the heir's body—the right, that is, to bring him up in such a way that he would become a worthy tenant. There followed, too, the right of disposal of the ward's marriage—an obvious development, so far as the female ward was concerned, for marriage ended her wardship and it was important that the lord should not be forced to take an enemy as his tenant; with less clear justification for the male ward, but nevertheless an established custom at any rate by the time of Henry II.[1]

In the twelfth and thirteenth centuries, and even later, these rights no doubt formed an important part of the revenues of the *mesne* lord; but, for him, reliefs and wardships cut both ways, since through them he lost at least as much to the king as he gained from his tenant. For the king, however, they represented clear gain, because he alone, as Holdsworth put it, was always lord and never tenant.[2] Moreover, that gain was particularly great, as even the smallest military tenure in chief entitled the king to a relief assessed on the whole of his tenant's lands, of whomsoever they were held, and similarly, in minority, to wardship of them all. It was thus as royal rights that these feudal incidents became mainly important, and in their exercise the crown evolved a regular system of procedure. Upon the tenant's death, the king became immediately

[1] F. Pollock and F. W. Maitland, *History of English Law*, 2nd. edn., vol. I, pp. 318-29; Holdsworth, vol. III, pp. 61-6.　　　　[2] *Ibid.* vol. III, p. 84.

2 COURT OF WARDS AND LIVERIES [CHAP. I

entitled to primer seisin, and a *diem clausit extremum* or other writ was issued out of the Chancery to an escheator for the taking of an inquisition post mortem.[1] If this found the heir to be of full age, he could then sue out his livery and obtain seisin; if a minor, his lands were taken into the king's hand until he should come of age.[2] Wards' lands were administered by the escheators, who accounted for their issues in the Exchequer.[3] Legal cases connected with the incidents of tenure in chief fell largely within the common law jurisdiction of the Chancery.[4]

Nevertheless, the scientific development of livery and wardship as a regular source of royal income dates from the Tudor period. Sir John Fortescue had already insisted, in *The Governance of England*, that the financial position of the monarchy must be improved, and after 1485 the demands of the nation state, both internal and external, made this essential. Moreover, Tudor financial policy was conditioned by a further fact: parliamentary taxation formed a relatively unimportant part of the king's revenues. The idea was current in the sixteenth century, and died hard in the succeeding age, that direct taxation was an emergency measure, granted by Parliament only in times of extraordinary expenditure such as foreign war or insurrection. The king was supposed, in the medieval phrase, to 'live of his own'; that is to say, for the ordinary day-to-day expenses of government he was very considerably dependent on income derived from the crown lands and from his feudal dues. Thus arose the paradox that the legal rights of livery and wardship continued, and were systematically extended, when the feudal structure, which had given them purpose and been their excuse, had ceased to exist. It is this fact which gives the history of the Court of Wards and Liveries its chief interest.

The statutory foundation of the Court dates only from the later years of Henry VIII's reign,[5] but the policy that it implied was begun by his predecessor. In his efforts to increase the yield of the feudal incidents Henry VII anticipated much of the practice, and something even of the machinery, of the Court itself.

The most characteristic feature of the new practice was the

---

[1] *Cal. of Inquisitions Post Mortem, Henry VII*, vol. i, Preface.
[2] In the case of males at twenty-one, of females at fourteen or upon marriage.
[3] E. R. Stevenson, 'The Escheator' in *The English Government at Work, 1327-36*, ed. W. A. Morris and J. R. Strayer, vol. ii.
[4] Holdsworth, vol. i, p. 453.
[5] 32 Henry VIII c. 46; 33 Henry VIII c. 22.

CHAP. I] HENRY VII AND HENRY VIII 3

sustained effort made by the crown to reveal descents and minor successions of land held in chief. To this end Henry VII used the inquisition post mortem with so much energy that, in his reign, the Chancery issued a writ for the holding of an inquisition wherever there seemed the slightest possibility of a finding for the king; this is proved by the number of inquisitions where, in the upshot, only a *mesne* tenure appeared.[1] Moreover, from 1491 to the end of the reign information obtained in this way was supplemented by a long series of commissions to inquire concerning concealments. These were very various in scope and character. Sometimes they initiated inquiries in a single county only,[2] sometimes in a pair, or even a group of counties;[3] some of them related solely to wardships and marriages,[4] some included lands;[5] some omitted wardships from the commissioners' terms of reference,[6] but others were comprehensive.[7] Again, there is evidence of record searches made on the king's behalf for information about tenures,[8] and Professor Dietz has pointed out that the two feudal aids which Henry sought in 1504 were desired by him not only for their immediate cash yield but also for their wider effects in establishing an up-to-date record of those who held lands in chief.[9] In the whole of this policy Henry VII was foreshadowing what was to be, for the hundred years of its existence, the principal preoccupation of the Court of Wards and Liveries.

Apart from illegal concealments, in the later middle ages evasion of the feudal incidents had taken place on a considerable scale with the growing popularity of the feoffment to uses. Descent of property from owner to heir was the essential condition of livery and wardship, and it was just this descent that the use contrived to avoid. The person in whose interest the use was made, the *cestui que use* as he was termed, had all the advantages of ownership with none of its disadvantages; he was protected against the feoffees to uses in equity, but nevertheless the legal seisin lay in them and not in him, so that upon his death the property did not descend. 'By

---

[1] *Cal. of Inquisitions Post Mortem Henry VII*, vol. I, p. ix.
[2] *C.P.R. 1485-94*, p. 351; *C.P.R. 1494-1509*, pp. 66, 249, 263, 459, 592.
[3] *C.P.R. 1485-94*, pp. 415, 478; *C.P.R. 1494-1509*, pp. 66, 204, 437-8, 457, 592, 627.
[4] *C.P.R. 1485-94*, p. 351.
[5] *C.P.R. 1494-1509*, pp. 66, 249.   [6] *Ibid.* pp. 263, 459.
[7] *C.P.R. 1485-94*, p. 415; *C.P.R. 1494-1509*, pp. 204, 437-8, 457, 459, 592.
[8] F. C. Dietz, *English Government Finance 1485-1558*, p. 29.
[9] *Ibid.* p. 28.

4 COURT OF WARDS AND LIVERIES [CHAP. I

keeping up a wall of joint tenants, by feoffment and refeoffment',
Maitland puts it, 'he can keep out the lord and can reduce the
chances of reliefs and so forth to nothing.'[1] This was especially
disadvantageous to the king as supreme landlord, and Henry VII
was clearly anxious to limit the extent of such evasion. The statute
of 1488-9 'against fraudulent feoffments to deprive the king of his
wards'[2] is interesting as a tentative move towards the position finally
achieved by Henry VIII's statute of Uses: it provided that, if the
cestui que use of lands held by knight service died intestate, his heir
should be in ward if a minor, and pay relief if of full age. What it
amounted to was that, in cases of intestacy, the use was, for certain
specific purposes, turned into a legal estate, and the old division
between legal and equitable ownership, so far as these same purposes were concerned, disappeared. Comparing the measure with
the statute of Uses, it is of course much more limited in its application; but the similarity of purpose is striking.[3]

Besides its effort to combat concealment and evasion, Henry VII's
policy had a more positive side. Professor Thorne has described
a number of ways in which Henry's Chancery operated to increase
the number of tenants in chief. Such an increase was, for instance,
a result of the practice of granting licences to alienate a portion, but
not the whole, of lands held in chief;[4] or again, the arrangement
whereby widow's dower was so assigned as to include some lands
held in chief had a similar effect,[5] and so, where there was descent
to coparceners, had the insistence that each should take a portion of
the *capite* lands.[6] The importance of usages of this sort was that
they extended the field from which the crown might expect to draw
valuable feudal incidents.

All this activity involved a growth of judicial business concerned
with prerogative rights. Much routine litigation, later to be dealt
with by the Court of Wards, was, in the later years of Henry VII,
disposed of by the Council Learned in the Law. It was before this
body that those who had wrongfully taken the profits of a ward's
or idiot's lands were summoned to appear,[7] and there that a tenant
in chief who had failed to sue livery might have to answer the

[1] *Equity*, edn. of 1920, p. 26.
[2] 4 Henry VII c. 17.
[3] For judicial interpretations of the statute see Constable, p. 20, *note* 48;
Staunford, f. 9.
[4] Constable, Introduction, p. xiii.   [5] *Ibid.* p. xxix.
[6] *Ibid.* p. xxxiii.   [7] P.R.O. D.L. 5/2, ff. 23, 24.

CHAP. I]   HENRY VII AND HENRY VIII   5

issue of his lands.[1] To the Council Learned were surrendered royal wards who had been retained without authority,[2] and those accused of embezzling them were brought before it.[3] On occasion, too, the Council Learned heard a complaint by a ward alleging wrongs committed against him.[4] Prerogative business also began to loom large elsewhere, and important cases in this connection were argued both in the common law courts[5] and the Exchequer Chamber.[6] A number of Inns of Court readings on the medieval *Prerogativa Regis* reflect the new recognition of the importance of the prerogative. It is significant that, while Professor Thorne mentions no less than eight such readings probably dating from Henry VII's reign, he has found none that can certainly be attributed to an earlier period.[7]

Lastly, and perhaps most interesting of all, Henry VII's reign saw the development of administrative machinery that was later to serve as a model for the Court of Wards and Liveries. Initially, it is true, sales of wardships were probably negotiated personally by the king or by Sir Reginald Bray acting on his behalf.[8] On the other hand, the administration of such wards' lands as were retained in the king's hand necessarily involved some delegation and the appointment of receivers. Thus in Henry's very first year a group of three receivers-general was appointed for the lands of royal wards in Yorkshire, Cumberland, Westmorland and Northumberland;[9] some ten years later the commissioners appointed to inquire concerning concealments in another group of counties were authorized to approve such revenues as resulted from their inquiries;[10] and in 1499 the king made the Bishop of Carlisle his receiver and surveyor of wards and marriages in Cumberland, Westmorland and Yorkshire.[11] By the close of the century, it is clear, the king's energy in

[1] P.R.O. D.L. 5/2, f. 29.
[2] *Ibid.* ff. 6, 11, 24, 42 for examples.
[3] P.R.O. D.L. 5/4, f. 153.
[4] P.R.O. D.L. 5/2, f. 12. On the Council Learned in general see R. Somerville, 'Henry VII's "Council Learned in the Law"', *E.H.R.*, vol. LIV.
[5] *English Reports*, vol. LXXII (Keilwey), pp. 210, 249, 352.
[6] *Select Cases in the Exchequer Chamber* (Selden Soc.), vol. II, p. 161.
[7] Constable, Introduction, pp. xlviii-li.
[8] Sums received for them appear in P.R.O. E.101/413/2/1, Sir Thomas Lovell's book of receipts, 2-5 Henry VII.
[9] *C.P.R. 1485-94*, p. 56.
[10] *C.P.R. 1494-1509*, p. 33; the counties were Lincoln, York, Leicester, Rutland, Stafford and Derby.
[11] P.R.O. E.101/415/3, *memoranda* 1 Oct. 15 Henry VII.

6 COURT OF WARDS AND LIVERIES [CHAP. I

these matters was bearing fruit, the Chamber accounts for 1499 containing much fuller details than previously.[1] They include, for instance, a list of some seventy-five wards—some with a note of value and offers by prospective purchasers, others with the marginal comment *vend'*. Again, an adjacent entry lists forty odd names of persons who had failed to sue out livery since their ancestors' decease, and amongst memoranda of the same date are many other items relating to livery, wardship, marriage and idiots. Miscellaneous though these last are, they present a picture of intense activity—the seizure of wards on the king's behalf and the subsequent competition to purchase them, offers sometimes being made through Bray, with whose wife a female ward was on occasion lodged: in that competition to buy wardships the queen herself sometimes joined.

This increased business made desirable a more formal organization than had at first sufficed. So long as Bray lived, the old personal methods continued in use, and wardship administration was not differentiated from other prerogative business. In 1503, however, Sir John Hussey was appointed to oversee, manage and sell royal wardships,[2] and he very soon succeeded in establishing an office to assist him in this work. A surviving declaration of receivers' accounts for the year 1502-3 includes wards' side by side with other accounts;[3] in 1503-4 they are separate,[4] and the two years following they are rendered by a single receiver-general, William Lychefelde.[5] This represents clearly enough the stages in the establishment of a wardship office. The functions of that office —with its master, receiver-general, auditor and particular receivers in each county—are described in a memorandum of Henry VIII's reign. According to this, it was the master's—that is Hussey's— duty to deliver to the auditor each term a list of the king's wards to enable the particular receivers to answer the profits of their lands.[6]

[1] P.R.O. E.101/415/3, *memoranda* 1 Oct. 15 Henry VII.
[2] *C.P.R. 1494-1509*, p. 334. W. C. Richardson, 'The Surveyor of the King's Prerogative', *E.H.R.*, vol. LVI, pp. 61-2, brings out the significance of Hussey's appointment, but curiously misses Lychefelde's accounts which are the proof of specialization.
[3] P.R.O. E.36/247, declarations of divers accounts, 18-19 Henry VII.
[4] *Ibid.* declarations of divers lands in the king's hand by reason of minor age, 19-20 Henry VII.
[5] P.R.O. E.36/212, declaration of account of William Lychefelde, 20-21 Henry VII; E.36/248, *do.*, 21-2 Henry VII.
[6] See below, Appendix 1.

CHAP. I] HENRY VII AND HENRY VIII 7

Hussey also provided similar lists for the king,[1] which no doubt gave Henry some means of checking the declarations of accounts to which he repeatedly set his sign-manual. Moneys received by Lychefelde were paid into the King's Chamber.[2]

Yet despite this evidence for a high degree of organization, the extent to which specialization took place in the last decade of Henry VII's reign must not be exaggerated. Although Hussey had an over-all responsibility for sales of wardship, this side of his activities is not reflected in Lychefelde's accounts. The master may well have taken the initiative in arranging sales, but the only record of them is in the bonds for payment of the purchase price which are listed amongst other obligations delivered to the treasurer of the King's Chamber by various of Henry's ministers.[3] Fines for liveries are similarly recorded.[4] The conclusion thus seems clear that, in contrast with the income from wards retained by the crown, that from sales and from liveries continued to be collected in the older, less formal way. An incidental effect of this variation of practice is to make it impossible to calculate the value of livery and wardship to Henry VII in any given year of his reign, for we know, of course, only the face value of the bonds and not what they actually realized.[5]

Nevertheless, although certain figures are lacking, it need not be doubted that by these last years of Henry VII, the period of Empson and Dudley, livery and wardship had become very productive indeed. It is true that some of the more extravagant stories

---

[1] P.R.O. E.36/214, the kynges boke of paymentis, 21 Henry VII—1 Henry VIII, 635.

[2] P.R.O. E.36/212, pp. 65-72 and E.36/248, pp. 83-90.

[3] F. C. Dietz, *English Government Finance 1485-1558*, pp. 33-4, 38-40.

[4] *Ibid.*

[5] The figures (to nearest pound) available for 1504-5 and 1505-6 are—

    1504-5   Issues of wards' lands 5,110 *l.*
                    Arrears of wards' lands 2,143 *l.*
                    (P.R.O. E.36/247, pp. 159 *seq.*)
                    Bonds for sales of wards 1,867 *l.*
                    Bonds for special liveries 2,025 *l.*
                    (Dietz, *op. cit.* p. 39.)
    1505-6   Issues of wards' lands 6,434 *l.*
                    Arrears of wards' lands 2,094 *l.*
                    (P.R.O. E.36/248, pp. 83-90.)
                    Bonds for sales of wards 2,177 *l.*
                    Bonds for special liveries 1,205 *l.*
                    (Dietz, *op. cit.*, p. 40.)

8 COURT OF WARDS AND LIVERIES [CHAP. I

of the extortions of the two *fiscales judices* are exaggerated.[1] But writing a century later, and in the light of experience of Elizabeth's and James I's impositions, Bacon and Coke both stressed the sufferings of tenants in chief under Henry VII,[2] and the preamble to one of Henry VIII's earliest statutes is their justification for doing so.[3] Perhaps it may be said that Henry VII anticipated not only the practice of the Court of Wards and Liveries, but some of its unpopularity too.

It was thus under Henry VII that livery and wardship took on the new character that they were to retain until the abolition of the feudal tenures in 1660; Henry VII was the innovator, and his son did little more than formalize his father's system and set it on a statutory basis. Indeed, so far from being the inventor of the new policy, in the first years of his reign Henry VIII to some extent let it lapse. Shortly before his death Henry VII had been forced, by the unpopularity of Empson and Dudley, to issue a proclamation that persons should be admitted to traverse inquisitions by which they were wronged.[4] This was ratified by the new king, and passed through Parliament as an 'act concerning untrue inquisitions procured by Empson and Dudley': it provided that persons were to be admitted to traverses upon untrue inquisitions of the previous reign, notwithstanding the fact that they had been forced to sue out their liveries on the basis of those inquisitions.[5] Meanwhile, to prevent the recurrence of false inquisitions, action was taken to secure due publicity: escheators and commissioners were to sit in open places and take such evidence as was offered in public.[6] With the characteristic Tudor gesture of sacrificing an unpopular servant, Henry allowed proceedings to be taken against Empson and Dudley, and their execution followed. All this must have looked very like the abandonment of Henry VII's policy, and it is small wonder that in 1510 it was rumoured that Sir John Hussey was out of his office of master of the wards.[7]

In fact that rumour was not true. Hussey held his office and with it a yearly fee of 100 *l.*, which he continued to receive until

---

D. M. Brodie, 'Edmund Dudley: Minister of Henry VII', in *T.R.H.S.*, 4th Series, vol. xv.

[2] Bacon, vol. vi, p. 218; Coke, *Fourth Part of the Institutes*, edn. of 1669, pp. 196-7.

[3] 1 Henry VIII c. 8.

[4] Coke, *Fourth Part of the Institutes*, edn. of 1669, p. 196.

[5] 1 Henry VIII c. 12.   [6] 1 Henry VIII c. 8.   [7] *L. & P.*, vol. I, no. 392.

CHAP. I]   HENRY VII AND HENRY VIII   9

1513,[1] when he was succeeded as master by Sir Thomas Lovell.[2] Henry filled up other appointments too. In 1509 he made John Daunce receiver-general[3] and Thomas Robertes auditor.[4] Potentially most important of all, the terms of Lovell's grant of office in 1513 gave him the right to appoint feodaries,[5] and for many counties they are known to have been appointed.[6] These officers were later to prove absolutely basic to the efficient administration of livery and wardship, and in them the Court of Wards and Liveries put its whole trust.

Hussey's continuation in office, and these further appointments —especially of accounting and local officers—would at first sight suggest that the reaction from Henry VII's policy was short-lived indeed, and that Henry VIII very soon adopted, and even developed, his father's system. Yet it is improbable that that was the case. A memorandum on wardship, unfortunately without date but probably belonging to about 1520, after describing Henry VII's organization of a wardship office adds that 'ther hath no like ordre be takyn' since his time,[7] thus implying that the old king's machinery of account was discontinued, and that the new king's appointments of a receiver-general and auditor were not at first effective. This is also rendered likely by the fact that wards' accounts were originally brought within the scope of Henry VIII's general surveyors.[8] It is thus pretty clear that there was a reversion to the old, unspecialized administrative methods that had obtained prior to 1503. In one sense, of course, the point is academic. In 1514 John Daunce was appointed one of the two general surveyors,[9] and it is no doubt unimportant whether, during the next two years, he took wardship accounts as general surveyor or as receiver-general. But the transference of accounting for wards' lands from the general surveyors to the Exchequer, which took place two years later, was surely a retrograde step.[10] Moreover, the memorandum made a serious indictment of the policy pursued in these early years of Henry VIII: it regarded as a rash alienation of capital the practice that had grown up of selling wards' lands along with

---

[1] B.M. Add. MS. 21481, ff. 31, 44, 69.
[2] *L. & P.*, vol. I, no. 2055/104.   [3] *Ibid.* no. 257/22.
[4] *Ibid.* no. 190/43.   [5] *Ibid.* no. 2055/104.   [6] *Ibid.* no. 2222/12.
[7] See below, Appendix I.
[8] *L. & P.*, vol. I, no. 709/14; 3 Henry VIII c. 23.
[9] *L. & P.*, vol. I, no. 3499/49.
[10] 6 Henry VIII c. 24.

B

10   COURT OF WARDS AND LIVERIES   [CHAP. I

wardship of the body, and in general demanded a rigorous control of sales.[1]

The exact date at which Henry VIII, by tightening up the administration and returning to his father's methods, took his first step towards the foundation of the Court of Wards cannot be stated definitively. Sometime before New Year's Day 1518-19 Sir Richard Weston was joined with Lovell in the mastership of the wards,[2] and in 1518, too, Daunce got a new patent of the office of receiver-general, this time holding it jointly with Roger Wigston.[3] Again it may be significant that, in 1519, the Venetian ambassador, Giustinian, spoke of Henry's wealth as deriving in part from the *Court* of Wards.[4] On the whole, however, it seems more reasonable to connect the reform with the appointments of 1520. In that year, Lovell having given up the mastership on account of age and pressure of business, Sir Edward Belknap was set in his place at Weston's side.[5] Yet another receiver-general was also appointed in 1520, Thomas Magnus, the archdeacon of the East Riding of Yorkshire.[6] His account for the year 1523-4 survives, and is the earliest of the second series of receiver-general's accounts.[7] In 1521 there was a new grant of the auditor's office, to Thomas Robertes and John Peryent, both experienced men.[8] In other ways Weston's second period as master saw developments—for one thing, there is an interesting provision in the patent which he and Belknap obtained, authorizing them to convoke the Council Learned; for another, it seems likely (though the evidence is not easily interpreted) that Weston endeavoured to control indiscriminate sales of wardships and leases of wards' lands;[9] again, there was certainly an attempt at this time to get better service out of escheators.[10]

The final phase of wardship administration prior to the statutory foundation of the Court came with the mastership of William Paulet, for the first part of which he held office jointly with Thomas

---

[1] See below, Appendix I.
[2] *L. & P.*, vol. III, p. 1534.
[3] *L. & P.*, vol. II, no. 3914.
[4] *C.S.P. Ven.*, ii, 559.
[5] *L. & P.*, vol. III, no. 1121/10.
[6] *Ibid.* no. 1036/23.   [7] P.R.O. Wards 8/72.   [8] *Ibid.*
[9] P.R.O. Ind. 10217 (1), calendar of bargains: the wards' names listed for 13-17 Henry VIII, unlike other years, have no entries of committees' names or purchase prices. P.R.O. Wards 9/148, moreover, is an entry book of bargains for wards left unsold by Weston to his successors.
[10] *L. & P.*, vol. III, no. 3692.

CHAP. I]   HENRY VII AND HENRY VIII   11

Inglefield.[1] Belknap had died in 1521,[2] but in September 1525 Weston was still master, though offering to throw up the office if made steward of the Duchy of Lancaster.[3] Inglefield probably succeeded him at Easter 1526,[4] and Paulet joined Inglefield in the November following.[5] Their joint mastership lasted until 1537, after which Paulet continued in office alone.[6] For this period much more record material is available than at any previous time, though its state of preservation is unequal.[7] It leaves no room for doubt that Paulet, and to a less extent Inglefield, were the creators of the administrative tradition that the Court of Wards inherited.

On the financial side, certainly, the influence of Paulet was predominant, for he held, in addition to the mastership, the office of receiver-general. His accounts in that capacity[8] took on very much the form and appearance that was to become common to those of the Court's receivers-general during the century of its working— though, unlike those, Paulet's did not yet include receipts from sales of wards. Of these a separate record was kept, which was still authenticated by the treasurer of the King's Chamber when he actually received the bonds for payment of the purchase price.[9] But the title of the book in which the account of sales was kept shows that the masters were now entirely responsible for negotiating them.[10] About the productivity of Paulet's office a little may be said. On the basis of three of his accounts that survive in fair condition, it may be stated that the issues of wards' lands were reaching an annual average of nearly 4,500 l.—a figure that is 1,000 l. a year less than the yield in Lychefelde's receiver-generalship earlier in the century.[11] On the other hand, despite the forebodings of the

[1] Or Englefield; he was grandfather of Sir Francis Englefield, master of the Court under Mary.   [2] *E.H.R.*, vol. LVI, p. 67.
[3] *L. & P.*, vol. IV, no. 1646.   [4] P.R.O. E. 36/246.   [5] *Ibid.*
[6] See his accounts listed in next note.
[7] The following records (P.R.O. unless otherwise stated) have been noted as containing material for this period:
Legal. Wards 9/223, in Wards 4/1, Bod. MSS. Rawl. A. 150 and A. 396, process books; in Ind. 10218, list of pleadings; in Wards 15/1, loose pleadings.
Administrative. Wards 9/197, list of wards; Wards 9/147, 148, 151, entry books of bargains; Ind. 10217 (1), calendar of bargains; Wards 9/149, entry book of receipts for sales of wards; E. 36/246, bills for wards sold; Wards 9/187, entry book of leases; Wards 9/114, 179, 286, entry books of indentures; Wards 9/578, entry book of particulars for liveries.
Financial. Wards 11/3/9, 8/107, 8/73, 9/361, 8/74, receiver-general's accounts.
[8] See note above.
[9] P.R.O. Wards 9/149, under 22 Henry VIII, note by Brian Tuke.
[10] P.R.O. Wards 9/149.   [11] See above, pp. 6-7.

12 COURT OF WARDS AND LIVERIES [CHAP. I

memorandum cited above, sales of wardships became exceedingly productive, in the years 1528-30 averaging 4,153 *l.*, and in 1534-6 3001 *l.*[1]

In this period there were also rapid developments in the judicial business of the mastership, perhaps initiated by Inglefield, who was a justice of the Common Pleas. The former practice of submitting cases *ad hoc* to the Council Learned was now abandoned, and from at least 1528 the masters were sitting regularly in Westminster palace for the conduct of judicial business.[2] Much of what came before them was inherited from the jurisdiction of Henry VII's Council Learned—it was before them that intrusions on wards' lands were answered,[3] defaulting accountants brought to a reckoning,[4] the king's wards surrendered.[5] But their process books show a movement, gradual but definite, into the forms and action of a formal court of law, forbidding a defendant's departure until he has made answer,[6] making an injunction against proceeding elsewhere,[7] and entertaining a growing number of suits between private individuals.[8] The masters were now assisted in the conduct of judicial business by an attorney,[9] the immediate ancestor of the attorney of the wards, who was to be one of the most important officers of the Court.

For the rest, Paulet's mastership saw a great increase in the general business, neither specifically financial nor judicial, of wardship and livery. To shoulder part of the burden that this imposed the office of clerk of wards was created,[10] and very much closer liaison than formerly was established with the feodaries, the process books being full of instructions conveyed to them—to certify wards' lands,[11] to bring in relevant records,[12] and to undertake the hundred and one tasks that were involved in wardship administration in the localities. In addition to the wardship organization, there were livery officials, who were clearly in close touch with Paulet and his officers.[13] Sir Thomas Nevell and Serjeant Robert Norwych were appointed overseers of liveries in 1529, the latter

[1] Calculated from P.R.O. Wards 9/149.   [2] P.R.O. Wards 9/223, f. 2.
[3] Bod. MS. Rawl. A. 396, p. 38.   [4] P.R.O. Wards 9/223, ff. 20-1.
[5] *Ibid.* f. 2.   [6] Bod. MS. Rawl. A. 150, p. 77.   [7] *Ibid.* p. 25.
[8] Listed in P.R.O. Ind. 10218.
[9] P.R.O. Wards 8/73, Henry See; P.R.O. Wards 8/74, William Porteman.
[10] P.R.O. Wards 8/107 John Aile. . . (gone); P.R.O. Wards 9/361, Robert Skynner; P.R.O. Wards 8/74, Robert Rawson.
[11] P.R.O. Wards 9/223, f. 3.   [12] *Ibid. passim.*
[13] Bod. MS. Rawl. A. 396, p. 32.

CHAP. I] HENRY VII AND HENRY VIII 13

being succeeded six years later by Sir Richard Riche, and he for a short time by Inglefield himself and then in 1537 by Serjeant John Hynde.[1]

A modern biographer states that, in 1532, no less a person than Thomas Cromwell was master of the wards,[2] but so far no confirmatory evidence of this statement has been found. Certainly it was to Cromwell that Inglefield wrote in February of that year, thanking him for procuring the writer's recompense for the mastership of the wards;[3] again it was Cromwell who, in 1534, ordered the sheriff of Yorkshire that the persons to inquire after the death of Sir J. Denham should be resident near the lands the deceased had held.[4] On the other hand, these facts perhaps only indicate what is clear enough already—that Henry VIII's administrative system was not rigidly formalized, and that a man so influential as Cromwell might have his finger in every pie. They do nothing to minimize the importance of Paulet.

It remains to explain the factors which caused Henry to place the administration of wardship and livery on a statutory basis, and which resulted in the definitive erection of the Court in 1540. Firstly this was in any case little more than a formalizing of existing arrangements. Again, the financial difficulties of the king, consequent upon his expensive foreign policy, combined with the unpopularity of loans and benevolences to necessitate the efficient collection of his feudal revenues. This involved striking at the whole machinery of uses, so often made the means of avoiding payment of feudal exactions. Two royal bills of 1529 would have had far-reaching effects and gone to the root of the difficulty, but they were dropped—perhaps because of opposition in Parliament.[5] Later the general rule was made that the use was forfeited if the *cestui que use* was guilty of treason.[6] It was becoming increasingly obvious that the law must be made to reflect actuality, and that the nominal and substantial ownership, so long separated by the practice of conveyancers, must be reunited.[7] The statute of Uses[8] was at once the product of the desire to make livery and wardship more profitable by preventing settlements which deprived the king of his

---

[1] *L. & P.*, vol. IV, no. 5978/15; *ibid.* vol. VIII, no. 632/34; *ibid.* vol. XII, no. 795/27.
[2] R. B. Merriman, *Life and Letters of Thomas Cromwell*, vol. I, p. 143.
[3] *L. & P.*, vol. V, no. 799.   [4] *L. & P.*, vol. VII, no. 383.
[5] Holdsworth, vol. IV, pp. 450-3.   [6] 26 Henry VIII c. 13.
[7] F. Pollock, *The Land Laws*, pp. 88-95.   [8] 27 Henry VIII c. 10.

14 COURT OF WARDS AND LIVERIES [CHAP. I

rights, and the immediate cause of the erection of the Court of Wards and Liveries. The rebels of the Pilgrimage of Grace had no illusions as to its effect and included it amongst their grievances,[1] associated significantly enough with a demand for remedy against escheators who found false inquisitions and extorted fees.[2] But although the power to devise, which had been abolished by the statute, was partially restored by the two statutes of Wills,[3] the king's rights were now secured. The Court was established to deal with the consequent increase in the business of livery and wardship.[4]

There was another, and exceedingly interesting, cause of this growth of business. The act by which the Court of Augmentations was established[5] provided that that court, in granting out the abbeys and their lands, should reserve to the crown a tenure in chief by knight's service; and although, when the reserved rent was found to press hard on the purchasers of 'smale quylettes', its size was reduced,[6] nevertheless any tenure in chief by knight's service, however small, brought a man's lands within the royal grasp so far as livery and wardship were concerned. Henry Spelman, elaborating his odd theory of sacrilege and its consequences, regarded this as the thin end of the royal wedge that was to prove such a curse to the families who had acquired monastic lands. It increased to a great extent the number of tenures held directly to the king, and Spelman even goes so far as to make it the principal cause of the setting up of the Court—'These tenures, by being by this means multiplied in such excessive manner, the king's former officers, that before could span their business with their hand, could not now fathom this with both their arms. The greater harvest must have greater barns and more labourers'.[7] Actually, the process of increasing tenures in chief does appear to have been another reason why the Court was necessary.

The Court of Wards and Liveries rested on two statutes—the acts of Parliament 32 Henry VIII c. 46 and 33 Henry VIII c. 22. The first established the Court of Wards as a court of record, with a seal to be kept in the custody of the master. The king's wards and their lands were placed under the survey of the new Court, and accounts of such were to be made to it, instead of to the Exchequer;

---

[1] M. H. and R. Dodds, *Pilgrimage of Grace*, vol. I, pp. 103, 114, 364.
[2] *Ibid.* vol. I, p. 368.   [3] 32 Henry VIII c. 1; 34 Henry VIII c. 5.
[4] Holdsworth, vol. IV, pp. 449-80.   [5] 27 Henry VIII c. 27.
[6] 35 Henry VIII c. 14.
[7] *History and Fate of Sacrilege*, edn. of 1846, p. 175.

CHAP. I]   HENRY VII AND HENRY VIII   15

no process was to issue from the Exchequer for matters under the survey of the Court of Wards. Many of the details of the enactment related to the officials of the Court and these, along with other matters within its scope, will more properly be discussed later. One provision must, however, be noted: it was arranged that, upon a ward reaching full age, his livery must not be passed without reference to the Court. The close connection of wardship and livery was thus apparent from the start, and it soon became obvious that the two could be most efficiently administered in conjunction. Accordingly, a year after the establishment of the Court of Wards, the office of master of the liveries was united to it, in the second statute on which the Court, as it will be studied in subsequent pages, was based. As in the case of the general surveyors, Henry VIII placed his father's organization upon a statutory basis; but of all the new revenue courts, the Court of Wards and Liveries was to have the longest existence.

CHAPTER II

THE OFFICERS OF THE COURT

INSTITUTIONS are made by the men who serve them, and the personnel of the Court may well be the first matter for comment. The two statutes which brought the new machinery into existence provided that the king should appoint the principal officers, and that these were to be the master, surveyor-general of the liveries, receiver-general, attorney, two auditors, two clerks of the wards, clerk of the liveries, usher and messenger.[1] In fact, for the first half of its existence the Court found a single auditor and a single clerk of the wards sufficient for the business of these offices, and the statutory officers thus numbered at first nine, and only later eleven. Except for the clerks, usher and messenger they were reckoned judges of the Court, and it seems to have been usual to relieve the pressure of business by causing affidavits to be sworn before any one of those considered to hold judicial office.[2] Again, when Charles I attempted to remove the Court to Oxford and the auditors failed to obey his summons, it was held that, in so far as their duties were judicial, it was not permissible for them to attend by deputy.[3] Nevertheless, all the officials had heavy administrative duties and, with the exception of the attorney, the balance of their functions was executive rather than legal.

The first master was William Paulet, in 1551 created Marquis of Winchester—a choice that implied continuity of policy, for he had been master of the wards since 1526[4] and surveyor of the king's widows and governor of idiots and naturals in the king's hand since 1531.[5] On the accession of Edward VI he was re-appointed by the Council, with the proviso, however, that all officers were to be sworn and new patents made out except for those holding for life.[6] After his resignation in 1554, the mastership was held by Sir Francis Englefield; but, being a staunch Catholic,

---

[1] 32 Henry VIII c. 46; 33 Henry VIII c. 22.
[2] See bundles of affidavits, P.R.O. in Wards 10/44 etc.
[3] B. M. Egerton MS. 2979, f. 30. See Curle's case, Coke, *Reports*, vol. VI, pp. 3-7.
[4] See above, p. 11. [5] *D.N.B.* Paulet, William. [6] *A.P.C. 1547-50*, p. 27.

CHAP. II]   THE OFFICERS OF THE COURT   17

soon after Elizabeth came to the throne he was deprived of the seal of the Court[1] and ordered to deliver up such of its records as remained in his custody.[2] After a short interval in which Sir Thomas Parry held office, in 1561 Cecil began his long reign over the Court, which lasted until his death in 1598.[3] About his mastership a contemporary panegyrist was enthusiastic, describing him as 'allwaies most carefull both of her majesties profitt and prerogatyve, & to maintaine the priviledges & authoritie of the court';[4] and though, as will be seen later, the period of his administration was not one of high revenues, much of the productivity of later years had its origin in his reforms.[5] The fact seems indisputable that, despite all his other duties and interests, Burghley was an able and efficient master.

The long rules of Paulet and Burghley, Tudor government servants *par excellence*, stand out in sharp contrast to the more rapid succession of Stuart masters. Already after the death of Burghley, Elizabeth seems to have experienced some difficulty in filling the position. The old statesman died on 4 August 1598, and for over nine months the office was vacant, so that all judicial proceedings in the Court were in abeyance.[6] In the autumn of 1598 it appeared that Essex would be the new master, and, as a contemporary wrote, 'the voice of all the land bestowed' the position upon him.[7] A correspondent of his secretary urged him to see to it that none but himself became secretary to the Court, so certain did it seem that the earl would be master.[8] Essex himself went so far as to seek detailed information about the Court from Sir William Fleetwood, the receiver-general,[9] who passed on the query to his personal clerk, Edward Latimer, in a highly confidential letter—'I woulde not haue any manne but yourselfe priuie here unto for A thousande poundes.'[10] But whether because he was not offered the mastership on the same terms as Burghley, or that he scrupled at the strictness of the oath (both rumours were current), Essex never took office; no doubt behind the whole episode is the beginning of his quarrel with the queen.[11] Thomas Owen, a judge in the Common

---

[1] *A.P.C. 1558-70*, p. 29.   [2] *Ibid.* p. 47.

[3] An account of the succession of masters down to 1599 appears in *C.S.P. Dom. 1598-1601*, p. 204.   [4] Peck, vol. I, p. 20.   [5] See below, ch. III.

[6] *C.S.P. Dom. 1598-1601*, p. 204.   [7] H.M.C., *Cowper*, vol. I, p. 24.

[8] H.M.C., *Salisbury*, vol. VII, p. 531.   [9] *C.S.P. Dom. 1598-1601*, p. 102.

[10] P.R.O. Wards 14/3/20, papers of Edward Latimer.

[11] *C.S.P. Dom. 1598-1601*, p. 110.

18 COURT OF WARDS AND LIVERIES [CHAP. II

Pleas, was mentioned as a possible choice, but he died[1] and, to everybody's surprise, Sir Thomas Fortescue refused the position in the spring of 1599.[2] In one way and another, it was not until 21 May that Robert Cecil succeeded his father,[3] though as early as 1591 Burghley was said to be planning that he should do so.[4]

The interregnum of 1598-9 is interesting for the proof it affords that the mastership was certainly not a sinecure, for the absence of a master made it impossible for the Court to fulfil anything like its normal functions. At the opening of the Michaelmas term after Burghley's death, the surveyor, attorney, auditor and clerk of the wards held conference in the council chamber and determined to have collected out of the statutes information as to what judicial and financial business could, and could not, be transacted without a master. Some of the resultant memoranda have survived, with the endorsement that they were considered by the lord keeper, lord chief justice, attorney-general and attorney of the wards, and were afterwards to be shown to the queen by the lord keeper. The upshot was unsatisfactory—as has been seen, the hearing of cases was held up, and the remaining officers sat for routine business only, such as the taking of affidavits and commissions, in the council chamber and not in court; moreover, even the administrative procedure of the Court was inconvenienced—ordinary financial process had to be taken for sealing to the new lord treasurer's house.[5] A rather similar situation arose in 1612, when, towards the end of Robert Cecil's life, he sought to leave London for Bath; on that occasion very precise arrangements as to the business that might be done without him were conveyed by the master's letter to the Court, and these were thereupon incorporated in one of its decrees.[6] The significance of both incidents lies in the light they throw on the master's position: he was very clearly no mere figurehead, but a working member of the Court, heavily involved in all its day-to-day activities.

The interim between the death of Burghley and the appointment of his son marked the beginning of difficulties over the mastership which were to be accentuated under the Stuarts. Robert Cecil himself enjoyed a certain measure of success, but his period of

---

[1] *D.N.B.* Owen, Thomas.   [2] H.M.C., *Salisbury*, vol. IX, p. 173.
[3] *C.S.P. Dom. 1598-1601*, p. 204.   [4] *C.S.P. Dom. 1591-4*, p. 97.
[5] Details in this paragraph are based on P.R.O. Wards 14/3/20, papers of Edward Latimer.
[6] P.R.O. Wards 9/91, f. 1.

CHAP. II]   THE OFFICERS OF THE COURT   19

office was marked by the increasingly obvious incompatibility between the effort to increase the Court's revenues and the need to check its growing unpopularity. This was the point made in the *Apology for the late Lord Treasurer* by Sir Walter Cope, himself afterwards master of the Court,[1] and perhaps the realization of the impossibility of his task accounted for Cecil's attitude towards the negotiations for the abortive great contract.[2]

Cecil's successor, Sir George Carew, died in 1612, the year of his appointment.[3] Sir Walter Cope, the next master, was also rapidly carried off by death; but in any case he was said to be likely to lose his place since his want of dignity made the Court less profitable than before.[4] Sir William Knollys, master in 1614 and created Viscount Wallingford during his tenure of office, was deposed for maladministration in 1618.[5] Even Lionel Cranfield, whose business talents were certainly useful in the Court, ended his career under a cloud—his activities as master were among the matters for which he was censured at the time of his impeachment in 1624.[6] There was some doubt as to who should follow him, both Rudyerd, the surveyor,[7] and Pye, the attorney,[8] being considered as candidates. In fact, the appointment went to Sir Robert Naunton, a former surveyor of the liveries and the author of the *Fragmenta Regalia*, who proved the longest survivor of the Stuart masters, holding office from 1623 to 1635. In the latter year, hearing that a commission was to be issued to inquire concerning his health and whether he was able to serve in the position any longer, he declared himself ready to surrender his patent without any such commission, should the king be unwilling to give him a term in which to recover.[9] The same year he died, and the succeeding masters were Francis, Baron Cottington (1635-41),[10] and William, Viscount Saye and Sele,[11] the last master with the exception of Cottington again, whom the king reappointed at Oxford.[12]

There were several reasons to account for the unsatisfactory nature of the Stuart masters of the Court. First, James and Charles were genuinely unlucky in their choice; as has been seen, sickness

---

[1] Printed in John Gutch, *Collectanea Curiosa*, 1781, vol. I, pp. 119-33.
[2] See below, ch. VII.   [3] *D.N.B.* Carew, George.
[4] *C.S.P. Dom. 1611-18*, p. 246.
[5] F. C. Dietz, *English Public Finance 1558-1641*, p. 171.
[6] See below, pp. 147-8.   [7] *C.S.P. Dom. 1623-5*, p. 292.   [8] *Ibid.* p. 330.
[9] *C.S.P. Dom. 1634-5*, p. 562.   [10] *D.N.B.* Cottington, Francis.
[11] P.R.O. Wards 9/431, f. 373.   [12] Steele, no. 2523.

20   COURT OF WARDS AND LIVERIES   CHAP. II]

and death played their part in striking down several who held the position. Again, this was the time when the crown needed to increase its income by every means at its disposal; administration of the revenues of livery and wardship was stricter, and the duties of the master inevitably more unpopular and more exacting. But there is a further reason which throws some of the responsibility on to the kings themselves. With the appointment of Carew to succeed Salisbury in 1612, James seems to have made a deliberate change in the type of man chosen. Bacon had sought the mastership without success,[1] and perhaps a touch of his disappointment appeared in the *Directions for the master of the wards*[2] that he probably compiled in this same year. In them he clearly expects the master to attend to certain purely routine matters, 'being a meaner person'. Contemporaneously, Chamberlain reflected, in a letter to Carleton, how out of countenance with themselves Burghley and Salisbury would be, could they see their successors.[3] The speech made by Carew on becoming master is also significant in this connexion. The king, he said, 'meaneth to be as it were Mr. of the Wards himself, and those whome he useth to be but his substitutes and moove wholy by his impulsion, wᵗin the circle of his owne motion'.[4] James especially never understood the virtue of delegating responsibility nor possessed the Tudor ability to get the best out of his servants.

Next in seniority to the master was the surveyor-general of the liveries, an official who, like the master himself, is older than the Court. Indeed, just as Paulet, the first master, so John Hynde, the original surveyor, had previous experience of the business of his office, for the year before the Court was set on a statutory basis as Serjeant Hynde he was hearing cases.[5] Hynde was the first of a distinguished line of lawyers who held the position of surveyor-general; a reader at Gray's Inn and recorder of Cambridge, he had been considered amongst the best counsel of the day.[6] Robert Keilwey, who succeeded him in 1547, was also a man of standing in the legal profession. Made reader at the Inner Temple in the year of his appointment to the surveyorship, and serjeant in 1552, he was the author of a learned collection of *Reports*; perhaps equally

---

[1] Holdsworth, vol. v, p. 241.
[2] Bacon, vol. xi, pp. 286-8.
[3] T. Birch, *Court and Times of James I*, vol. i, p. 208.
[4] P.R.O. S.P. 14/69, no. 69, discourse to the Court; c.f. Bacon's *Directions*.
[5] Bod. Rawl. MS. A 396, p. 196.   [6] *D.N.B.* Hynde, John.

CHAP. II]   THE OFFICERS OF THE COURT   21

important when the establishment and maintenance of a tradition was so urgently necessary, Keilwey enjoyed a long term of office, right down to his death in 1581.[1] Thomas Seckford, the next surveyor, was relatively old at the time of his appointment, having been reader at Gray's Inn as early as 1555 and treasurer of the inn ten years later.[2] He only held the surveyorship for some seven years, and when he died the position seems at first not to have been filled. The receiver-general's accounts for the years 1589 to 1590 mention no payment to a surveyor, and then Richard Kingsmill, already serving as attorney of the wards, was promoted.[3] Kingsmill, a bencher of Lincoln's Inn, had in some ways a rather unhappy period of office, for he became involved in the controversy that arose between the clerks of the wards and the liveries. The clerk of the wards, indeed, alleged that Kingsmill had broken with previous custom in granting continuances of liveries without having them entered of record in the wards' office of the Court. This Kingsmill sharply denied to be an innovation, and though the details of the controversy—and, much more, its rights and wrongs —are obscure, it leaves to some extent the impression that the Tudor surveyors enjoyed perhaps a little more independence than their successors in Stuart times.[4]

There was, too, another distinction between the earlier and the later surveyors—a difference in the type of man appointed. Sir Cuthbert Pepper, Kingsmill's successor and Elizabeth's last surveyor, was in the old tradition—a reader, and later treasurer, of Gray's Inn;[5] so too was Sir Roger Wilbraham, the diarist, who followed Pepper in 1607, after a legal career that had taken him to Ireland as solicitor-general and that had included a period as master of requests.[6] But Naunton, surveyor for a short time in 1617, was not a lawyer, and Sir Humphrey May the year following, though a member of the Middle Temple, had made a political, and not a legal, career.[7] That was true also of Benjamin Rudyerd, the last surveyor of the liveries, who held the office from 1618 until the Court's suppression. He was called to the bar from the Inner

[1] *D.N.B.* Keilway, Robert.
[2] *Ibid.* Seckford, Thomas; and *Pension Book of Gray's Inn 1569-1669*, p. 500.
[3] P.R.O. Wards 9/386, r.g.a. 30-2 Eliz.
[4] P.R.O. Wards 14/3/20, controversy between Hare and Churchill.
[5] *Pension Book of Gray's Inn 1569-1669*, pp. 109, 500.
[6] *Camden Miscellany*, vol. x, pp. vi-viii.
[7] P.R.O. Wards 9/413, r.g.a. 16 Jas. 1; *D.N.B.* May, Humphrey.

22   COURT OF WARDS AND LIVERIES   [CHAP. II

Temple in 1600, but then, according to his contemporary, Sir James Whitelocke, 'he left the studye of the law, and betooke himself to travell, and, getting into the good opinion of the Earl of Pembroke and other noblemen, was put into the place of Surveyor of the Court of Wards, and afterwards knighted.'[1] Rudyerd's qualities, and his versatility, are not in question. The friend of Ben Jonson, a poet himself, and energetic in colonial enterprises, he had a varied and interesting career; nor is evidence lacking that he showed reasonable application to his duties in the Court. Nevertheless, the appointment of this kind of man to the surveyorship is not without significance: what had been originally a technical office to be held by an experienced lawyer had become a prize for the courtier or politician.[2]

The principal legal officer of the Court was the attorney, and, indeed, Carew, on being made master, disclaimed a deep knowledge of the common law himself, stating that this was rather the attorney's function.[3] In the hundred years of the Court's existence there were fifteen attorneys, and they are perhaps more conveniently listed in a footnote than in the text.[4] There are, however, some points that may be made about them. According to Coke, the attorney of the wards, like the attorney-general and solicitor-general, was chosen by the king from amongst those who were double readers of the Inns of Court;[5] this implies that they were benchers of their inns

[1] Quoted in John Hutchinson, *Notable Middle Templars*, p. 211.
[2] *D.N.B.* Rudyerd, Benjamin.
[3] P.R.O. S.P. 14/69, no. 69, discourse to the Court.
[4] Attorneys of the Court of Wards and Liveries:

Name	Date of Appointment	Reference
Thomas Polsted	1540	*L. & P.*, xv, no. 1027/15.
John Sewster	1541	*Ibid.* xvi, no. 580/34.
Richard Goodrich	1546	*Ibid.* xxi, part 1, no. 970/23.
Nicholas Bacon	1547	*Ibid.* xxi, part 11, no. 771/13.
Robert Nowell	1561	*C.P.R. Elizabeth, 1560-3*, p. 6.
Richard Onslow	1568	P.R.O. Ind. 16772, f. 251.
Thomas Wilbraham	1571	*Haydn's Book of Dignities*, p. 494.
Richard Kingsmill	1572	P.R.O. Ind. 16772, f. 309.
James Morris	1589	P.R.O. Wards 9/386.
Thomas Hesketh	1597	*C.S.P. Dom. 1595-7*, p. 390.
Henry Hobart	1605	*C.S.P. Dom. 1603-10*, p. 239.
James Ley	1608	*D.N.B.*
Walter Pye	1621	*C.S.P. Dom. 1619-23*, p. 218.
Henry Calthorpe	1636	*D.N.B.*
Rowland Wandesford	1637	P.R.O. Ind. 16793, f. 233.

[5] Dugdale, *Origines Juridiciales*, p. 144 (citing Coke).

CHAP. II]   THE OFFICERS OF THE COURT   23

before being made attorney, and in fact most of them can be shown by independent evidence to have been so. They were men with solid experience behind them of legal work in the common law, duchy or prerogative courts—Goodrich, for instance, had been attorney of the Court of Augmentations,[1] Nicholas Bacon its solicitor;[2] Onslow had for a time been solicitor-general,[3] and Hesketh held contemporaneously with the attorneyship the position of attorney and king's serjeant at Lancaster under the auspices of the Duchy.[4] Again, the list of attorneys includes three recorders of London.[5] Moreover, it is perhaps interesting to note the positions held by the attorneys not only prior to their appointment in the Court of Wards, but also subsequent to it. For some of them the attorneyship was simply a rung in the ladder to high judicial or political office: Nicholas Bacon left it to become lord keeper,[6] Hobart was later on lord chief justice of the Common Pleas,[7] Ley afterwards lord treasurer.[8] Some had parliamentary careers, notably Richard Onslow, who was speaker in 1566,[9] and James Morris, who was bold enough to incur Elizabeth's displeasure and get himself thrown into the Tower as a member of the parliament of 1593.[10] Robert Nowell's claim to distinction was of another character: the brother of the more famous Alexander and Lawrence Nowell, he spent much money on poor scholars, amongst them the poet Spenser.[11] All in all, the attorneys of the wards were an interesting and able succession of officials, learned in the law but with interests by no means confined to it.

Two of the attorneys, Sir Nicholas Bacon and Sir James Ley, are worthy of special mention, not so much because of their subsequent careers as because of their great interest in questions of wardship. Bacon's attorneyship has two distinctions—first, it was during his period of office that Staunford wrote and dedicated to the attorney of the wards his classical account of the crown's rights, the *De Prerogativa Regis*;[12] second, it was Bacon who framed the *Articles devised for the bringinge up in vertue and lerninge of the*

---

[1] *D.N.B.* Goodrich, Richard.
[2] *Ibid.* Bacon, Nicholas.   [3] *Ibid.* Onslow, Richard.
[4] I am indebted to Mr Robert Somerville for this piece of information.
[5] Richard Onslow (*D.N.B.*) Thomas Wilbraham (*Records of the Society of Lincoln's Inn, Black Books*, vol. I, p. 375) and Henry Calthorpe (*D.N.B.*).
[6] *D.N.B.* Bacon, Nicholas.   [7] *Ibid.* Hobart, Henry.
[8] *Ibid.* Ley, James.   [9] *Ibid.* Onslow, Richard.
[10] J. R. Tanner, *Tudor Constitutional Documents*, p. 557.
[11] *V.C.H., Lanc.*, vol. VI, p. 504 note.   [12] See below, pp. 67-8.

24 COURT OF WARDS AND LIVERIES [CHAP. II

Queenes Majesties wardes,[1] one of the rare indications throughout the history of the Court of any serious interest in the welfare of the wards. Ley is said, soon after he had become attorney, to have obtained a privy seal authorizing him to act within the Court as attorney-general on the king's behalf; according to Wood, this had not previously been the custom, but succeeding attorneys kept the privilege that Ley had won for them.[2] Ley was also the author of a tract on the Court, and made a collection of cases heard before it.[3]

The statute erecting the Court provided for two auditors to be its chief financial officers, but till towards the close of Elizabeth's reign it seems that one auditor sufficed. The first to hold this office was Sir John Peryent,[4] who had indeed been auditor of the wards for the best part of twenty years before the statute was passed[5] and who was, therefore, the oldest and most experienced official carried over from the old organization. Peryent, however, in that pre-statute period, had employed as a clerk a man named William Tooke,[6] and in 1544 the office of auditor was granted to the two of them in survivorship.[7] Thus William Tooke succeeded to it in 1551,[8] and from that time until the end of the Court's existence the Hertfordshire family of Tooke kept the position in their hands. William died in 1588 at the good old age, according to his memorial brass in Essendon Church, of eighty-eight. He had nine sons and three daughters, and his second son, Walter, succeeded him as auditor. Walter Tooke's formal, copperplate signature is one of the most familiar hands to anyone working in the Court's records for the end of Elizabeth's or the beginning of James I's reign. That makes the more pathetic the quavering, sick man's signature that he appended to his letter of 18 November 1609 to Cecil, seeking permission for his son to act as deputy because of his own sickness.[9] This was no doubt Walter's third son, John, who did in fact succeed to the auditorship in 1610.[10] By this time the second auditorship was in existence, and for some

---

[1] See below, pp. 120-1.   [2] *Athenae Oxenienses*, ed. P. Bliss, vol. II, col. 441.
[3] *A Learned Treatise Concerning Wards and Liveries*, 1642 (see below, p. 68). *Reports of Divers Resolutions in Law Arising upon Cases in the Court of Wards etc.*, 1659 (see below, pp. 68, 89).
[4] Provision for his continuation was made in 32 Henry VIII c. 46.
[5] *L. & P.*, vol. III, no. 1451/10.   [6] P.R.O. Wards 8/74, r.g.a. 28-9 Henry VIII.
[7] *L. & P.*, vol. XIX, part 2, no. 340/19.
[8] He first received the fee in 5 Edw. VI: P.R.O. Wards 9/365, r.g.a. 1 Edw. VI-I Mary.   [9] P.R.O. S.P. 14/49, no. 40, Walter Tooke to Salisbury.
[10] *C.S.P. Dom. 1603-10*, p. 594.

CHAP. II]   THE OFFICERS OF THE COURT   25

years at the beginning of Charles I's reign John and his sixth son, Thomas, held the two positions.[1] James Tooke, who was one of the auditors at the time of the Court's dissolution, was not a son of Thomas, but still a member of the Hertfordshire family; he, or another of the same name, had been feodary of London and Middlesex.[2]

The appearance of a second auditor dates from 1589, when a new patent was granted to Walter Tooke, on this occasion joining with him William Curle.[3] Curle's name does not figure in the receiver-general's accounts before the year ending 1600, but a list of officials of the Court, which is at least six years earlier than that, brackets him with Tooke as auditors.[4] In 1603 Edward Curle, William's son, seeking the reversion of his father's place, asserted that by the examples of the times offices were not likely to be hereditary;[5] but in fact in 1615 Francis Curle succeeded, and the second auditorship was thus in the Curles' hands, all told, for over a quarter of a century. It then appears to have passed to Charles Maynard, who held it until the dissolution of the Court.[6]

In the latter part of the Court's existence, the other financial office, the receiver-generalship, showed the same tendency as the auditorship to lodge in a single family. The Tudor receivers were Philip Paris (1541-5), John Beaumont (1545-51), William Dansell (1551-81), John Battisforde (1581-4), George Goring (1584-94) and William Fleetwood.[7] Thereafter the office remained in the Fleetwood family until the final days of the Court. William Fleetwood held it for some fifteen years, and though persistently in debt to the crown was nevertheless succeeded by Miles Fleetwood, his son. When Miles Fleetwood died, in March 1640,[8] his eldest son— another William—became receiver-general; and on his following the king to Oxford, and being sequestered of his office by Parliament for so doing,[9] a younger brother, Charles Fleetwood, was appointed in his place.[10] The family principle could not be pushed much further!

---

[1] Fees paid to them both from 22 Jas. I: P.R.O. Wards 9/414, r.g.a. 16-22 Jas. I.   [2] *Visitations of Hertfordshire*, Harleian Soc., p. 167.
[3] P.R.O. Ind. 16776, 31 Eliz., f. 1.
[4] P.R.O. in Wards 10/16, list of officials of Court.
[5] H.M.C., *Salisbury*, vol. xv, p. 371.   [6] *C.S.P. Dom. 1625-6*, p. 533.
[7] For the succession of receivers-general, see P.R.O. *Wards Guide*, pp. 24-7.
[8] P.R.O. Wards 9/431, f. 240.   [9] *H.C.J.*, 11 Dec. 1643.
[10] *D.N.B.* Fleetwood, Charles.

C

26 COURT OF WARDS AND LIVERIES [CHAP. II

In comparison with the positions so far discussed, the office of clerk of the wards was of less dignity; yet it is difficult to escape the impression that the clerk was one of the most influential of the Court's officials because of the important executive and co-ordinating functions that he possessed. More even than other institutions, the Court of Wards depended for its effective action on good record keeping, and what it owed in this connection to successive clerks is clear even today when many record series are broken and partially dispersed. As with the auditorship, two clerks of the wards were envisaged in the statute, but at first one proved enough, and, as Thomas Anton sufficed for the business during a period of thirteen years, he was appointed sole clerk in 1553.[1] Anton's successor, Ralph Bossevile, obtained his patent of appointment five years later,[2] and his son Henry, who in 1560 was joined with his father in survivorship, followed his father in office in 1580.[3] The Bosseviles thus covered between them the greater part of Burghley's mastership, and it may be fancied that they fitted in well with his conservative administration of the Court. Both were substantial men, made associates of the bench of Lincoln's Inn,[4] but neither has left in the records the impression of the vigorous and thrusting activity of the clerk who came after them.

This was John Hare, almost certainly the most effective of the clerks of the wards. Actually the office of clerk was granted jointly to John Hare and his brother Hugh,[5] and the latter continued to share the fees due until in 1604 John obtained a new patent with his son Nicholas in survivorship.[6] But there is no evidence that Hugh played an active part. His hand does not figure in the drafts and documents of the period, at least recognizably, as his brother's does; and it is perhaps significant that, when a commission issued to take the oaths of officers, Hugh was returned as not taking the oath by reason of absence.[7]

John Hare, on the other hand, was very active indeed. Related by marriage to the Tookes,[8] he had obtained a post, probably through their assistance, as one of the minor attorneys of the

---

[1] *C.S.P. Dom., Addenda 1547-65*, p. 432.
[2] *C.P.R., Philip and Mary 1557-8*, p. 428.
[3] *C.P.R., Elizabeth 1558-60*, p. 421.
[4] *Records of the Society of Lincoln's Inn, Black Books*, vol. I, pp. 363, 440.
[5] P.R.O. Ind. 16776, 32 Eliz., f. 4.   [6] *C.S.P. Dom. 1603-10*, p. 152.
[7] P.R.O. in Wards 10/16, list of officials of Court.
[8] *C.S.P. Dom. 1547-80*, p. 672.

CHAP. II] THE OFFICERS OF THE COURT 27

Court, and this he was holding in 1589.[1] At the beginning of Hilary term 1589-90 he was admitted as clerk of the wards,[2] and for nearly a quarter of a century gave devoted service to the Court. He was clerk at one of the most important times in the Court's history, when every nerve was strained to increase its revenue and yet when an agitation against its extortions had developed. Studying the records of this period, one finds it impossible to believe that Hare himself was not behind many of the reforms. At least he was a tireless official; his crabbed, but very distinctive, handwriting is all over the records—criticizing, suggesting, altering, endorsing. He was energetic in improving the administration, as one note in his hand shows—'Whilst there is now idle tyme all the Kallenders wolde be made up and perfected. That for wardes & leases at lardge is behynde at least 3 or 4 yeres wch wolde now be perfected. The last fyle of offices & I thinck the former alsoe are unentred wch is not well.'[3]

Like many another zealous administrator, he did not avoid—perhaps even he provoked—opposition. Through the last decade of the sixteenth century there dragged on a complicated dispute with the clerk of the liveries. Hare seems to have fired the first shot directly after becoming clerk when, in submitting to Burghley a list of thirty-nine wards who had reached full age without a grant of their wardship having been made, he complained that nevertheless the clerk of the liveries permitted the liveries of such to go forward without the clerk of the wards' certificate that their wardships had been duly granted.[4] The clerk of the liveries being then a minor, this, and perhaps other provocations, led one of his father's executors to charge Hare in open court that he had done more wrong to the clerk of the liveries than was ever done to any of the queen's wards.[5] If there was substance in the charge, Hare had indeed worked quickly, for it was made before he had held office for two years. Thereafter the battle developed—the granting of continuances of liveries without their being entered of record in Hare's office, and in general the custody of livery records, being the main questions at issue. Both sides claimed that their opponent's

[1] P.R.O. S.P. 12/224, no. 90, names of officers of Exchequer and Court of Wards.
[2] P.R.O. Wards 9/267, flyleaf.
[3] Note on an undated letter—P.R.O. in Wards 10/25.
[4] P.R.O. Wards 9/315, flyleaf.
[5] *C.S.P. Dom., Addenda 1580-1625*, pp. 329-30.

28   COURT OF WARDS AND LIVERIES   [CHAP. II

practice led to loss of revenue; the clerk of the wards went so far as to assert that the clerk of the liveries was no officer of the Court, the clerk of the liveries to bring in the surveyor on his side.[1] The upshot of a confused business seems to have been in Hare's favour: he seems to have secured both the points for which he had fought,[2] and we know from a chance reference that the clerk of the liveries was sequestered of his office.[3]

Later, in 1604, Hare even got across the master of the Court;[4] and, five years later, he informed Cecil that there were many ill practices in the administration, though rather pathetically he begged not to be named as the informer of them.[5] However, he was not held responsible for the misbehaviour of his under-clerk, Godfrey Hyrst, in 1610,[6] and in any case it is perhaps wrong to stress too much his quarrels; more to the point was his all-embracing energy. It was, for instance, wholly typical that when, in 1610, the abolition of the feudal tenures was mooted he should himself draft an act providing for an alternative system of securing revenue—with the added proviso that, under a new name, the Court of Wards should continue to supervise its collection.[7] His death in 1613 was probably a greater loss to the Court than that of any of the Stuart masters or other officers of the Court.

In September 1604 John Hare had obtained a new patent of the clerkship, this time in survivorship with his son, Nicholas, who therefore became sole clerk on John's death,[8] and appears to have remained so until 1618: indeed in that year it was ruled by the master, attorney and chief justice of the Common Pleas that, when the grant of the clerkship was made in survivorship, there need not always be two clerks of the Court.[9] It is unlikely, however, that Nicholas Hare actually served as clerk, his fee being paid to Richard Chamberlain as his deputy.[10] Chamberlain, along with Hugh Audley, had already obtained a grant of the reversion of the clerk's office,[11] and in June 1618 the new pair obtained a patent granting the actual office.[12]

Richard Chamberlain was of an Oxfordshire family, the Cham-

---

[1] P.R.O. Wards 14/3/20, controversy between Hare and Churchill.
[2] *C.S.P. Dom. 1598-1601*, pp. 395-6.   [3] C.U. MS. Hh. 4. 7, f. 101.
[4] H.M.C., *Salisbury*, vol. xvi, p. 128.   [5] *C.S.P. Dom. 1603-10*, p. 484.
[6] B.M. Lansdowne MS. 608, f. 44.   [7] P.R.O. S.P. 14/55, no. 60, draft act.
[8] *C.S.P. Dom. 1603-10*, p. 152.   [9] *C.S.P. Dom. 1611-18*, pp. 519-20.
[10] P.R.O. Wards 9/413, r.g.a., 11 Jas. I.   [11] *C.S.P. Dom. 1603-10*, p. 152.
[12] P.R.O. Ind. 6805, signet office docquet, June 1618.

CHAP. II]   THE OFFICERS OF THE COURT   29

berlains of Shirburn, and owned lands in Warwickshire;[1] from the last decade of the sixteenth century, when he held a minor office in the Court,[2] he gave a long lifetime of service to its interests. Even after the dissolution of the Court in 1645 he remained the vigilant guardian of its records; his vivacious, and often very angry, letters, written to his deputy (or so he chose to regard him) at Westminster during this latter period, have survived.[3] His last appearance is in a petition, soon after the Restoration, to Charles II, seeking payment of his pension.[4] He claims to be 'above one hundred and tenn yeares of age', but since in 1650 he had been content to give his age as 'fourscore and fourteen years old, and somewhat older',[5] the latter figure is perhaps the pardonable exaggeration of a very old man. He certainly seems to have been well over a hundred.

Audley, though appointed at the same time as Chamberlain and known to have shared with him Hare's old chambers in the Inner Temple in 1619,[6] seems to have taken less part in administrative business than his colleague.[7] Chamberlain subscribes one of his letters with his name and the phrase 'first before Mr Awdly in my patent', and he was clearly not the man to tolerate a rival. Audley, moreover, was interested in the Court simply for what he could get out of it; he was a private financier, using official opportunities to line his own pocket.[8] When Charles I took the courts to Oxford, Chamberlain followed him, and indeed his house, Nutman's End, was garrisoned for the king.[9] On 11 December 1643 the office of clerk of the wards was sequestered by Parliament from Chamberlain and Audley,[10] and the following May it was granted to Miles Corbett.[11]

Of the remaining statutory officers—the clerk of the liveries, the usher, and the messenger—little need be said. As to the first of them, however little there may have been in John Hare's argument that the clerk of the liveries was no true officer of the Court, it is

---

[1] Dugdale, *Antiquities of Warwickshire*, pp. 81, 757.
[2] P.R.O. in Wards 10/16, list of officials of Court.
[3] P.R.O. in Wards 10/1, Chamberlain correspondence.
[4] P.R.O. S.P. 29/20, no. 6, petition of Richard Chamberlain, Oct. (?) 1660.
[5] P.R.O. in Wards 10/1, Chamberlain correspondence.
[6] *Inner Temple Records*, vol. II, p. 115.
[7] It should be added, however, that it is simply an impression from the records I have seen.   [8] See below, p. 35.
[9] *Diary of Richard Symonds*, Camden Soc., 1859, p. 191.
[10] *H.C.J.*, 11 Dec. 1643.   [11] B.M. Add. MS. 34253, f. 30.

30 COURT OF WARDS AND LIVERIES [CHAP. II

noteworthy that he was the only one of the principal officers not to receive a fee from the Court's revenues. George Paulet, presumably the master's brother, was one of the first to be clerk of the liveries;[1] thereafter, having passed to two other grantees, the office from 1561 became quasi-hereditary in the Cooke family,[2] and despite the troubles at the end of Elizabeth's reign a Cooke was holding it at the time of the Court's dissolution.[3] The usher was in charge of the actual premises of the Court; if a description dating from the last decade of the sixteenth century is to be believed, there was also a gentleman usher with ceremonial duties, but no mention has been noted of his payment.[4] The messenger was responsible for the delivery of writs directing appearance, though he had at least one pursuivant to assist him;[5] to his custody, on occasion, debtors were committed.[6]

The minor offices in the central administration increased with the formalization of procedure and the growth of business. A paper dating from the last decade of the sixteenth century mentions between thirty and forty names,[7] and a further increase in personnel almost certainly occurred under the Stuarts.

Thus, on the legal side, the Court had its common attorneys, inferior officers who are not, of course, to be confused with the attorney of the wards himself. From 1576 at any rate there were two of these minor attorneys,[8] whose position was firmly established some five years later by an order of the Court relating to them. Suitors, it seems, had not welcomed the innovation of having officially sponsored attorneys of this kind. Now, however, they were forced to employ them, alike in their own interest and for the avoidance of waste of the Court's time through inexperienced handling of cases by outside attorneys and solicitors. Henceforth the clerk of the wards was to receive no bill, answer, replication or rejoinder except through one or other of the recognized attorneys, and from this time forward all pleadings in the Court bear the signature of one of them in the left hand bottom corner. No

---

[1] *C.P.R. Edward VI*, vol. IV, p. 195.
[2] *C.P.R. Elizabeth* 1560-3, p. 250.   [3] See below, p. 165.
[4] New College MS. no. cccxxv, *Briefe Collection of the . . . Courts*. I am indebted to my colleague, Mr R. L. Rickard, for this reference.
[5] *Ibid*. two pursuivants mentioned, the messenger perhaps himself being one.
[6] P.R.O. Wards 14/6/11, orders of 12 Feb., 24 Eliz.
[7] P.R.O. in Wards 10/16, list of officials of Court.
[8] P.R.O. S.P. 12/110, no. 19, Description of the Courts of Justice in England by Alexander Fisher.

[CHAP. II   THE OFFICERS OF THE COURT   31

appearance in Court was to be permitted until one of the attorneys had been retained and, once retained, he might take a fee of 3s. 4d. per term as long as the suit remained undetermined.[1] A third attorney seems to have been added at some date between 1601 and 1625,[2] while ten years later a fourth attorneyship was created.[3] As a young man, as has been noticed, John Hare held one of these positions;[4] and amongst those holding office under Charles I John Winthrop, later governor of Massachusetts, may be noticed.[5] The attorneys were not appointed by patent, but at the master's discretion, and the forthright Richard Chamberlain was sceptical as to their claim to be considered officers—'The four attorneys . . . made by the Master of the Court are no more attorneys in that Court than the Lord Mayor of London's horse is.'[6]

Financial officials also increased in number as accounting became stricter and a stronger effort was made to bring in arrearages. In 1594 William Fleetwood, the receiver-general, nominated Edward Latimer as his clerk, authorizing him to sign bonds and acquittances on the receiver's behalf.[7] This was a personal appointment; Latimer would be paid by Fleetwood and had no claim for fees on the Court's revenue. Besides Latimer, Fleetwood had a teller named Richard Richardson.[8] From James I's time, moreover, there dates the office of clerk remembrancer, Richard Perceval, later joined by William Radcliff,[9] and afterwards Michael Humfrey[10] holding it. In 1629 a man named Alexander Stafford obtained a similar position.[11]

But it was the multiplication of offices under the clerk of wards and the auditors that was the most striking feature of the Court's internal economy. In the reign of Charles I there were twelve clerks in the auditor's office alone.[12] These were not statutory officials,

[1] P.R.O. Wards 14/6/11, orders of 14 June 23 Eliz.
[2] A third attorney was admitted on 31 May 1625, but it is not known whether this was the first appointment to such a position (B.M. Lansdowne MS. 608, f. 65).
[3] P.R.O. in Wards 10/38, docquet of appointment to fourth attorneyship.
[4] P.R.O. S.P. 12/224, no. 90, names of principal officers of Exchequer and Court of Wards, 1589.
[5] D.N.B. Winthrop, John; and see G. W. Robinson, *John Winthrop as Attorney*.
[6] P.R.O. in Wards 10/1, Chamberlain correspondence.
[7] P.R.O. Wards 14/3/20, papers of Edward Latimer.
[8] P.R.O. Wards 9/387, f. 508.
[9] P.R.O. Wards 9/413, r.g.a. 11 and 13 Jas. I record payments to the two.
[10] *A.P.C. 1617-19*, p. 344.
[11] *C.S.P. Dom. 1629-31*, p. 56.   [12] B.M. Egerton MS. 2978, f. 79.

32 COURT OF WARDS AND LIVERIES [CHAP. II

and Chamberlain makes the point that the statute assigns the clerk 'to all the business and labour in his office himself', his assistants only receiving what he allowed them to take out of his own fees.[1] The multiplication of clerks probably meant, however, a corresponding increase in the number of fees taken of the subject; the growth in personnel, therefore, was a contributory cause of the Court's unpopularity. In the Commons debates on tenures in 1609-10 it was complained that 'much of the money goes to Officers clerks';[2] in a later debate, in 1614, a member returned acrimoniously to the same subject—'he hath known the Clerk of the Wards sit there in a rug Gown; now Twenty Clerks; and where Clerks increase, the grievance of the subject groweth.'[3] When Cranfield was master, he created a new officer, a secretary who acted for him in many connections, having control of his signature-stamp; but this secretary was never a legal officer of the Court and his life did not exceed two years.[4]

Such were the men who staffed the Court of Wards and Liveries. But behind the lists of office-holders, and the sketches of their careers, lie questions of a more general character—what kind of man sought office with the Court, and what factors operated to induce him to do so? To these problems we may perhaps give tentative answers.

The typical Court of Wards official was essentially an administrator, whose talents (and frequently they were not inconsiderable) were directed to the efficient conduct of the Court's business. The Court was his main, though not always his sole, sphere of public service, and he was not, generally speaking, a politician. To this rule there were of course exceptions. It is perhaps more widely applicable, for instance, to the Tudor than to the Stuart officers of the Court, for in the latter period the impression is left that the Court had more careerists than previously, men like Audley whose concern was less what they could give to it than what they could get from it. Again, so far as the mastership was concerned, those who held it were often public figures, with a framework to their

[1] P.R.O. in Wards 10/1, Chamberlain correspondence.
[2] *H.C.J.*, 13 July 1610.
[3] *Ibid.* 14 May 1614.
[4] See below, pp. 36, 147. The secretary was probably Nicholas Herman; at any rate he frequently conveyed the master's wishes to the officers of the Court (see P.R.O. in Wards 10/23, miscellanea)

CHAP. II]   THE OFFICERS OF THE COURT   33

careers that was quite external to the Court of Wards: it would obviously be impossible, for example, to describe the historical significance of Burghley or Robert Cecil simply in terms of their conduct of the Court. Yet it was the first master, William Paulet, who was in many ways the archetype of the Court of Wards official: serving successively Henry VIII, Edward VI and Mary, when asked how he survived the changes of the period, he replied 'Ortus sum ex salice, non ex quercu'.[1] In their attitude to wider questions of public concern, officials like John Hare and the Tookes were perhaps more of the willow than the oak, and hence the permanence of tenure that they enjoyed and the continuity of policy that they were able to maintain in the Court. The successful government servant must inevitably have something of the facile talent of the vicar of Bray.

Another influence on official mentality was the strong family interest that existed in several of the branches of the Court's administration. The succession of Tookes as auditors, of Fleetwoods as receivers-general and Cookes as clerks of the liveries has been noted; moreover, the practice of granting offices to father and son in survivorship probably made for a system of unofficial apprenticeship and for continuity of practice. Lists surviving from the end of Elizabeth's and from Charles I's reigns also show that younger members of the Tooke family found employment as clerks in the auditors' office or elsewhere in the administration.[2] A further feature of this traditionalism is also noteworthy. Throughout the Court's history there was remarkably little migration or promotion from one office to another: John Hare was a minor attorney before becoming clerk of the wards, Kingsmill was attorney before obtaining the surveyorship, Naunton surveyor and later master—but these are the sole exceptions noted to the general rule. The picture left in one's mind is of a fairly highly departmentalized organization.

The services rendered to the crown by the principal officers of the Court were of great financial value, and their own emoluments were proportionately high, far exceeding the fees and diet which appear regularly in each receiver-general's account.[3] In themselves these would be quite inadequate remuneration for the men of real distinction who filled some of the offices, due allowance being made

---

[1] Naunton, *Fragmenta Regalia* (Arber's English Reprints), p. 25.
[2] P.R.O. in Wards 10/16, list of officials of Court; B.M. Egerton MS. 2978, f. 79.   [3] See also, for a list of fees, c. 1574-8, Bod. MS. Rawl. A. 297.

34 COURT OF WARDS AND LIVERIES [CHAP. II

for the contemporary value of money. Thus Burghley and Cottington alike received only 233 *l. 6s. 8d.* at the time when they held
the mastership;[1] Ralph and Henry Bossevile and Richard Chamberlain had fees for the clerkship of wards of only 20 *l.*[2] There was, it
is true, a steady increase in the receiver-general's fee. Sir William
Dansell in the reign of Edward VI had 100 *l.* fee and 50 *l.* diet
yearly,[3] a sum afterwards increased by 43 *l. 6s.* 8d.,[4] later increased
to 210 *l.*[5] and in 1609-10 again increased 'in respect of keeping
more servants for the safetie of his Ma^{ts} Treasure and Bonds and
attendance given in terms and vacations',[6] so that in 1638 Sir
Miles Fleetwood received 276 *l.* 13*s.* 4*d.*[7] Nevertheless, in themselves the fees mentioned in the accounts are relatively small and
in no way represent the real value of the positions.

That value is of its nature impossible to assess with any precision,
but it almost certainly stood high, especially for the master of the
Court. First and foremost he stood to gain from those seeking
appointment to positions in the administration. A note amongst
the Latimer papers of 1598 makes it clear that the gift of feodaryships and of the positions of minor attorney were officially in his
hand;[8] but unofficially he must have had the predominant influence
in the appointment to even the statutory offices, and men were
willing to pay considerable sums for these.[9] Then again, the master
was well placed to secure grants of wardship. Burghley's contemporary biographer claimed that he only retained three wards
for himself during the whole period of his mastership,[10] and that is
borne out by the entry books of sales of wards amongst the Court's
records. On the other hand, Mr J. Hurstfield has pointed out that
certain important wardships of noblemen left minors at this time
are nowhere entered as having been granted, and he suspects
Burghley of having had effective enjoyment of these.[11] However this
may be, Mr Hurstfield has certainly put his finger on another
source of profit enjoyed by Burghley. The *Compleat Statesman*, as
Burghley's life was called, maintained that, granting sixty to eighty
wards a year, Burghley 'never tooke benefitt, but of two, or three,

---

[1] P.R.O. Wards 9/380, f. 55; Wards 9/430, f. 96.   [2] *Ibid.*
[3] H.M.C., *Salisbury*, vol. I, p. 136.   [4] *Ibid.*   [5] *Ibid.*
[6] P.R.O. Wards 9/430, f. 96.   [7] *Ibid.*
[8] P.R.O. Wards 14/3/20, papers of Edward Latimer.
[9] See below, p. 38.   [10] Peck, vol. I, p. 21.
[11] J. Hurstfield, 'Lord Burghley as Master of the Court of Wards, 1561-98' in
T.R.H.S., 4th Series, vol. XXXI, pp. 103-4.

CHAP. II] THE OFFICERS OF THE COURT 35

or perhaps foure in a yere, (or very few more).'[1] But Mr Hurstfield has proved beyond all reasonable doubt that, in the last three years of his life, Burghley received 3,000 *l.* from private suitors for wardships, who paid a mere 906 *l.* as the official prices for them.[2] The possibilities that this opens up are enormous. If Burghley, essentially a moderate man, was making profits on this scale, what are we to expect of the Stuart masters? One of them, Viscount Wallingford, had an official grant for a time of 2,000 *l.* a year from the Court's revenues or the choice of the best ward, except noblemen, falling in any year;[3] even when he surrendered the patent by which he enjoyed this advantage, he received *in lieu* of it a pension of 2,000 *marks.*[4] But this sort of privilege aside, it is the unofficial and unrecorded rake-off about which it would be so interesting to know.

Lower down the hierarchy, the other officers also used their positions to obtain grants of wardships. In Elizabeth's reign, for instance, three members of the Tooke family—William, Walter and William junior—had between them no less than twenty-eight; Keilwey, the surveyor, had five; his successor, Seckford, four; William Fleetwood, the receiver-general, four; and Marmaduke Servant, the usher, three; even Richard Chamberlain, at that time a very junior official, secured one.[5] Later officers, especially Hugh Audley, were perhaps less easily satisfied. It was said that as often as he put off his hat to the master of the Court, he gained a young heir,[6] and his own estimate of the value of his office is significant— 'It might', he said, 'be worth some thousands of pounds to him who would go, after his death, instantly to heaven; twice as much to him who would go to purgatory; and nobody knows what to him who would adventure to go to hell.'[7] Again, the officers might secure especial privileges in connection with wards committed to them: certainly Rogers, the usher, seems to have done so when, by his influence with Wallingford, as a petitioner asserted, he obtained leave to cut his ward's woods to the value of 1,400 *l.*—it is true that the wood sale was made to raise money to purchase adjoining lands, but no security was taken that the proceeds would be so applied, and Rogers took them to his own use.[8]

---

[1] Peck, vol. I, p. 21.　　　　　　　　　　[2] Hurstfield, *op. cit.*, p. 108.
[3] *C.S.P. Dom. 1611-18*, p. 405.　　　　[4] *C.S.P. Dom. 1619-23*, p. 159.
[5] Calculated from P.R.O. Wards 9/150, B, list of bargains.
[6] *The Way to be Rich, According to the Practice of the Great Audley*, 1662, p. 14.
[7] *Ibid.* p. 12.　　　　　　　　　　[8] H.M.C., *Report*, vol. IV, p. 124.

36   COURT OF WARDS AND LIVERIES   [CHAP. II

Perhaps the greatest part of the value of positions in the Court, however, lay in the fees taken from the subject at every stage in the suing out of a livery and the securing of a wardship, and indeed at every point in the manifold business of the Court. An order early in James I's reign had sought to limit these;[1] but when, towards the end of the reign, commissioners were appointed to inquire into the oppressive fees exacted by the courts as a whole, precise details for the Court of Wards leave no doubt as to how extensive the fees had become.[2] The fees charged were often twofold—a payment to an under-clerk for drafting or engrossing an instrument, and a further payment, often greater, to one or other of the statutory officers for giving it his official sanction. The clerk of the wards took very heavy toll, his fees being set out under no less than forty-eight separate heads; the two auditors also did well, since much of both sides of the Court's business, livery and wardship, passed through their hands and each of them was entitled to take 2s. for signing the copy of any record other than offices.[3] The charges for a special livery were particularly high, being, according to Coke, 'no benefit to the King, but to fill the purses of Clerks and Officers'.[4] It was one of the charges proved against Cranfield that he had duplicated one of these fees for livery, taken before his time by the surveyor only.[5] Another charge was that he had permitted his secretary to take fees for forwarding suits; and though he was not found guilty on this count, the accusation is given point by a sentence used by Thomas Powell, writing at this time. The petitioner for a lunatic, he urged, should see that the master's secretary registered his application for the grant—'And withall it will not be amisse, that you use means to make the said Secretary mindfull of you in your absence'.[6] The truth is that the system on which wardship and livery were administered left some room for bribery of officials beyond their recognized fees, although from 1610 the petitioner for a wardship had to swear that he had given no bribe to obtain his grant.[7]

---

[1] P.R.O. Wards 14/3/20, orders of 11 May 1 Jas. I.
[2] Bod. MS. Tanner 287, ff. 11-26; printed below, Appendix III.
[3] See also B.M. Egerton MS. 2978, f. 78 etc., certificate of fees of auditors and clerks of the Court, temp. Charles I.
[4] *Fourth Part of the Institutes*, edn. of 1669, p. 199.
[5] *State Trials*, vol. II, col. 1248.
[6] Powell, p. 210.
[7] P.R.O. in Wards 10/72 & 73, several examples amongst miscellaneous documents.

CHAP. II]   THE OFFICERS OF THE COURT   37

Despite their many opportunities for lawful perquisites, the officers of the Court, indeed, sometimes behaved dishonestly. There are on record several cases of proved peculation and a greater number of allegations (difficult to prove, or disprove, at this distance of time) of corrupt practice. So far as actual embezzlement goes, the receiver-general, since he was the officer who actually handled moneys received, was most likely to be guilty. Early in the Court's history, John Beaumont, Edward VI's receiver-general, concealed in his arrearages various sums totalling, in money and bonds, more than 21,000 *l*.[1] A later receiver-general, George Goring, did much the same, and on his death in 1594 these moneys could only be recovered by sale of his lands and goods.[2] This difficulty over Goring led to a tightening up of the system. On 6 June 1594 the queen wrote to the new receiver-general, William Fleetwood, arranging for the regular payment of the Court's income into the Exchequer at Easter and Michaelmas, and on the same date Burghley was instructed to make terminal, or more frequent, views of money in the receiver-general's hands.[3] Even this royal intervention did not prove very effective, for William Fleetwood himself was later in debt to the queen on four successive years of his account,[4] and was sequestered of his office in 1609.[5] Miles Fleetwood, too, seems to have been accused by the auditor and the clerk remembrancer of retaining moneys.[6] There were also possibilities of corruption, though of a less spectacular kind, on the legal side of the Court's administration. The attorney, Hesketh, for instance was alleged by Lord Sheffield in 1601 to be very partial—'a thing, God knows, too ordinary in this time';[7] and Pye and Chamberlain, attorney and clerk, were accused by a defendant of all sorts of improper actions on the plaintiff's behalf.[8] But these and other similar allegations it would be hard to follow up. We should not make the mistake of expecting from the sixteenth and seventeenth centuries, the public morality of our own day; but, when all is said, the opportunity for sharp practice was great, and there were certainly some who took it.

[1] F. C. Dietz, *Finances of Edward VI and Mary*, p. 80.
[2] H.M.C., *Salisbury*, vol. IV, p. 528.
[3] P.R.O. Wards 14/3/20, papers of Edward Latimer.
[4] Coke, *Reports*, vol. IV, pp. 479-80; Ley, *Reports*, p. 50.
[5] P.R.O. Wards 9/405, f. 412.   [6] Sackville MS. 454.
[7] H.M.C., *Salisbury*, vol. XI, p. 242.
[8] *C.S.P. Dom., Addenda, 1625-49*, p. 496.

38   COURT OF WARDS AND LIVERIES   [CHAP. II

Some indication of the value of positions in the Court is provided by the sums which men offered to secure them. On Goring's death, Walter Hickman attempted to secure his office for a brother, William Hickman; he wrote to Burghley in support of William's candidature, 'you shall have 1,000 *l*. and my Lady Dixie, my brother's wife, will with many thanks send unto my good lady your wife 100 *l*. to buy her four coach horses'.[1] Rather later it was alleged that Audley paid 3,000 *l*. for his office,[2] and Buckingham, though he denied it, was said to have sold the mastership to Cranfield for 6,000 *l*.[3] Values must have risen sharply in the subsequent period, for Hanchett claimed that he paid 4,000 *l*. for the comparatively insignificant position of usher,[4] and that office was said to be worth 450 *l*. a year in the last days of the Court's existence.[5] The rating of officers for loans also provides evidence as to their wealth,[6] and pensions give a final pointer. Elizabeth Fleetwood, for instance, received an annuity of 250 *l*. after her husband's death.[7] More important, in the proposed pension list after the dissolution of the Court 5,000 *l*. compensation was suggested for the late master, 4,000 *l*. for the receiver-general, 4,000 *l*. for the two auditors, 1,000 *l*. for the usher and 750 *l*. for the messenger.[8] Chamberlain claimed to have been allowed 1,500 *l*., though this sum had not been paid to him;[9] Audley said that 'his ordinary losses were as the shavings of his beard, which only grew the faster by them: but the loss of this place was like the cutting off of a member, which was irrecoverable'.[10]

In the localities the significant feature is the development of the feodary as the executive officer of the Court in each county. The feodaries were appointed by patent on the master's choice. They were required to find sureties for good behaviour: an example of sureties in a surviving formulary book, for instance, shows Philip Glacocke junior, the feodary elect of Essex, producing as his

---

[1] H.M.C., *Salisbury*, vol. IV, p. 531.   [2] *The Way to be Rich*, p. 12.
[3] B. Whitelock, *Memorials of the English Affairs*, edn. of 1853, vol. I, pp. 15, 18.
[4] H.M.C., *Report*, vol. XIII, App. 1, p. 512.
[5] H.M.C., *Report*, vol. VI, p. 218.
[6] P.R.O. S.P. 12/224, no. 90, names of principal officers of Exchequer and Court of Wards, 1589; S.P.16/52, no. 61, list of officers of Chancery, Common Pleas, Exchequer and Court of Wards, 1627.
[7] H.M.C., *Report*, vol. I, p. 34.   [8] *H.C.J.*, 16 April 1662.
[9] P.R.O. S.P. 29/20, no. 6, petition of Richard Chamberlain, 1660.
[10] *The Way to be Rich*, p. 16.

CHAP. II]   THE OFFICERS OF THE COURT   39

sponsors a member of Lincoln's Inn, a kinsman in the county concerned, and another in Lombard Street.[1] Once he was vouched for in this way, the feodary's letters patent of appointment could then be issued. There are in existence two entry books of such appointments, covering the period 1597-1645,[2] and also, for 1619, an odd file of the master's orders to make patents for feodaryships.[3] After an order of the Court of 1599 had set on foot an inquiry as to which feodaries had taken the oath and which had not,[4] subsequent orders of 1600 and 1603 provided *inter alia* that, even after appointment, no feodary should act until he had taken an oath before the master, and the oath had been recorded in court and on the back of his patent.[5] An example of the bond that the feodary had to make for good service has also survived.[6] On occasion there was interference by the crown in favour of a particular candidate, as in 1599 when Sir John Stanhope wrote in support of the appointment of a certain Humfrey Weare as feodary of Devonshire, ordering the clerk of the wards to 'make staye of the proceedinge of any other for the obtayninge of that office untill you shall heere further of her Maties pleasure in that behalfe'.[7]

In some cases, the characteristic sixteenth-century device of doing duty by deputy was adopted—Walter Tooke, for instance, since his duties of auditor kept him in London, appointed Thomas Newre to act in his place as feodary of Hertfordshire;[8] but this practice was to some extent checked by the order of 1600, forbidding deputies to exercise the office unless specifically allowed by the Court to do so, and their appointment placed on record.[9] It seems to have been the practice for such authorizations of service by deputy to be made over the signature of the attorney of the Court,[10] but it is interesting that less feodaries than escheators seem to have had deputies.[11]

Feodaries' patents of appointment became void by the death of either the grantee or the king who had made the grant, or they

---

[1] P.R.O. in Wards 10/27, formulary book.   [2] P.R.O. Wards 9/275 & 276.
[3] P.R.O. in Wards 10/35, file of orders to make patents.
[4] P.R.O. Wards 14/6/11, orders of 28 June 1599.
[5] P.R.O. Wards 14/6/11, orders of Hil. 42 Eliz.; Wards 14/3/20, orders of 11 May 1 Jas. I.
[6] P.R.O. in Wards 10/27, formulary book.
[7] P.R.O. in Wards 10/8, letter from Stanhope to clerk of wards.
[8] P.R.O. in Wards 10/35, draft appointment of Thomas Newre, 32 Eliz.
[9] P.R.O. Wards 14/6/11, orders of Hil. 42 Eliz.
[10] P.R.O. Wards 9/275 & 276, back of volumes.   [11] *Ibid.*

40 COURT OF WARDS AND LIVERIES [CHAP. II

could be voided by surrender. Also feodaries were removable at the discretion of the Court for neglect of duties, opposition to the king's title or because, in the contemporary phrase, they had become 'desperate and insoluant'.[1] In James I's reign allegations were heard in Court against Chomley the feodary of Lincoln, and, despite the fact that they do not appear to have been proved, the master clearly had his suspicions and Chomley lost his office.[2] At this time, too, the feodary of Warwick, Humphrey Colles, having got indebted to the crown, was dismissed.[3] Again, there is in existence a letter from Naunton to Audley, instructing him to draw up an order for the sequestration of the feodary of Leicestershire.[4]

The duties of the feodary were various and, as time went on, increasing. Primarily his concern was with the descent of property held of the crown in chief. He had to be present at the taking of every inquisition post mortem, to see that reasonable values were found and, generally, in Coke's phrase 'to doe his uttermost indeavour to manifest the truth concerning the King's Tenures';[5] for this purpose he was to be given adequate notice—one order says twenty days,[6] another fifteen[7]—of the day and place of each inquisition. Other important duties followed, if the inquisition found the heir to be a minor and the wardship to belong to the crown. The feodary had then, within thirty days, to make a survey of the state of the ward, in stock, leases, ready money or otherwise;[8] he had also to survey the lands and certify their value, this function becoming particularly vital from the last years of Elizabeth's reign onwards, with the effort to secure higher values than those found in the inquisitions. In 1600 feodaries were ordered not to state land values at any lower point than the best value in the queen's reign,[9] and six years later than the best value since the foundation of the Court.[10] The feodary's survey became, much more than the inquisition, the basis for fixing the fine for the sale of wardship, and yet for this responsible work he was to take no fee.[11]

---

[1] P.R.O. in Wards 10/27, formulary book.
[2] C.U. MS. Dd. 13. 28, ff. 15, 18.   [3] P.R.O. Wards 9/88, f. 487.
[4] P.R.O. in Wards 10/38, letter from Naunton to Audley, 1631.
[5] *Fourth Part of the Institutes*, edn. of 1669, p. 202.
[6] P.R.O. Wards 14/6/11, orders of Hil. 42 Eliz.
[7] P.R.O. Wards 14/3/20, orders of 11 May 1 Jas. I.
[8] P.R.O. Wards 14/6/11, orders of Hil. 42 Eliz.   [9] *Ibid.*
[10] *Ibid.* orders of Hil. 1606.
[11] P.R.O. Wards 14/3/20, orders of 11 May 1 Jas. I.

CHAP. II]　　THE OFFICERS OF THE COURT　　41

The feodary had a host of other duties. He had to certify vacancies in livings where the advowson belonged to a ward in his county, to notify the Court when any estate in, or annuity from, a ward's lands ceased; he had to cause manor courts to be kept, and to assist the sheriff in the serving of process for debt.[1] Above all, before February each year he had to complete his account up to the Michaelmas previous;[2] from the beginning of Elizabeth's reign good series of his accounts survive.[3]

How much labour was involved in the execution of this work it is not easy to determine. In the course of two years (1638-40) the feodary of Oxfordshire attended twenty-six inquisitions and made thirteen surveys;[4] in connexion with both there were no doubt many days' labour as well as riding over the county. It must also be borne in mind that the office involved regular visits to London. The *Instructions* of 1622 stated that the feodary was to attend the clerk of the Court or the master's secretary at the end of every term.[5] Ralph Wilbraham, the feodary of Chester and Flint since the beginning of James I's reign, surrendered his patent because his age made it difficult for him to give attendance in London, and it was decreed that a new patent should be issued to his kinsman, Henry Dewes, 'one that is here Termelie at London'.[6]

To one side of the feodary's activities it is necessary to return. The most interesting feature of the new official is his gradual tendency to supplant the escheator in the whole business consequent on the death of a tenant in chief. From his first emergence in the thirteenth century, the escheator had dealt with such matters in the localities; and as late as 1589 detailed rules were drawn up in the Exchequer for his accounting, and other, functions.[7] Bacon, writing probably in the first decade of the seventeenth century, still stressed the escheator's importance and gave a description of his duties in traditional terms—

Every shire hath an officer called an escheator, which is an office to attend the king's revenue, and to seize into his majesty's hands all lands escheated, and goods or lands forfeited, and therefore is called escheator; and he is to inquire by good inquest of the death of the king's tenant,

---

[1] P.R.O. Wards 14/6/11, orders of Hil. 1606.　[2] *Ibid.* orders of Hil. 42 Eliz.
[3] They are listed in P.R.O. *Wards Guide*, p. 9.
[4] P.R.O. in Wards 10/66, inquisitions found in co. Oxford.
[5] *Foedera*, vol. XVII, p. 401.　　　　　[6] P.R.O. in Wards 10/23.
[7] P.R.O. E.368/457, L.T.R. Memoranda Roll, Mich. 31 Eliz., *communia*, m. 66.

D

42   COURT OF WARDS AND LIVERIES   [CHAP. II

and to whom the lands are descended, and to seize their bodies and lands for ward if they be within age, and is accountable for the same; he is named by the lord treasurer of England.[1]

From this period, too, there date lists, found amongst the Sackville papers, of persons certified by the justices of assize as fit to be escheators.[2] Yet by the time Bacon's account was written the escheator's powers were dwindling, and it is his last sentence that gives the key to the older official's decline. Appointed by the Exchequer, the escheator was never *persona grata* to the Court of Wards. The title of a rough memorandum of the year 1607 strikes the right note of antithesis—'Feodaries of the Court of Wardes and Liveries against th' Escheators of th' Exchequer'.[3] Appointed annually, the escheator had no chance against the feodary who was a permanent official; and by 1645 the office of escheator had quite declined from its former importance.

This decline is especially clear in the escheator's loss of control over the taking of inquisitions post mortem. It has already been seen that the escheator was forced to give notice to the feodary of any inquisition post mortem that he intended to take, and the latter's right to inform the Court of any default in this connexion placed him in a position of superiority over his colleague.[4] Moreover, in the sixteenth century there was a growing habit of taking some inquisitions, at least, not before the escheator alone but before commissioners appointed *ad hoc*. In 1589 the Exchequer endeavoured to secure that the escheator should at least be a member of the quorum of such commissions, both 'for the encouragement of gentlemen of credit to undertake the office of Escheator' and 'because two officers are likely to deal more uprightly than one'.[5] But the Court of Wards by no means always followed this practice. Perhaps this was primarily due to the escheator's slackness, as in a case reported where he had delayed to find an inquisition upon a writ of *mandamus*, and a commission of *supersedeas*, omitting him, had therefore been awarded;[6] but the use of commissions seems to have been the considered policy of the Court. As a critic in 1617 put it, 'the Court endevors utterlie to exterpate that office, & confer

[1] Bacon, vol. VII, p. 780.
[2] H.M.C., *Sackville*, vol. I, pp. 319-23.
[3] B.M. Lansdowne MS. 166, f. 247.
[4] P.R.O. Wards 14/6/11, orders of Hil. 42 Eliz.
[5] P.R.O. E. 368/457, L.T.R. Memoranda Roll, Mich. 31 Eliz., *communia*, m. 66.   [6] C.U. MS. Dd. 13. 28, f. 9.

CHAP. II] THE OFFICERS OF THE COURT 43

all the business to be done in the Cuntrie to the trust of one man, which is the feodarie'.[1] The new official was encouraged at every turn. He is said frequently to have nominated the commissioners, endeavouring when he did so to leave out the escheator.[2] Certificates of subsequent feodaries leave no doubt as to the superiority of their position—in 1635 Edward Wenyeve, the feodary of Suffolk, reporting on an inquisition taken after the death of a certain John Auger, said, 'But I conceiving such theire verdict to be contrary to trewth and the evidence given, and it being within the yeere, did there uppon cause the Escheator to forbeare to take a verdict, and to adiorne the Jury.'[3] The subordination of the escheator to the feodary is also suggested by the bitter, and rather cryptic, remark of a speaker in the debate of 1614—'A Clerk's Clerk's Clerk Escheator; and hath attended, and pulled off the Feodary's Boots.'[4]

The question naturally arises as to what type of men became feodaries, and from what grade of society they were recruited. The orders of 1600 and 1603 place a ban on the employment of retainers or household servants as feodaries,[5] and the fact that it was necessary to introduce a provision of this sort rather suggests that some feodaries, at least, were of a lower social class than had been the escheators. Much evidence for this is, however, lacking,[6] and the typical feodary met with is described as either esquire or gentleman. One such, Humphrey Colles, feodary of Warwickshire, has been charmingly described in a recent paper: a local gentleman of antiquarian tastes—and how well placed, with his feodary books, he was to gratify them!—he helped Simon Archer and Dugdale in their researches.[7] To some extent the office was no doubt held by younger sons, and remoter connexions, of persons of influence; in 1570, for instance, Sir Thomas Gresham wrote to Burghley soliciting the feodaryship of Somerset for John Coles who married his niece.[8] There are cases, too, of young men probably serving an apprenticeship as feodaries in the hope of obtaining positions in the central administration. But the problem of the feodary is one that can only be settled on the basis of local studies.

---

[1] B.M. Hargrave MS. 358, f. 7.   [2] *Ibid.* f. 4.
[3] P.R.O. in Wards 10/38, certificate of Edward Wenyeve.
[4] *H.C.J.*, 14 May 1614.   [5] P.R.O. Wards 14/6/11 and Wards 14/3/20.
[6] See however an extract from Goodman, Bishop of Gloucester, printed by C. Hill and E. Dell, *The Good Old Cause*, p. 122.
[7] Philip Styles, *Sir Simon Archer*, Dugdale Soc. Occasional Papers, no. 6, p. 24. But for Colles see also above, p. 40.   [8] *C.S.P. Dom. 1547-80*, p. 394.

44 COURT OF WARDS AND LIVERIES [CHAP. II

The feodaries were paid a retaining fee of 40s. yearly, together with 20s. portage money on every 100 l. of revenue that they brought into Court;[1] they also submitted each year petitions for the allowance of charges and expenses incurred in the course of their duties.[2] This would seem to have left them to a great extent dependent on fees taken from the subject, and this inevitably led to some unpopularity. In 1614 a member of the House of Commons moved that they be tied to certain fees, instancing a case where a feodary had taken 20 l. 'of a mean man';[3] at another time Chomley, the feodary of Lincoln, took 10 l. to execute a writ of *diem clausit extremum*.[4] Remuneration by perquisites was, as ever, open to objection; but it is natural to feel a certain amount of sympathy with the feodaries. John Goodhand, the feodary of the West Riding of Yorkshire, accused in Star Chamber of various extortions, admitted that, having only 40s. from the king, he had accepted extra, voluntary fees, and asserted that this practice was allowed by the Court.[5] A few years previous, another feodary had been condemned in Star Chamber for exceeding the ordinary fees, and in 1634 the feodaries petitioned the king that they were now liable to action, taken by those whom they had offended when about their duties. The opinion of the attorney-general was sought, and he recommended that the subject should allow the feodary 40s. for every inquisition taken, whether the finding was for or against the king—'Where of late some of them haue required to haue there victuall and horsemeat paid for, I doe not thinke fitt it shold be allowed them saue onely for there dinners for otherwise they will growe burdensome with there many attendants.'[6] Subsequently individual feodaries thought it wise to seek for pardon of offences committed in their official capacity, and even some escheators followed their example.[7] An indication of the value of various feodaryships in the Court's final days is given by the sums that

---

[1] Bod. MS. Rawl. A. 297, f. 30.

[2] Various petitions for allowances in different bundles of P.R.O. Wards 10; the petitions were originally filed as vouchers to the receiver-general's account.

[3] *H.C.J.*, 14 May 1614.

[4] C.U. MS. Dd. 13. 28, f. 15.

[5] *C.S.P. Dom. 1635-6*, pp. 212-13.

[6] B.M. Add. MS. 26729, f. 245.

[7] Feodary of Salop and Montgomery, *C.S.P. Dom. 1638-9*, p. 75; feodary of Surrey, *C.S.P. Dom. 1637*, pp. 193, 378; feodary of Lincoln, *C.S.P. Dom. 1637-8*, p. 144; escheators of Surrey and Sussex, *C.S.P. Dom. 1637*, p. 378.

CHAP. II] THE OFFICERS OF THE COURT 45

were proposed as compensation after its dissolution, although in fact the proposal was rejected by Parliament.[1]

Of the local and particular receivers, who form the lowest rung in the administrative ladder, little need be said. Appointed by the master, and accounting to the feodary of the county where the lands for which they were responsible were situated, they probably differed little from the ordinary manorial and estate bailiffs and collectors of the period.[2]

The whole organization of wardship and livery provides a detailed picture of sixteenth and seventeenth century administrative methods, not the least interesting feature of which is the hierarchy of officials by whom the machinery was worked. With them tradition counted for much. The law on which their system was based was medieval, and on to that they had built their own stereotyped procedures, so that they no doubt thought it a recommendation when a new master could claim, like Sir Walter Cope, that he had 'lived under the shadowe of this Courte almost 40 yeares'.[3] Yet they were not altogether prisoners of their system. There were independent and energetic personalities among them, who, as such men must, played their part in shaping the institution in the service of which they spent their lives.

[1] *H.C.J.*, 21 Dec. 1660. The table of values is as follows:—Somerset 150 *l*; Devon 200 *l*.; London, Middlesex and Pembroke 400 *l*.; Gloucester 150 *l*.; Cornwall 100 *l*.; Shropshire and Montgomery 60 *l*.; Sussex 150 *l*.; Surrey 100 *l*.; Radnor, Brecon and Glamorgan 50 *l*.; Stafford 70 *l*.; Essex 200 *l*.; Berks 50 *l*.; Kent 200 *l*.; Norfolk 150 *l*.; Derby 50 *l*.; Monmouth 50 *l*.; Nottingham 50 *l*.; Oxford 100 *l*.

[2] Their accounts are listed in P.R.O. *Wards Guide*, p. 2.

[3] P.R.O. S.P. 14/69, no. 68. *C.S.P. Dom. 1611-18*, p. 135, assigns both this paper and P.R.O. S.P. 14/69, no. 69, to Sir George Carew; but, as Mr C. A. F. Meekings has pointed out to me, the two are quite dissimilar, and I prefer his suggested attribution of the former to Cope.

CHAPTER III

THE REVENUES OF THE COURT

THE Court of Wards and Liveries was primarily a financial court, and perhaps its main historical significance lies in the part that it was able to play in counteracting, to some extent, the financial embarrassment of the monarchy, consequent upon the price rise and other factors. The statute founding the Court provided that its revenues should be paid yearly to the treasurer of the King's Chamber,[1] but in fact there developed a system of direct allocations to those departments of the royal administration that required money, the bills and warrants on which such payments were made being preserved as vouchers of the receiver-general's accounts.[2] These allocations were in part constant, in part variable. From 1563 there was a statutory assignation of 10,000 *l.* yearly to the cofferer of the royal Household,[3] and for many years the Wardrobe, too, received a regular sum of 2,000 *l.* Early in Elizabeth's reign heavy payments were made for Ireland, Berwick and the Works;[4] the use that the queen made of the Court is well illustrated by an order for payment, directed to it in 1602, when the government required money for the Spanish war and for Ireland—'As usual', wrote Elizabeth, 'we wish to meet such accidents by supplying the Exchequer from the Court of Wards or Duchy of Lancaster.'[5] In the meantime, too, the defalcations of the receiver-general, Goring, had resulted in his successor being ordered to pay into the Exchequer each Easter and Michaelmas whatever had not been allocated, and paid, elsewhere; about this *remaine*, as it was called, there was a good deal of correspondence (some of it rather acrimonious) in the years 1594-8.[6]

Under the Stuarts, pensions and gifts from the Court's revenues were a serious drain. In 1611, for instance, John Viscount Haddington and his wife obtained an annuity of 1,000 *l.*;[7] six years

---

[1] 32 Henry VIII c. 46 (xxiii).
[2] P.R.O. in Wards 10/4, 5, 7, 8, 16-19, 21, 25-9, 31-4, 36-47, 53, 61-4, 67, 76-9, 84—files of vouchers of r.g.a.; but many of these are incomplete.
[3] 5 Eliz. c. 32.   [4] F. C. Dietz, *English Public Finance 1558-1641*, pp. 303-4.
[5] *C.S.P. Dom. 1601-3*, p. 247.
[6] P.R.O. Wards 14/3/20, papers of Edward Latimer.
[7] *C.S.P. Dom. 1611-18*, p. 57, where for 'Thos.' read 'the'.

CHAP. III] THE REVENUES OF THE COURT 47

later the Earl of Montgomery had a gift of 4,000 *l.*;[1] in 1624 Buckingham was assigned a pension of 1,000 *l.*,[2] Sir Edward Villiers one of 500 *l.*,[3] Sir Thomas Edmondes one of 750 *l.*[4] The year following, the dowager Duchess of Lenox obtained an annuity of 2,100 *l.* for her life and the life of her two sons, as well as two cash payments of 3,350 *l.*[5] and 1,000 *l.*[6] Another heavy annuity was that of the Earl of Bristol, who got 2,000 *l.*[7] From time to time there seem to have been spasmodic efforts to put the brake on, and the payment of pensions was, for a few months at least, suspended.[8] But no permanent improvement was made. The commissioners for retrenchment found that in a single year 27,051 *l.* had been expended in this way,[9] and in a period of just over two months in the spring of 1638, while moneys received by the Court totalled 9,779 *l.*, a sum of 1,288 *l.* was paid out in pensions.[10]

In answer to these demands the revenues from wardship and livery rose enormously, though by no means consistently, through the hundred years of the Court's existence. It is possible to trace in detail the developing revenues of the Court in the receiver-general's accounts. A general view of these[11] suggests that, so far as its productivity was concerned, the Court went through three phases. An initial period of steady and rapid development was followed, through the greater part of Elizabeth's reign and the opening years of James I's, by static and even declining revenue; only in the second decade of the new century did there begin that rise which, in the 'twenties and 'thirties, was to reach astronomical heights.

The increase during the first period is very much what might be expected. In 1542 the nett revenue stood at a mere 4,434 *l.*; but with the Court getting into its stride and livery fines as an added and developing source of income,[12] the first three years of Edward VI saw nett revenues of 7,613 *l.*, 6,600 *l.* and 9,125 *l.*, and by the beginning of Elizabeth's reign these figures had been

---

[1] *C.S.P. Dom. 1611-18*, p. 446. [2] *C.S.P. Dom. 1623-5*, p. 301.
[3] *Ibid.* p. 300. [4] *Ibid.* p. 314. [5] *Ibid.* p. 495.
[6] The second payment in 1628, *C.S.P. Dom. 1628-9*, p. 202.
[7] *C.S.P. Dom. 1631-3*, p. 90. [8] Sackville MS. 7610.
[9] H.M.C., *Cowper*, vol. I, p. 291. [10] *C.S.P. Dom. 1637-8*, p. 421.
[11] For a description of the receiver-general's accounts and abstracts of revenues in selected years see Appendix II. Tables in that appendix give references for such figures as are quoted below without a separate reference.
[12] The statute 33 Henry VIII c. 22 brought liveries within the purview of the Court, but in 34 Henry VIII fines for liveries only brought in 38 *l.*

48 COURT OF WARDS AND LIVERIES [CHAP. III

multiplied threefold to 20,290 *l.* in 1559, 23,286 *l.* in 1560, and 29,551 *l.* in 1561.

What at first sight is so extraordinary is the succeeding phase and the Court's failure under Burghley, and to some extent under his son too, to achieve high revenues. So far as Burghley is concerned, Mr Hurstfield has addressed himself to this problem and struck a nice balance between the effect of corrupt practices on the one hand and statesmanlike moderation on the other in keeping down the Court's receipts.[1] Whatever the cause, the estimate that William Fleetwood's clerk, Edward Latimer, made for Essex in 1598—'the Revenue . . . hath been of late yeeres . . . 1600 *li.*'[2]—is higher than the level shown in the accounts immediately prior to Burghley's death. The period of nine months without a master that followed, and above all the rumour that the Court was to be put down and the resultant effort to conceal wardships until such time as it was, no doubt accounted for the persistence of low revenues into the new reign.[3] It is difficult to believe that Robert Cecil, any more than his father, was conducting an all-out drive for higher income. Even as late as 1607 the nett revenue had only advanced to 17,810 *l.*; the year following it was 17,319 *l.* There is evidence that from the start of the reign Salisbury was looking favourably on the possibility of abolishing wardship in exchange for a fixed annual payment to the crown; certainly in the negotiations for the great contract he played the part of honest broker.[4] Again, he showed in his policy some regard for the ward's welfare even at the expense of the Court's profits: it is significant, for instance, that Cope says he found the month's pre-emption allowed to the ward's friends a hindrance to increased revenue.[5]

Such would seem to be the background of the surprisingly low yield of these middle years of the Court's existence. Yet it would

[1] J. Hurstfield, 'Lord Burghley as Master of the Court of Wards, 1561-98', *T.R.H.S.*, 4th Series, vol. XXXI.

[2] P.R.O. Wards 14/3/20, papers of Edward Latimer; another copy of the memorandum in Wards 10/10.

[3] P.R.O. S.P. 14/52, no. 88—Observations on an intended petition 'In this last yere, since his Majestie came to the Crowne from the 18th of March before the late Majesty's death, untill the 18th of March last there hath not half soe many graunts of wards passed the Master of the Wards hands, as did in the yere before, notwithstanding this great mortality; euery man, in hope that something wold be done in this matter (which hath bene held in expectacion ever since his Majestys coming to the crowne) having indevoured to ceale their tenures, or at least forborne to make suite for their wardships.'

[4] See below, p. 144.   [5] John Gutch, *Collectanea Curiosa*, 1781, vol. I, p. 127.

CHAP. III] THE REVENUES OF THE COURT 49

be unjust to Burghley and Salisbury, and still more so to John Hare, their clerk of wards, not to recognize that it was on the administrative improvements of their period of office that the possibility of the higher revenues of the Court's later days was based.

One interesting feature of the early years of the seventeenth century is the number of widely varying estimates of the value of wardship that were made at this time. In 1600 Thomas Wilson said that it was reckoned to bring the queen, in an average year, between 20,000 *l.* and 30,000 *l.*,[1] and in a paper drafted some three years later the higher of these two figures is quoted for the bare fines and rents from wardships and marriages, fines of liveries and dowers.[2] The debates of 1609-10 produced other estimates—Sir Julius Caesar asserted that wardships were worth 60,000 *l.*,[3] Hakewill suggested that the king received nearly 45,000 *l.* 'for wardships and the dependances thereupon',[4] and Salisbury put forward the more modest figure of 21,000 *l.*[5] The wide divergences between these figures were no doubt partly due to lack of information, and bad guessing, on the part of some of their authors; but partly too they arose from the different bases on which the calculations were made, the higher estimates probably including other feudal revenues, not administered by the Court. Then again, it may be that these were made with an eye on potentiality rather than actuality.

If so, the income of the Court in later years abundantly justified them. The second decade of the century saw the beginning of the last great rise of nett revenues. Despite Salisbury's diffidence about them, the *Instructions* of 1610 proved profitable. 'Then were articles invented', said Coke later on, 'that helped the king to all his revenues, and tied the officers to their own fees and places. The king's revenues prospered well then.'[6] Bacon's *Directions for the master of wards*, dating from the year following, are further evidence of the effort to expand revenue,[7] and later *Instructions* had the same end in view. By 1613-15 nett revenues were standing at about 23,000 *l.* to 25,000 *l.*; the figures for 1617-22 show yet further

[1] 'The State of England', *Camden Miscellany*, vol. XVI, p. 28.
[2] P.R.O. S.P. 14/52, no. 88, observations on an intended petition.
[3] *P.D. 1610*, p. 12.
[4] G. W. Prothero, *Statutes and Constitutional Documents 1558-1625*, p. 345.
[5] *P.D. 1610*, p. xx.   [6] *State Trials*, vol. II, col. 1192.
[7] Bacon, vol. XI, pp. 286-8.

50 COURT OF WARDS AND LIVERIES [CHAP. III

increase to 29,386 *l.*, 26,051 *l.*, 27,990 *l.*, 35,644 *l.* and 30,759 *l.*[1] And even this return was small in comparison with the enormously high figures of nett revenue in Charles I's reign. The king's financial needs and his difficulty with Parliament made it essential for the full potentiality of his feudal income to be realized. Regardless of consequences, the Court was committed to a policy of maximum productivity. Its nett revenues in the last four normal working years lay between 66,000 *l.* and 83,000 *l.* per annum.

Such was the trend of nett revenues. Behind the increased productivity that the figures reveal lay long-term policies of the Court, some of which had been in operation, with varying success, since the earliest days of Burghley's mastership and even before. Perhaps the most constant of these was the Court's effort to keep track of tenants in chief so that they could be made to fulfil their obligations to the crown.[2] An early example of this determination to let none of the crown's tenants escape was the appointment of commissioners, in 1556-7, to make a calendar of records in the Exchequer at Chester relating to lands held by knight service in the county palatine.[3] Subsequently, the policy that this implied was generalized, and the duty of maintaining the necessary body of information was imposed on the feodaries. In 1570 they were briefed for their inquiries with notes from the records of the Court,[4] and some thirty years later they were instructed to compile their own feodary books.[5] Yet their task was difficult enough, for they were concerned with a vast body of tenants, everyone indeed who held the tiniest scrap of land, or even a reversion, by knight service in chief. It was inevitable that some should conceal their tenures and slip through the feodaries' net, entering upon their lands without an inquisition post mortem.

From early in Elizabeth's reign, therefore, the Court endeavoured to combat concealments of this sort by the encouragement of private informers, whose aid was enlisted by a species of bribery closely comparable to that employed in the discovery of concealed

---

[1] Calculated from r.g.a. in P.R.O. Wards 9/413 and 414.

[2] 'The crown had increasing difficulty in keeping track of its tenants-in-chief, and by the time of the Tudors the situation was wellnigh hopeless', writes Professor Plucknett (*Legislation of Edward I*, 105). Nevertheless, the Court made a bold effort to cope with that situation.

[3] P.R.O. Wards 14/3/20, draft order, 6 Feb. 3 and 4 Philip and Mary.

[4] P.R.O. Wards 14/6/11, order of 14 April 12 Eliz.

[5] *Ibid.* orders of Hil. 42 Eliz.

CHAP. III] THE REVENUES OF THE COURT 51

lands.[1] Payments were sometimes made to such informers—in 1572, for instance, Thomas Wood had 70 *l.* for bringing to light a concealed livery,[2] and six years later Paul Raynsforde received a number of substantial sums.[3] More frequently, however, the informer's reward was, so to say, in kind. Just as the man who revealed lands held by defective title might hope to obtain the grant of them, so those who revealed concealed tenures might expect a share of the mean rates if the heir was of age or a grant of the wardship on easy terms if he was a minor. Latimer's memorandum of 1598 recommended that this should be turned into a regular procedure, with the moiety of the mean rates or grant of the wardship as the normal reward to the informer.[4] To some extent this was achieved during the reign of James I, when the checking of concealments became a constant preoccupation of the Court. Good treatment of informers was promised in the *Instructions* of 1610;[5] the anonymous author of the *Collections for the King's Majesties service, in point of his highnes Prerogative* returned to the same theme in 1617, demanding that prosecutors for concealments should be given good terms;[6] and the *Instructions* of 1618 left the master free to grant concealed mean rates or wardships to those who revealed them 'in such sort as others maie be incouraged to imploy themselves in the like Service'.[7] The practice was established of considering one year without suit as constituting concealment, where formerly three years had been allowed. This shortening of the time permitted was one of the charges brought against Cranfield;[8] but actually it dates from the *Instructions* of 1610, and in any case Cranfield's reply had its point—'within 3 years, the ward might die, and the king lose the wardship'.[9]

Apart from definitely illegal concealments of the kind just considered, there were other loopholes through which the tenant in chief might escape his obligations, and these too the Court set itself to close. For some time past it had been the practice to except the duty of suing out livery from the scope of general pardons; but in 1589, at the Court's suggestion, the proviso was extended so that payment of primer seisins and mean rates also came within the

[1] M. S. Giuseppi, *Guide to the Public Records*, vol. I, p. 147.
[2] P.R.O. Wards 9/380, f. 140.   [3] P.R.O. Wards 9/384, r.g.a. 20 Eliz.
[4] P.R.O. Wards 14/3/20, papers of Edward Latimer.
[5] P.R.O. S.P. 14/61, no. 6, instructions.
[6] B.M. Hargrave MS. 358, f. 6.   [7] *Foedera*, vol. XVII, p. 69.
[8] *State Trials*, vol. II, col. 1241.   [9] *Ibid.* col. 1242.

52 COURT OF WARDS AND LIVERIES [CHAP. III

exception,[1] and in the general pardon of 1624 the proviso was again widened so that it included almost all duties arising from livery and wardship.[2]

Again, collusive conveyances of one sort and another, by which tenants avoided livery and wardship, also presented a problem. To some extent this could be tackled by means of legislation,[3] but for the most part it had to be dealt with by the Court in its judicial capacity, hearing the legal arguments for and against in particular cases. Fraud and covin of this kind loomed large, indeed, amongst the cases that came before the Court. Burghley was said by his biographer to have punished fraudulent conveyances,[4] and from the period immediately after his death West prints a commission to inquire into one alleged to be such and the inquisition in which the allegation is proved.[5] Latimer's memorandum[6] and the *Instructions* of 1610[7] are alike in stressing the Court's duty to suppress this type of fraud. Actually, its most dangerous manifestations were the lease for a long period of years and the long-term trust. About a case on the former of these topics, a lease for a thousand years with covenant by the lessor to make further assurance in fee simple whenever required, a contemporary did not hesitate to say that on its upshot turned the whole making or marring of the Court.[8] The difficulty was that it was quite often impossible to prove actual illegality. In 1606 the master and council are found stating, rather pathetically, about the whole question of long leases, 'they know not how this Court can helpe it otherwise than as usually they doe'.[9] Bacon, too, though he disapproved of long leases of land in chief, made to defraud the crown, termed them an abuse of the law and not definitely against it.[10] In Cotton's case, it is true, the judges assistant of the Court took their courage in both hands and ruled that the minor heir of an assignee of a lease for years who had died in possession should be in ward;[11] but a subsequent direction of the

---

[1] 31 Eliz. c. 16; see also P.R.O. S.P. 12/222, no. 103, remembrance from the auditor, 1589. In Ley, *Reports*, 6-7, it appears that mean rates were excepted in the pardons of 27 and 29 Eliz.

[2] 21 Jas. I c. 35.   [3] 13 Eliz. c. 5; 27 Eliz. c. 4.   [4] Peck., vol. I, p. 20.

[5] West, *Second Part*, ff. 319-22.

[6] P.R.O. Wards 14/3/20, papers of Edward Latimer.

[7] P.R.O. S.P. 14/61, no. 6, instructions.   [8] H.M.C., *Salisbury*, vol. XI, p. 438.

[9] P.R.O. Wards 14/6/11, orders of 5 May 1606.

[10] Bacon, *Works*, edn. of 1824, vol. IV, p. 155.

[11] *English Reports*, vol. LXXVIII, Godbolt, p. 116 (the date of the case was 10 Jas. I).

CHAP. III]   THE REVENUES OF THE COURT   53

Court, no doubt made under pressure of opinion, laid it down that a similar finding was not to be made again.[1]

Nor was it only through concealed tenures and collusive conveyancing that the crown might be defrauded. These aside, the possibilities for fraud in the inquisition post mortem were considerable—a tenant might be said to hold by a base tenure implying no duties to the crown, when really he held by knight service in chief; an heir might be declared of age, when he was not; the death of the ancestor might be post-dated to lessen the mean rates due; lands held by the deceased might be omitted; above all, the property concerned might be undervalued. Against any, and all, of these eventualities the Court had to guard, and it did so by securing that its own officers, the feodaries, should be present at every inquisition, holding a watching brief for the crown.[2] Everything depended on the feodaries, and Burghley went to the root of the matter when he wrote 'giving them strait charge, to looke better to the quenes service, for the increasing of her revennue'.[3] Of course not everybody agreed with the Court's policy of building up the power of the feodaries at the expense of the escheators; still less with its liking for inquisitions taken before commissioners instead of before the escheator alone. Individual feodaries were not, on every occasion, beyond reproach,[4] and the *Collections* of 1617 suggest that the practice of taking inquisitions before commissioners may even have been a retrograde move; commissioners were often partial, and even if feodary and escheator were of their quorum might 'overcrowe and outcountenance' them both. The author of the *Collections* states that it was sometimes impossible to get a jury for an inquisition, when any great man was interested against the king—a misfortune that has an odd fifteenth-century flavour about it. He saw the strengthening of the escheator's office as the obvious remedy for a difficult situation.[5]

The Court, however, continued to place its trust in the feodaries, but over them exercised an ever closer control. The *Additions of Instructions* of 1617 forbade the finding of any inquisition against the crown during the first year after the tenant's death, and made it the feodary's duty to acquaint the Court at once of any case of

---

[1] Notestein, Relf and Simpson, *Commons Debates 1621*, vol. v, p. 43.
[2] See above, pp. 40, 42-3.   [3] Peck, vol. I, p. 20.
[4] E.g. feodary concealing wards, H.M.C., *Salisbury*, vol. XIII, p. 114.
[5] B.M. Hargrave MS. 358, ff. 4-7.

54 COURT OF WARDS AND LIVERIES [CHAP. III

the sort that might crop up.[1] That this order was observed is proved by a surviving certificate of the feodary of Suffolk on an inquisition, taken in 1635 after the death of John Auger, where the jury proved difficult—'But I', wrote Wenyeve, the feodary,

conceiveing such their verdict to be contrary to trewth and the Evidence given, and it being within the yeere, did there uppon cause the Escheator to forbeare to take a verdict, and to adiourne the Jury to the two and twentyeth day of May next for the giueing in of theire verdict, And in the meane tyme doe humbly pray the directions of this Honorable Court heerein.[2]

The case is interesting not merely in itself, but for the considerable degree of centralization that it implies. The constant effort to make the inquisition post mortem reveal the best for the crown was undoubtedly a cause of increasing revenues.

Nevertheless, despite all the Court could do, the inquisition post mortem remained in some ways an inadequate basis for the calculation of the real value of a tenant in chief's property. For this reason, therefore, there was developed a system of checking the inquisition by a subsequent survey, or certificate, executed by the feodary in whose county the lands lay. Feodaries' surveys, indeed, had always been made, and the earliest of them antedate the Court itself, going back to the fifth year of Henry VIII's reign, in which feodaries were first generally appointed for wards' business. But initially the surveys seem to have been simply part of the policy of building up a careful record relating to lands held of the crown— that is to say, they had a long-term value in keeping track of royal tenures rather than an immediate purpose of returning higher values than those found in the inquisitions. That this was their original use is proved pretty clearly by the Court thinking it worth while, in 1553, to spend 30 l. in having them engrossed and indexed in books which include even the very earliest surveys of Henry VIII's reign;[3] and, in fact, a similar system of entry seems to have been continued until nearly halfway through Burghley's mastership.[4] But in the feodary's survey lay a greater potentiality than a mere establishing of the record.

The realization of that potentiality, like so much else that the

---

[1] *Foedera*, vol. XVII, p. 61.
[2] P.R.O. in Wards 10/38, certificate of Edward Wenyeve.
[3] P.R.O. Wards 14/5/3, vouchers to r.g.a. 1553.
[4] P.R.O. Wards 9/129-40 and others listed in *Wards Guide*, p. 31.

CHAP. III]   THE REVENUES OF THE COURT   55

Court was later to turn to profit, seems to date from the latter years of Burghley's administration and the period immediately succeeding it, when falling income acted as a challenge to those whose duty it was to administer the crown's feudal revenues.[1] An obvious use to which the feodary's survey, at this time and subsequently, could be turned was where the deceased tenant in chief held lands in more than one county. The practice of including such lands in a single inquisition was opposed by the Court, since the jurors had not, except for their own county, the necessary local knowledge on which to base their findings. An order of 1599 therefore forbade that any wardship should pass under these circumstances until supplementary surveys by the feodaries concerned were available in court.[2] An indication of how these were made is given by an endorsement on the certificate of the feodary of Gloucester, dated 21 October 1631, concerning the lands of Robert Straunge—'I could not make my Certificate sooner', he wrote, 'because the office was found in Wiltes and I had no notice of it until the very beginning of the tearme—the lands lay xx^{ty} miles from me.'[3]

But the real significance of the feodaries' surveys as a cause of increased productivity lay in the higher values found in them than in the inquisitions post mortem. Repeated orders of the Court leave no manner of doubt as to what was considered the feodary's duty in this connection: in 1599-1600 he was instructed to certify lands at no lower values than appeared in Elizabeth's reign,[4] in 1606 at values not less than the best since the erection of the Court.[5] Actually, in the years that followed he went—no doubt under pressure—far beyond these instructions. There developed the distinction between the survey proper, made where the heir was of full age, and the certificate or estimate, made where he was a minor. It is in documents of the second category (sometimes entitled, significantly enough, 'Certificate of the Improved Value')

[1] Peck, vol. I, p. 20.   [2] P.R.O. Wards 14/6/11, orders of 28 June 1599.
[3] P.R.O. Wards 5/15/2858. But the survey was not always made by the feodary of the county in which the lands lay, nor always perhaps on the ground. P.R.O. in Wards 1/118, order of 19 June 4 Charles I provided that, since the Court did not like the certificate of the feodary of Chester of the estate of the king's ward, Peter Warburton, the feodary of Middlesex was to make a new certificate; *ibid.* order of 5 June 9 Charles I arranged for lands late of Richard Broughton to be surveyed by the feodary of Bedford, since the feodary of Carmarthen was not in town.
[4] P.R.O. Wards 14/6/11, orders of Hil. 42 Eliz.   [5] *Ibid.* orders of Hil. 1606.

56 COURT OF WARDS AND LIVERIES [CHAP. III

that there occur the greatest increases over values found in the inquisitions. It does not at present seem possible to express these higher valuations in terms of an average proportionate increase: there would seem to have been so infinite a variation from case to case that an average would have little meaning. The examples listed below, however, give some idea of the fantastic raising of valuations that went on.[1]

In addition to the inquisition and the survey, the Court had still further information about values at its disposal. In petitioning for a grant of wardship, the prospective guardian had to enter his own confession of the ward's value, and, since the Court took care that the details of the feodary's survey should remain secret,[2] this was

---

[1] The following comparisons of values returned in inquisitions and surveys, and indeed much else of what I have written about the feodaries' surveys, I owe to my colleague Mr F. J. W. Harding, who has recently been working on this material. To 21 Eliz., as explained in the text above, feodaries' surveys are entered in books; for later dates originals only are available, and these are found in P.R.O. Wards 4 & 5 with many strays in Wards 10. The only means of reference to a portion of this enormous class is a partial calendar of Wards 5 where, in addition to feodaries' surveys, schedules and other valuation documents are also found.

SOME EXAMPLES OF INCREASED VALUES IN FEODARIES' SURVEYS

No. Wards 5	County	Name of Tenant	I.P.M. Value			Date	Survey Value			Date
			l.	s.	d.		l.	s.	d.	
5/1486	Chester	Leicester, Adam	69	4	8	34 Eliz.	74	0	10	34 Eliz.
14/2386	Essex	Colvill, John	1	5	0	41 Eliz.	5	0	0	4 Jas. I.
13/2247	Essex } Herts	Quarles, James	58	10	0	42 Eliz.	66	1	4	43 Eliz.
15/2880	Gloucester	Toms, John	2	0	0	45 Eliz.	2	10	0	45 Eliz.
13/2292	Essex	Walderne, John	4	5	4	6 Jas. I.	8	10	8	6 Jas. I.
15/2895	Gloucester	Ven, John	1	10	0	17 Jas. I.	30	0	0	17 Jas. I.
15/2776	Gloucester	Perks, Thomas	3	10	0	22 Jas. I.	53	0	0	22 Jas. I.
13/2159	Essex	Herris, Christopher	1	10	0	4 Charles I	23	0	0	4 Charles I.
13/2156	Essex	Hawkins, John	24	8	8	10 Charles I.	300	13	4	10 Charles I.
15/2781	Gloucester	Player, William	2	6	8	12 Charles I.	40	0	0	12 Charles I.

[2] P.R.O. Wards 14/6/11, orders of 5 May 1606; *Foedera*, vol. XVII, pp. 401-2, instructions of 1622.

CHAP. III] THE REVENUES OF THE COURT 57

an independent estimate—though, as may be guessed, it was usually lower than the feodary's valuation. In addition, comparison with records of previous inquisitions, and other record material in court, was made as a matter of course. The Court had thus four distinct sets of data for the final assessment of values—the inquisition post mortem, the survey, the petitioner's confession, and its own body of past records. It need hardly be emphasized that the importance of this assessment was that upon it depended the amount for which, if the heir was a minor, his wardship was sold and his lands leased or, if he was of age, the fine of his livery was fixed. Good values were the basis of high revenues.

So far our concern has been simply with total nett revenues and the general effect on them of the Court's policies. To establish the basis of the increased productivity of Stuart times, however, it is necessary to go further than this. The separate sections of the Court's revenue were differently, and unequally, affected by the policies that have been examined; and, in addition, each was subject to a whole set of conditioning factors peculiar to itself. As a result, the over-all increase in nett income that the century witnessed is to be accounted for rather by the great prosperity of certain of the Court's revenues than by the uniform development of them all.

Sums received from the sales of wardships and marriages were the part of the Court's revenues that prospered best. Standing at 1,117 *l.* in 1547, they had risen by the first year of Elizabeth's reign to 5,003 *l.* Under Burghley they fell away badly—nine years, chosen at random through the period of his mastership, show them varying between 2,500 *l.* and 3,500 *l.*; but they picked up again to something like the early Elizabethan level in the first decade of the new century. Then, after 1610, their rise is striking—to close on 14,000 *l.* in 1615, and even that seems small in relation to the figures reached under Charles I. Comparison between the average sales in the first three years of Edward VI's reign and the last three normal years' functioning of the Court under Charles gives the figure 1,271 *l.* on the one hand, and 39,819 *l.* on the other—roughly, about a thirty-one-fold increase on the century's working. Of course, not quite all of this vast growth of revenue was profit: the sum paid out in exhibitions for the maintenance of the wards had risen too, but while in 1547-9 this had averaged 412 *l.*, that is, a third of the receipts from the fines, in 1639-41 it was on an average

E

58   COURT OF WARDS AND LIVERIES   [CHAP. III

4,045 *l.*, only a tenth.[1] Putting the matter in another way, in these last years of the Court profits from sales of wardships and marriages accounted for something very near half of the total nett revenue.

The causes of this very great increase were various. First it is possible to trace, from Burghley's time onwards, a formalizing of the business of sales that was probably not without effect in securing higher prices. An order of 1570 provided that no bargain was to pass until it had been engrossed and signed by the hands of two of the council of the Court,[2] but in fact under Burghley the entry books do not always contain these signatures.[3] On the other hand, in Robert Cecil's large, formal entry book of sales, a fair number of items are signed on one side by the attorney and auditor and on the other by the master.[4] It is clear that in James I's reign the master played a greater part in the sale of wardships than previously: for a time, from 1612 to 1622, he was even present at the beating of the bargain and not merely at its conclusion.[5] Again, precautions were repeatedly taken against quasi-corrupt practices—from 1610 the applicant for a wardship had to take an oath that he had given no bribe to an officer of the Court to obtain it;[6] the *Instructions* of 1618 and 1622 alike limited sales to the council chamber and the sittings of the Court appointed for that purpose;[7] the *Instructions* of both 1610 and 1622 forbade the granting of wardships as rewards.[8]

Another factor that operated on the revenues from sales was the so-called rate. When it came to fixing the price of a ward, this was done with more or less conscious reference to the annual value of the lands that would eventually descend to him. While Burghley, however, was generally content to sell for a price something like one or one and a half times the yearly value of the lands,[9] the Latimer memorandum of 1598 recommended 'somewhat a better

[1] This agrees with a contemporary description of the Court's practice in B.M. Egerton MS. 2978, f. 80—'There is usually allowed an Exhibicion of 20s. out of every 10 *l.* rente towards the maintenance of the warde.'

[2] P.R.O. Wards 14/6/11, orders of 14 April 12 Eliz.

[3] P.R.O. Wards 9/156 generally has signatures; Wards 9/157 and 158, though similar in other respects, have not.

[4] P.R.O. Wards 9/160.

[5] Bacon, vol. XI, p. 287; but this practice was discontinued in 1622—*Foedera*, vol. XVII, p. 402.

[6] P.R.O. S.P. 14/61, no. 6, instructions of 1610.

[7] *Foedera*, vol. XVII, pp. 67, 401.

[8] P.R.O. S.P. 14/61, no. 6, instructions of 1610; *Foedera*, vol. XVII, p. 403.

[9] J. Hurstfield, *T.R.H.S.*, 4th Series, vol. XXXI, p. 113.

CHAP. III]   THE REVENUES OF THE COURT   59

fyne',[1] and Robert Cecil was not slow to take the hint, raising the rate to at least three times the yearly value.[2] His excuse for this was that inquisitions were not found at even a tenth part of the true value and, therefore, if purchasers paid thrice as much as before, they would not in fact be exceeding the rate of one year's real value of the lands.[3] This raising of the rate was undoubtedly a contributing factor to the higher yield from sales in the first and second decades of the century. Later, however, it seems to have been dropped as a regular practice, and indeed the improved values of feodaries' certificates rendered it unnecessary.

On any showing, there can be no doubt that really basic to the rise in revenues from sales of wardships were these certificates. Improved values of the kind listed above[4] found their immediate and most obvious reflection in larger sums demanded from purchasers.

Issues of wards' lands, that is, the sums received in rents from lessees of wards' property, also showed a high rate of increase during the century—though not so considerable a rise as sales for wards: in 1547-9 issues produced an average yearly return of 5,420 l.; in 1639-41 36,968 l.—a rise of just under sevenfold in contrast with the thirty-one-fold of sales. Moreover, until the later days of the Court, income trends under the two heads are curiously divergent. For the first half of Burghley's administration, a time when, as has been seen, the profits from sales fell, issues more nearly held their own, their drop not really coming till later; nor, having fallen, did issues rise as rapidly as sales under Robert Cecil and his immediate successors. These minor divergences are puzzling, but as to the general development of income from issues of wards' lands there is no mystery. Its increase was due to the same causes as the increased revenues from sales—improved administration, higher rates and, above all, the better values found by the feodaries. Nor is it surprising, on the other hand, that issues did

---

[1] P.R.O. Wards 14/3/20, papers of Edward Latimer.

[2] P.R.O. Wards 9/348, John Hare's excellent Abstracts of Sales of Wards offers material for comparison between Burghley's practice and his son's. Taking wards whose names begin with the letter A as a sample—

from 1589 to 1598 Burghley sold 32, the total yearly value of whose lands was 828 l., for 1010 l., i.e. at an average rate of a little under 1¼;

from 1607 to 1610 Cecil sold 14, the total yearly value of whose lands was 171 l., for 554 l., at an average rate of well over 3.

[3] John Gutch, *Collectanea Curiosa*, 1781, vol. I, pp. 126-7.

[4] See above, p. 56, note 1.

60 COURT OF WARDS AND LIVERIES [CHAP. III

not achieve the phenomenal growth of sales. A sale was a single action, completed, if not on the spot, at least when the purchaser made his final payment for the wardship and redeemed his bond to meet the agreed purchase price. Issues, on the other hand, were a long-term matter. Rents had to be collected from year to year: some lessees might default, and indeed the Court's great problem of arrearages showed how many did so. Again, it was asserted in 1612 that the feodaries, who received the rents of wards' lands from collectors, proceeded to swallow them up in their petitions for allowances.[1]

All but one of the other sections of the Court's revenue may be rapidly dismissed. Mean rates were never an important item, mainly because of the practice of granting a proportion of them to the suitor who discovered the concealment[2]—and indeed, sometime between 1598 and 1638, the proportion so allowed was increased from half to two-thirds.[3] Fines for leases, except in the difficult period at the end of the old and the beginning of the new century, when they may have been regarded as an easy source of revenue, did not amount to much either. The *Instructions* of 1610 laid it down that leases were to be made without fine,[4] and a dozen years later Cranfield's *Instructions* contemplated little or no fine.[5] But income from this source never quite disappeared, and in most years was good for a few hundred pounds, though it is clear that the Court quite properly preferred to get a good annual rent and waive the fine. Fines for contempt and for widows to re-marry produced an insignificant yield.

There remains for consideration the income from liveries, and this presents a great contrast with the revenues of wardship. Fines for liveries failed to maintain a steady level at any period of the Court's history; they were always subject to fluctuation from year to year. Nor was the increase on the century's working very great. In 1547-9 they averaged 2,363 *l.* a year, in 1639-41 3,798 *l.*[6]—a growth of not much more than 50% over the earlier value. Livery failed to realize its potentialities as a source of royal revenue.

[1] P.R.O. S.P. 14/69, no. 70, regulations for increase of revenue.
[2] See above, p. 51.   [3] *C.S.P. Dom. 1638-9*, p. 93.
[4] P.R.O. S.P. 14/61, no. 6, instructions.   [5] *Foedera*, vol. XVII, p. 402.
[6] From early in Charles I's reign the receiver-general began to show primer seisins as a separate item in his account. The figures for 1639-41, given in the text, are therefore a conflation of amounts shown under two heads—fines for liveries and primer seisins.

CHAP. III] THE REVENUES OF THE COURT 61

There were, indeed, several reasons why this was so. Perhaps the first of them was that the administration of livery business was never set on so sound a basis as wardship. The end of the struggle between the clerk of the wards and the clerk of the liveries was marked by a proposed settlement by the attorney and receiver which gave the custody of livery records to the clerk of the wards.[1] This was pretty certainly implemented, for, a quarter of a century later, amongst proposals for the improvement of revenue there figured the recommendation that all books and schedules of liveries should be moved from the treasury of the Court into the care of the clerk of liveries.[2] The clerk of the wards' victory in the quarrel between the two clerks is set down in a contemporary paper on the impediments to profits from liveries as a principal cause of declining profits;[3] and while it is difficult to substantiate this allegation, it may well have been that the effect of the controversy, and the ill feelings it left behind, was to cause liveries to be given less attention than the other side of the Court's activities. It is significant, for instance, that the improved values of the feodary's survey, which accounted for so much of the prosperity of wardship revenue, were applied more tardily, and less wholeheartedly, to the fixing of fines for liveries. As late as 1622 it was thought necessary to include in Cranfield's *Instructions* one to the effect that feodaries should make surveys upon liveries of full age as well as within age,[4] and the impression left by surveys of the lands of heirs of full age is that they returned lower values than was the case when the heir was a minor.[5]

Another unsatisfactory feature of the administration of liveries was the heavy drain of officers' fees. By a false economy the clerk of the liveries received no official emolument or allowance as the clerk of the wards did, and it may well have been that this caused him to concentrate more on what he could obtain for himself than for the crown. But, in any case, other officers—the master, the surveyor, the attorney and auditors—all took substantial sums from those who sued livery, and it was natural therefore that there should have been a greater increase in officers' fees than in royal revenues from livery. In 1617 it was claimed that the two stood

[1] *C.S.P. Dom. 1598-1601*, p. 395.
[2] P.R.O. S.P. 16/44, no. 2, suggestions for improvement of revenue, 1626 (?).
[3] C.U. MS. Hh. 4. 7, ff. 100-1. [4] *Foedera*, vol. XVII, p. 404.
[5] This impression is confirmed by Mr F. J. W. Harding, who has recently been working on the feodaries' surveys.

62   COURT OF WARDS AND LIVERIES   [CHAP. III

in the ratio of two to one—clerks receiving 6,000 *l.* yearly to the king's 3,000 *l.*;[1] and the high fees quoted in the Return of 1623 suggest that this may have been no exaggeration.[2]

Finally, a further hindrance to the growth of revenue arose from over-long continuances of liveries, the process sometimes being prolonged for ten or even twenty years.[3] The danger, as in the case of concealed wardships, was that the heir might die before the crown had received its dues—the livery 'maye sleepe untill the partie who ought to have sued it doe dye, & so the liverie be quite lost'.[4] Various orders of the Court attempted to meet this danger by making the suitor for a continuance take out a bond so that, if he died before livery was sued, his estate was answerable for a sum equivalent to the fine.[5] But the fact was that the whole business of continuances was an abuse, and it may have been (as Kingsmill, the surveyor of the liveries, alleged) that their principal *raison d'être* was to enrich the clerk of the wards.[6] Carew spoke against them, when made master in 1612;[7] they were attacked by a government bill in the Parliament of 1614,[8] and, that having failed to pass, the suggestion was made twelve years later that no heir of full age should have continuance for longer than three terms after his ancestor's death.[9] The commissioners for revenue, too, ordered the Court to check the abuse. Its failure[10] to do so was the largest single cause of the disappointing yield from liveries.

No less important than the attempt to increase the various sections of the Court's revenue was the effort to secure their efficient collection. Arrearages proved a problem that constantly exercised the Court. At its foundation, the master had been empowered to issue process against defaulting accountants, as was done in the Duchy Chamber of Lancaster,[11] and later an order of the Court instructed the attorney to ascertain from the master of

---

[1] B.M. Hargrave MS. 358, f. 32.   [2] See Appendix III.

[3] P.R.O. S.P. 14/69, no. 70, regulations for increase of revenue; for an example of a petition for continuance of livery, see West, *Second Part*, f. 333.

[4] B.M. Hargrave MS. 358, f. 15.

[5] P.R.O. Wards 14/6/11, orders of 12 Feb. 24 Eliz.

[6] P.R.O. Wards 14/3/20, controversy between Hare and Churchill.

[7] P.R.O. S.P. 14/69, no. 69, discourse to the Court.

[8] *H.C.J.*, 14 May 1614.

[9] P.R.O. S.P. 16/44, no. 2, suggestions for improvement of revenue.

[10] P.R.O. in Wards 10/40, order by the commissioners for revenue, 1626.

[11] 32 Henry VIII c. 46.

CHAP. III]   THE REVENUES OF THE COURT   63

the rolls the Exchequer's methods of levying debts so that similar procedures might be adopted.[1] Process normally began by a writ directing appearance before the Court; if this was disregarded, it was followed by writs of extent and attachment, successively directed to the sheriff of the county in which the debtor dwelt. The success or failure of the system, therefore, depended upon the sheriffs' efficiency, and from the early days of the Court sheriffs had been fined for not carrying out process.[2] In the later years of Elizabeth's reign the slackness of sheriffs resulted in considerable losses; and in 1586 it was found necessary to order them to make personal returns to their writs within four days of every term, and to answer any charge against them.[3] Five years later they were charged with the payment of such arrears as had arisen through their failure to execute process.[4]

Further, in this last decade of the century there was a great improvement in the method of issue of writs of extent and attachment. These had previously been despatched to the sheriffs along with enormous schedules on which were listed details of the persons against whom process was to be made.[5] For such inconveniently large documents there were now substituted what came to be called the black books of the sheriffs. There was a sheriff's book for each county, and in it the clerk of the wards entered details of persons against whom process was to be made for the recovery of debts. Each volume has two main divisions, headed (i) Extents and (ii) Attachments, the former being divided into Posted Arrears and Sheriffs' Fines, Bonds and Recognisances and Arrears, and the latter having the sub-heading Arrears. It was despatched to the sheriff along with writs instructing him to extend and attach such persons as appeared under the headings Extents and Attachments within the book. A note inscribed at the front of each of these volumes throws some light on the procedure that was followed— 'Shereif I pray you and the Courte also comandeth that you forbeare to write any thinge wᵗhin this book, But you are to write yoʳ retornes to the severall matters herein conteyned in a Rolle of

[1] P.R.O. Wards 14/6/11, orders of 12 Feb. 24 Eliz.
[2] P.R.O. Wards 9/233 and 247, and in composite volumes, Wards 9/199, 246 and 346.
[3] *C.S.P. Dom. Addenda 1580-1625*, p. 180.
[4] P.R.O. in Wards 10/83, file of writs commanding appearance and payment of arrears by sheriffs, 33 Eliz.
[5] P.R.O. in Wards 10/83, file of writs of attachment, 32 Eliz.

64 COURT OF WARDS AND LIVERIES [CHAP. III

parchment and to annex the same rolle to the writts wch do receave wth this booke.'[1] The clerk was supposed to issue process, both into the county where the debtor dwelt at the time the debt was contracted and into the county where the lands were situated.[2]

This was only part of a complex system of certifying and posting outstanding debts, which the Court built up with infinite care. As early as 1561 it ordered the auditor to deliver to the clerk of the wards a book of arrearages, digested into shires, so that the clerk might answer from time to time what process and return had been made.[3] Some twenty years later it instructed the clerk to make an abstract of debts on bonds, and to acquaint feodaries with what was owing in their counties.[4] But the elaboration of the system of dealing with arrearages dates from John Hare's clerkship at the end of the sixteenth century. Twice yearly the auditors certified such debts as remained unpaid, and these were then entered in the so-called books of arrears, abstracts of arrears and sheriffs' books; upon payment, the auditors issued a docket of discharge, and the debt was noted in each series of volumes as being exonerated. Unpaid bonds were included within the scope of this system of process, and the certificates of those remaining undischarged were brought up to date. There are good series of all these sets of entry books, the contents of which, being notes of identical debts, duplicate each other.[5]

The feodaries, as might be guessed, were extensively used to assist in the levying of arrears. They were expected to consult the process books at regular intervals, and to certify each Easter what they had been able to do towards bringing in outstanding debts.[6] It was the feodary, too, who was responsible for serving the initial privy seal to a defaulting accountant, and only when this was not observed was process directed through the sheriff.[7] On occasion even the messenger of the Court was utilized—in 1581-2 arrangements were made for him to bring into Court such debtors as dwelt in, or had recourse to, London.[8]

[1] P.R.O. *Wards Guide*, p. 47.
[2] P.R.O. in Wards 10/31, draft of writ of extent.
[3] P.R.O. Wards 14/6/11, orders of Mich. 3 & 4 Eliz.
[4] *Ibid.* orders of 12 Feb., 24 Eliz.
[5] P.R.O. *Wards Guide*, pp. 42-51.
[6] P.R.O. Wards 14/6/11, orders of Hil. 42 Eliz. For a stiff letter to certain of them, as early as Mary's reign, see P.R.O. Wards 9/516, f. 312.
[7] P.R.O. Wards 14/6/11, orders of Hil. 1606.
[8] *Ibid.* orders of 12 Feb. 24 Eliz.

CHAP. III]   THE REVENUES OF THE COURT   65

All this suffices to show how sustained an attempt the Court made to collect its revenues. Yet the task was an enormous one, and it would be a mistake to over-estimate the success that was enjoyed. Even a dozen years after John Hare's reforms, there was some truth in the allegation that 'all the king's debts are in process'.[1] In 1606 the master and others were appointed as commissioners to find out all sums owing in the Court,[2] and in 1619 Bacon wrote to Cranfield, by that time master, that the king was offended by the delay in collecting debts, and urging a similar commission.[3] Meantime, however, there had been at least a partial confession of failure. In the same year as the first commission, it was decided to write off arrearages dating from before the twentieth year of Elizabeth's reign, or alternatively to grant them to such private individuals as cared to prosecute them.[4] This practice of grants from the arrearages was continued in later times—Buckingham, for instance, had 1,000 *l.* from them,[5] and a number of individuals received grants of the same sort from Charles I.[6] If the Court's continuous pressure for the return of high values seems unduly grasping, it is perhaps well to remember that it had to reckon on a considerable proportion of what was owing never, in fact, being paid.

In studying the financial policy of the Court of Wards the question naturally arises as to how burdensome its exactions were found by the subject. The answer to that is found in the agitation against the Court, which is dealt with in a later chapter. Here, however, two points may be made. First, it was not merely the crown that profited from wardship and livery—the throng of petitioners for wardships and informers of concealed liveries proves that. Second, there can be no doubt that the officers of the Court recognized the danger of pressing the king's claims too hard. The successive *Instructions* of James I's reign are an odd mixture of care for the Court's profits and for the ward's welfare: the set which precedes Ley's *Learned Treatise* sums up what must have been the intention of all conscientious administrators of the system, to take

[1] *C.S.P. Dom. 1601-10*, p. 484.
[2] *Ibid.* p. 331.
[3] H.M.C., *Report*, vol. IV, p. 299.
[4] P.R.O. Wards 14/6/11, orders of 5 May 1606.
[5] *C.S.P. Dom. 1623-5*, p. 301.
[6] *C.S.P. Dom. 1636-7*, p. 319.

66 COURT OF WARDS AND LIVERIES [CHAP. III

'speciall care that our just and reasonable profits may be raised . . . and that neverthelesse our Tenants may be moderately charged, and our Wards may be educated in Religion'.[1] Unfortunately, as will be seen, and as may be guessed, the two sides of this policy were generally quite incompatible.

[1] Ley, *Learned Treatise*, preceding text.

CHAPTER IV

THE ADMINISTRATION OF LIVERY
AND WARDSHIP

THERE is plentiful evidence of procedure in matters of livery and wardship. The law on the subject was discussed in general works like Fitzherbert's[1] and Brooke's[2] *Abridgements*, and much of its detail is to be found in the *New Natura Brevium*.[3] More specifically, both before and after the erection of the Court efforts were made to draw together the law of tenures in chief and present it as a whole. Such a synthesis was one of the aims of Littleton's *Tenures*,[4] a work valuable in itself, and still more so as the basis of. Coke's *First Part of the Institutes*,[5] which is a commentary on it. Moreover, the development of prerogative action under the early Tudors directed interest to the *Prerogativa Regis* of Edward I—a document which, though probably no statute, neatly summed up the king's rights[6]—and from early in Henry VII's reign this was the topic for an important series of Inns of Court readings, much of the learning of which has recently been made accessible in Professor S. E. Thorne's edition of one of them, Robert Constable's *Tertia Lectura* of 1495.[7] Also looking to the *Prerogativa Regis*, and even more direct in its bearing on livery and wardship, was William Staunford's *Exposicion of the Kinges Prerogative*, originally made in 1548.[8] Staunford, indeed, dedicated this book to Nicholas Bacon, then attorney of the wards: 'I have alwayes meant this my deuyse unto you', he wrote in his dedication, 'which I could not doe or practise so well uppon anye tytle as uppon this that appertayneth unto your office of Attourneyshippe of the wardes and liueries'. Certainly the *Exposicion*—its first half a commentary, chapter by chapter, on the *Prerogativa Regis*, its second an account of procedure consequent on the death of a tenant in chief—must have

---

[1] First edn. 1516; edn. of 1577 cited in this chapter.   [2] 1568.
[3] First edn. 1534; edn. of 1652 cited in this chapter.
[4] Written probably *c.* 1475-80.   [5] First edn., 1628, cited here.
[6] F. W. Maitland, *Collected Papers*, vol. II, pp. 182-9.
[7] *Prerogativa Regis*, ed. S. E. Thorne.
[8] Edn. of 1567 cited in this chapter.

67

68 COURT OF WARDS AND LIVERIES [CHAP. IV

been invaluable alike for officials and for pleaders in the Court. It was probably a copy of this work that was purchased by the usher, upon the attorney's command, in 1597.[1]

Yet it was not until the very last days of the Court of Wards that the most complete account of livery and wardship was published. Sir James Ley's *Learned Treatise Concerning Wards and Liveries* exists in a number of manuscript copies,[2] and was printed in 1641 and 1642, and reissued along with his *Reports* in 1659. In the epistle dedicatory to the 1642 edition it is stated that the book was written by Ley for his own use when he was attorney of the Court, and was published for the use of anyone intending to practise as counsel there. It owes much to Staunford and the reporters, but it is very clearly the product of Ley's own ripe experience.[3]

For the rest, amongst the records of the Court and elsewhere there are several minor, but interesting, sources of information. Three formulary books have come to light—one of them earlier than the Court's foundation;[4] another with the title *Liber president' special' 1589* and, in another hand, *The escheators office*;[5] a third dating from Stuart times.[6] There is an attractive little treatise on the practice of the Court by 'W. R. Sergeant at Law' and possibly by other hands,[7] and an invaluable notebook recently located contains, amongst other important matter, *Diverse Cases for Liveries* by the same author.[8] This last volume also includes a note, *The manner of obtayninge A grant of A Ward*, of which other recensions appear elsewhere.[9] Several copies of a set of *Rules for Liveries*, most probably antedating the Court, have also been noticed.[10]

---

[1] P.R.O. in Wards 10/78, vouchers of r.g.a. 39 Eliz.

[2] C.U. MS. Ff. 4. 22, Gg. 3. 26, Ll. 3. 2 and 3; B.M. Harleian MS. 736, no. 2. From descriptions kindly furnished to me by the Acting Librarian of the Inner Temple in 1940, it appears that Inner Temple Petyt MSS. 517 and 538. 32 are further copies of Ley's treatise. Most of these MSS. are entitled *Instructions for the Master of our Wards and Liueryes*, the *Instructions* of 1618 preceding the treatise.

[3] The printed edn. of 1642 is here cited as Ley, *Learned Treatise*.

[4] P.R.O. Wards 9/169.

[5] P.R.O. Ind. 17396.

[6] P.R.O. in Wards 10/27, formulary book.

[7] B.M. Harleian MS. 1323, f. 189 etc. 'W. R.' was most likely William Rastell, the son of the printer of More.

[8] P.R.O. Wards 14/6/11, notebook.

[9] B.M. Harleian MS. 1938, f. 29; a similar set in Powell, pp. 212-16.

[10] P.R.O. Wards 14/6/11; Bod. MS. Carte 124, ff. 517-25; B.M. Harleian MS. 1323, f. 189 etc.; C.U. MSS. Gg. 3. 26, ff. 91-4, and Hh. 4. 7, f. 17, etc.; P.R.O. Wards 9/169, f. 1.

CHAP. IV] ADMINISTRATION 69

Finally, the series of Stuart *Instructions* to the master and council of the Court contain much that is useful.[1]

The present chapter attempts to set out, from such sources and from incidental references in the Court's records, the procedure that followed upon the death of the king's tenant. Of course the Court's practice was not static, but developing; nevertheless, it is possible to give an account of the administration that is true in its essentials for the greater part of the period of its existence.

The keystone of the whole procedure was the office, or inquisition, found upon the death of the king's tenant. In general terms Ley states its purpose to be twofold—'first for the dignity of the King's person, who cannot take nor depart with any inheritance or freehold but by matter of record. Secondly because it puts the King presently upon the office found in actuall and full possession of the Wards lands, and the profits thereof since his Ancestors death before any service[2] or entrey by the Escheators, which actuall possession the King hath not before Office'.[3] It is true that by the medieval common law seizure went before inquisition,[4] and that the wording of the writs of *diem clausit extremum, mandamus* and so on continued to suggest that this was possible; but actually from the passing of the statute *de Escaetoribus* onwards the practice had been otherwise. Constable, writing at a time when the royal prerogative was steadily widening its scope, admitted that there was some doubt as to whether the king could seize lands without office, though he could seize the ward's body;[5] Coke, a century later, declared definitively that the escheator must not take lands into the king's hand prior to the finding of an office.[6] Thus the inquisition post mortem was normally the essential preliminary to the descent of property held in chief; only in a comparatively few cases, where a pardon or special livery had been sued, was it eliminated.

The inquisition was usually taken on the authority of a writ or

---

[1] 1610, 1617, 1618, 1622: P.R.O. S.P. 14/61, no. 6; *Foedera*, vol. XVII, pp. 61, 66, 400; Ley, *Learned Treatise*, preceding text.
[2] C.U. MS. Ff. 4. 22, f. 41, has 'seizure'—clearly a better reading.
[3] Ley, *Learned Treatise*, pp. 73-4.
[4] Staunford, f. 14.   [5] Constable, p. 33.
[6] *Second Part of the Institutes*, edn. of 1669, p. 689; see also Coke, *Reports*, vol. IV, p. 476.

70   COURT OF WARDS AND LIVERIES   [CHAP. IV

commission, issuing out of the Chancery,[1] upon the warrant of the master, surveyor, attorney or receiver of the Court of Wards and Liveries. The question arises, therefore, how the Court became informed of the tenant's death, and it appears that this did not occur in one way alone. Where the heir was of age, the responsibility was primarily his own; it was held to be his suit to have the land '& nul auter meane ordinarie',[2] so that he acquainted the Court of his ancestor's death and perhaps, for his pains, secured favourable commissioners. This was, for instance, the aim of Emanuel Scroope, when he wrote to the clerk of the wards in 1610, 'I haue sent my sarvant this bearer to sewe forth a Commissyon for fynding an offyce after the death of my Father. And I pray you admyt thes four Commissyoners who I do asseur you upon my nothe are no Recusantes. . . .'[3] So long as the heir was conscientious, or even careful, he might be relied on to give the necessary information.

For the rest, the escheator, and more particularly the feodary, of the county where the property lay were expected to warn the Court and, since inquisitions meant fees for them, had a financial interest in doing so. Thus there are contemporary letters from both officials, seeking writs to find inquisitions—'Mr Audley', wrote the feodary of the West Riding of Yorkshire in 1635, 'I desire you to make me a warrant for a writt of *mandamus* after the death of Thomas Ellis whose heire is of full age to my knowledge.'[4] Where the heir was a minor, a petitioner for his wardship would seek an inquisition at his own charge and obtain the writ, binding himself to deliver it to the feodary concerned.[5] This practice was encouraged by the Court because of the number of wardships that it revealed,[6] but it was obviously open to abuse and in 1603 it was found necessary to issue an order that a suitor for a concealed wardship should establish reasonable probability before obtaining a writ or commission.[7] In any case, the practice might work in an opposite direction from that desired—according to the *Collections* of 1617, many sought writs with no intention of prosecuting the matter.[8]

---

[1] Or other court with authority, such as the Palatinate courts.
[2] Dyer, *A.N.C.*, f. 170.
[3] P.R.O. in Wards 10/51, letter from E. Scroope, 1 Feb. 1610.
[4] P.R.O. in Wards 10/37, letter from J. Goodhand, 22 Aug. 1635.
[5] P.R.O. in Wards 10/69, bonds to deliver writs to feodaries, 1 Eliz.
[6] See above, p. 51.
[7] P.R.O. Wards 14/3/20, orders of 11 May 1 Jas. I.
[8] B.M. Hargrave MS. 358, f. 11.

CHAP. IV] ADMINISTRATION 71

The successful working of the system depended, like so much else in the wards' administration, upon the energy and efficiency of the feodaries.

Writs directing the taking of inquisitions fell into two classes—those which ordered the normal inquiry post mortem, and those issuing upon some defect in a former inquisition.

Of the former class the most usual was the *diem clausit extremum*,[1] which was used when information of the death was received within reasonably short time; this was usually sought by the heir, and was delivered to him. When a year and a day had passed without an inquisition, and the question arose who had held the lands during that period, the more peremptory *mandamus*[2] issued; it was also used where a previous inquisition was for any reason found void.[3] Special cases were met by particular writs—*certiorari*,[4] if the escheator having taken an inquisition had not returned it into the Chancery at the time of his death; *devenerunt*,[5] if the heir had died in wardship; *datum est nobis intelligi*,[6] termed by Fitzherbert 'another writ of *diem clausit extremum*',[7] where the escheator had died or had been removed from office after receiving a writ, but before taking an inquisition upon it.

The latter class of writs was in use largely because the king could not traverse inquisitions as the subject was able to do,[8] and had therefore to seek remedy against inaccurate or imperfect findings by the taking of a new office, most frequently upon a writ of *melius inquirendum*.[9] On the other hand it should be noted that, in one very important way, the growing use of the *melius inquirendum* represented a decrease in the king's claims. The old common law principle had been that 'the best must be understood for the king', and such phrases as *sed per que servicia Juratores ignorant* and *de quo tenetur Juratores ignorant*, occurring in inquisitions, had been interpreted as meaning a tenure in chief of the crown.[10] But this obviously unfair interpretation was checked by statute,[11] though it was held that if the uncertain inquisition was pre-statute no *melius inquirendum* should issue.[12] Two other writs of this second

[1] *N.N.B.*, p. 624, for the form of the writ.
[2] C.U. MS. Ff. 4. 22, f. 33; Ley, *Learned Treatise*, has a misprint 'memorandum' for 'mandamus'.   [3] See below, pp. 105-6.   [4] *N.N.B.*, p. 628.
[5] For an inquisition upon a *devenerunt* see West, *Second Part*, f. 322.
[6] Staunford, f. 52.   [7] *N.N.B.*, p. 627.   [8] See below, p. 76.
[9] *N.N.B.*, pp. 632-3.   [10] Bacon, vol. VII, pp. 549-50.
[11] 2 Edward VI c. 8.   [12] Dyer, *A.N.C.*, f. 155; see also below, pp. 105-6.

72 COURT OF WARDS AND LIVERIES [CHAP. IV

class may be mentioned. Where some of the ancestor's lands had not been included in the inquisition, or indeed where the specific phrase *et non habet plura terras sive tenementa* had been omitted, a further office was ordered upon the writ *que plura*;[1] if an escheator had been discharged before taking an inquisition, his successor might be instructed by an *amotus*[2] to have the question reconsidered.

Should the king prefer to do so in a particular instance, he was free to have the inquisition post mortem taken before specially appointed commissioners instead of the escheator.[3] If, for instance, an escheator was 'affectioned', which perhaps meant unwilling to urge findings favourable to the crown, a commission with *supersedeas* arranged for the inquisition to be taken before others.[4] The Court of Wards never fully trusted the escheator—an Exchequer official, and a considerable number of inquisitions was directed to be taken before commissioners instead of before the escheator alone, an order of 11 May 1603 providing that those on the commission were to be of the county concerned and men of integrity.[5] Such Commissions exhibit similar varieties to the writs upon which they were based, and they fall into the same two categories.

Generally speaking, it was the practice of the Court of Wards that an inquisition should be taken by virtue of writs or commissions of the kinds described, and the escheator's power to find *virtute officii* was restricted. Inquisitions without writ were only allowed upon lands of not more than 5 *l.* yearly value,[6] and even this narrow privilege of the escheator was regarded with jealousy. Prior to the statute 2 Edward VI c.8, if such inquisitions were uncertain, they were void outright and no *melius inquirendum* lay;[7] and in 1612 Carew on becoming master showed himself ready to remedy any oppression to the subject that might result from them.[8] The old *Rules for Liveries* stated the extreme position that 'of dutie A man shall neuer haue Liuery but if an office bee found for him by writt, and not by vertue of office found by the Escheator without writt'.[9] Again, the practice of letting liveries of lands under 5 *l.* yearly value be sued without any inquisition at all, and simply

---

[1] *N.N.B.*, p. 632, for the form of the writ.   [2] Bod. MS. Carte 124, f. 520.
[3] Constable, p. 44.   [4] Bod. MS. Carte 124, f. 520.
[5] P.R.O. Wards 14/3/20, orders of 11 May 1 Jas. I.
[6] 33 Henry VIII c. 22.
[7] *Second Part of the Institutes*, edn. of 1669, p. 691.
[8] P.R.O. S.P. 14/69, no. 69.   [9] Bod. MS. Carte 124, f. 520.

CHAP. IV]　　　　ADMINISTRATION　　　　73

upon warrant of the Court, was perhaps another method of depriving the escheator of his independent rights in this connexion.[1]

The responsibility for arranging the holding of an inquisition rested mainly upon the escheator, except where it was taken before a commission from which he had been deliberately excluded. It was his duty to notify the feodary in advance of the time and place at which it was proposed to take evidence,[2] and he had also to summon the heir or his representatives, as well as the tenants of the lands concerned, to attend, an order of the Court of 1608 specifying that the heir or his friends should have twenty days warning.[3] Some examples of the escheator's warning notices have survived. One dated 1609, from the escheator of Wiltshire, not only orders the addressee to be present in person but also to bring with him all his evidences concerning the lands under consideration.[4] The escheator of London took to issuing his summons on printed forms.[5] Having informed feodary, heir and tenants of the time and place appointed for taking the inquisition, the escheator had then to see that the sheriff was instructed to impanel a jury.[6]

These preliminaries satisfactorily accomplished, when the escheator actually came to take the inquisition he opened it with a charge to the jury, urging them to conceal or hide nothing, 'but the truthe to say & not spare nether for affeccion loue dred feare or envy'.[7] Then he caused the crier to proclaim that if there were any king's serjeant, king's attorney, or other manner of person with information to give, he should come in and be heard.[8] This was no doubt the feodary's cue. The feodary had a right to demand to see all relevant evidences a few days before the inquisition, and, if agreement between him and the heir was reached, a document was probably submitted to the jury ready drawn; if not, then both sides would state their case, the feodary appearing for the king's claim.[9] Either way it was important that the jury should themselves be in a position to know the truth of the evidence before them— hence the Court's opposition to inquisitions on lands outside the single county in which they were taken, and its practice, where a man held lands in several counties, of holding an inquisition in one

---

[1] Ley, *Learned Treatise*, p. 56.　　　　[2] See above, p. 40.
[3] P.R.O. Wards 14/6/11, order of 9 Oct. 1608.
[4] P.R.O. in Wards 10/31, summons to attend an inquisition.
[5] P.R.O. S.P. 15/43, no. 114, blank form ordering attendance at inquisition.
[6] P.R.O. Ind. 17396, f. 21, writ from escheator to sheriff.
[7] *Ibid.* f. 24, Eschetors chardge.　　[8] *Ibid.*　　[9] H.M.C., *Salisbury*, vol. x, pp. 414-15.

F

74 COURT OF WARDS AND LIVERIES [CHAP. IV

and securing details of his lands elsewhere from special surveys made by the feodaries.[1]

The honesty of the jury, too, was a matter of great importance. Legislation, some of it medieval, existed to ensure genuine findings: inquisitions were to be taken in towns openly, before people of good fame.[2] Even so, juries were sometimes troublesome, especially when the inquisition touched the interests of some man of substance in the locality: it is not difficult, for instance, to imagine what the young Earl of Hertford had in mind when, in 1557, he wrote to Sir John Thynne, who had managed the protector's business affairs, to say that he wanted a friendly jury.[3] In case of difficulties of this sort, the escheator was entitled to adjourn to take advice[4]— indeed, after 1617, where a finding against the crown within a year of the tenant's death was involved he was forced to take this course.[5] There were restrictions on his power to adjourn a jury into the Court itself—in 1603 an order provided that he might not do this without certifying its obstinacy,[6] and a little later it is pretty clear that, except at their own request or at the master's command, the jurors could not be adjourned into Court at all.[7] Bearing in mind the fate of that Rutland jury of the end of Elizabeth's reign who were adjourned into the Court and ordered to appear there *de die in diem* until further order taken, the new ruling was perhaps merciful.[8] In any event, if a jury proved hopelessly biased against the crown, it was always possible to issue a commission superseding the original writ or commission, for this involved automatically the impanelling of a new jury.[9]

When the findings had been agreed by the jury, to remove the possibility of subsequent forgery they were engrossed in a pair of indentures, one of which was taken by the foreman of the jury and one by the escheator; the latter was to see to it that the foreman received his counterpart upon a statutory pain of 100 *l.*,[10] nor, until the engrossments were made, was the writ ordering the inquisition held to be fully executed.[11] The escheator had the further

---

[1] Ley, *Reports*, pp. 31-2.

[2] 34 Edward III c. 13; 8 Henry VI c. 16; 1 Henry VIII c. 8.

[3] *Wilts Arch Mag.*, vol. xv, pp. 193-4; note that he also sought the feodary's favour.   [4] P.R.O. Ind. 17396, f. 63, instructions for an escheator's office.

[5] *Foedera*, vol. XVII, p. 61, additions of instructions.

[6] P.R.O. Wards 14/3/20, order of 11 May 1 Jas. I.

[7] C.U. MS. Dd. 13.28, f. 15.   [8] P.R.O. Wards 9/527, orders Mich. 44 Eliz.

[9] H.M.C., *Salisbury*, vol. IV, p. 298.   [10] 1 Henry VIII c. 8.

[11] Dyer, *A.N.C.*, f. 170.

CHAP. IV]   ADMINISTRATION   75

duty of returning the inquisition into the Chancery within one month,[1] whence it was passed to the clerks of the Petty Bag, who transcripted it into the Court of Wards.[2] The Court thus built up a body of records, which became the basis of the crown case at the taking of later inquisitions.

For all his work in connexion with the taking of an inquisition post mortem the escheator was entitled to a fee of 40s., with a further 6s. 8d. for engrossing it;[3] the feodary might also take 40s.,[4] and the sheriff for impanelling the jury 3s. 4d.[5]

Inquisitions post mortem followed a common form, and the information they were expected to furnish falls, broadly speaking, under three heads—the position, extent and value of the lands of the deceased; of whom they were held, and by what tenure; the name and age of the heir. The importance of the first and third of these is self-evident: if the heir was of age, the findings regarding the value of the property were relevant in assessing the fine to be paid for livery; if he was a minor, then the same set of facts helped to determine the fee for composition of wardship. It is worth while spending a moment, however, on the second head. In this connexion it was necessary that the office should specify not only whether the lands were held of the king or not, but also by what tenure they were held of him, for different tenures involved different incidents.[6]

[1] 8 Henry VI c. 16.
[2] Hence there are, among the Public Records, duplicate sets of inquisitions post mortem. See P.R.O. *Lists and Indexes*, vols. XXIII, XXVI, XXXI and XXXIII.
[3] P.R.O. Ind. 17396, f. 61, fees belonging to the escheator's office.
[4] C.U. MS. Dd. 13. 28, f. 17.   [5] P.R.O. Ind. 17396, f. 61.
[6] The following table, constructed from details in Ley, *Learned Treatise*, shows the principal tenures of the crown and the incidents of each:

Tenure	*Incident*
Knight service in chief	ward, marriage, primer seisin, relief, licence to alienate; prerogative wardship and primer seisin of all other lands held of common persons.
Grand serjeanty	as to knight service in chief.
Socage in chief	relief, primer seisin, livery, licence to alienate.
Petty serjeanty	as to socage in chief.
Common knight service	ward, marriage, relief, livery; but no licence to alienate, nor prerogative wardship of other lands, nor primer seisin.
Common socage	relief only.

Where land was held of the crown as of some manor, honor or lordship, this was a common tenure and not in chief, unless the manor etc. of which it was held had been anciently annexed to the crown. See Staunford, f. 29; Dyer, *A.N.C.*, ff. 44, 58; Ley, *Reports*, p. 52; Constable, pp. 10-13, 24.

76   COURT OF WARDS AND LIVERIES   [CHAP. IV

Even if it was never returned, an office found for the king remained a valid title for him until it was discharged by matter of as high a nature, such as livery. This made the subject's right to traverse an inquisition, if he were wronged by it, the more important;[1] it was his best chance of having the findings re-examined and perhaps adjusted. Apart from medieval legislation, Morton's *Articles* of 28 October 1477 provided for traverse,[2] and so did the statute 2 Edward VI c.8. Even so, the dice were heavily weighted against the man who set out to overthrow the king's title. Only when that was based solely on the inquisition, and on no other matter of record, was a traverse allowed;[3] and in answering it, the crown enjoyed the further advantage of being able to maintain its own title or disprove that of the traverser, whichever seemed the easier.[4] Nor were officials friendly to the traverse. It was one of the chief complaints against Empson and Dudley that traverses were not allowed by them;[5] and even after the setting up of the Court, they were only permitted upon bill of licence to traverse, the plaintiff paying costs should the case be adjudged against him. Something of the arduousness of traversing an inquisition may be gathered from the repeated postponements of even a case that was ultimately successful.[6] What it amounted to was that the practice of the Court acknowledged, but rather discouraged, traverses. Coke claimed as late as 1625 that its refusal to allow them, except by bill, was a restraint of the common law.[7]

If the inquisition found the lands to be held in chief and the heir of age, he had to proceed to sue out his livery. If he failed to do so, he lost the profits of his lands, and was unable to dispose of them or to endow his wife from out of them—in a word, he was legally an intruder.[8] In theory this was the position until he had done homage and actually received seisin; but in practice he was given six months grace in which to prosecute his livery,[9] and the

---

[1] 34 Edward III c. 14.   [2] Bod. MS. Carte 124, f. 517.
[3] Staunford, f. 61.   [4] *Ibid.* f. 65.
[5] See above, pp. 7-8.   [6] West, *Second Part*, ff. 313-18.
[7] *Commons Debates in* 1625 (Camden Soc.), p. 17. For examples of the bill to traverse see Ley, *Reports*, p. 26; West, *Second Part*, f. 324. Where no question of the rightness of the inquisition arose, but a right as against a previous tenant never executed, it was necessary to proceed by *monstrance de droit*; where the king seized land without any colour of legality, then the only possibility was to petition him (Staunford, ff. 70-2).   [8] Ley, *Learned Treatise*, p. 50.
[9] C.U. MS. Ff. 4. 22, f. 30; the reading in *Learned Treatise*, p. 51, '6. 3. moneths', is obscure.

CHAP. IV]   ADMINISTRATION   77

period could be extended from six months at the discretion of the Court,[1] upon payment of a fee of 6s. 8d.[2] During the 'continuance' of his livery, that is, from the time when it was tendered[3] until the time when it was finally sued out, the heir was in full enjoyment of his lands; the danger of over-long continuances, that in the meantime the heir might die and the profits from livery be lost, has been seen above, and also the Court's effort to counteract this by taking out bonds for ultimate payment of the fine due.[4] The heir's tender of livery had to include all his lands, and it was not permissible to sue livery by parcels.[5]

The Court recognized, and distinguished between, several different forms of livery. (i) Where the yearly value of the property did not exceed 5 l., a general livery *under value* might be sued; as has been seen, this was not necessarily preceded by an inquisition, but could pass on warrant of the Court alone. (ii) When the yearly value fell between 5 l. and 20 l. the general livery *above value* was often used, carrying with it rather higher fees than the first.[6] There were inherent in this form of livery, according to Coke, two dangers: firstly, the heir, having based his tender of livery upon the inquisition, must never afterwards query or deny any of its findings; secondly, his tender must include every parcel of land that the king ought to have, whether it had been detailed in the inquisition or not.[7] The general livery was fatally easy to overturn; its suing out 'dangerous, tedious and chargeable'.[8] (iii) The most significant development, therefore, was the increased use of special liveries, which could only be sued if the lands were worth more than 20 l. per annum, or at least were confessed at a value greater than 20 l. per annum. The special livery was granted upon payment of a fine, rated at half a year's value. It pardoned all that had been wrongfully done in the way of entry or intrusion, and gave the heir the profits of his land immediately, remitting the mean rates; but the last privilege was illusory, since these were, in fact, paid before the Court would grant a special livery.[9] The greatest benefit of the special livery was to the heir who had been in ward; for it, he did not need to have proved his age, and indeed

---

[1] Ley, *Learned Treatise*, p. 52.   [2] *C.S.P. Dom. 1598-1601*, pp. 395-6.
[3] For the form of a tender of livery see B.M. Harleian MS. 1323, f. 204.
[4] See above, p. 62.   [5] Ley, *Learned Treatise*, p. 59.   [6] *Ibid.* p. 61.
[7] *First Part of the Institutes*, f. 77.
[8] *Second Part of the Institutes*, edn. of 1669, p. 693.
[9] Ley, *Learned Treatise*, p. 63.

78   COURT OF WARDS AND LIVERIES   [CHAP. IV

this form of livery might even be granted during minority as, in a classical case, the Duchess of Buckingham had found out to her cost—the king had granted her a certain ward for so long as the child happened to be in his hand; when, afterwards, he made the ward a special livery, the duchess had no remedy.[1] But, on wider grounds, this method of suing livery enjoyed an increasing popularity. Once accomplished, it was eminently safe: it left far less possibility that the king might re-seize the lands upon some technical defect. On the other hand, Coke's enthusiasm for it was qualified—'the fees and charges are so great and the Bonds and Covenants etc. so many, so intricate, and dangerous, as it were worthy to be redressed, for the ease and quiet of the fatherlesse, and widow'.[2] (iv) Lastly, there was what amounted in law to a livery, the pardon sometimes granted by the king before the finding of an inquisition to an heir who had entered upon his ancestor's property;[3] such a pardon was granted either by act of Parliament or by letters patent under the great seal.[4]

Whichever form of livery was adopted, the process of suing it was complicated. After tendering his livery before the surveyor, the heir had to take the tender, along with a copy of the inquisition and, at least in the later days of the Court, the feodary's survey, to the clerk of the liveries; from him he obtained a schedule, which was carried to the auditors to enable them to cast the rates of full age. Not until these had been compounded for, and (if a special livery was being sued) the fine paid, would the clerk of the liveries make the indentures of livery, the heir binding himself to enrol the livery in the auditors' office within six months and to observe the covenants of the indenture. Only when all this had been done was the warrant issued for the livery to pass under the great seal. The patent had to be sought within three months after the making of the warrant, and the heir had to take the oath of supremacy and allegiance, though this might be done by commission.[5] Meanwhile homage was no doubt done, or respited, for this was yet another hurdle that the heir had to take before he obtained the final writ of livery, ordering the escheator to put him in possession.[6] Also,

[1] Bod. MS. Carte 124, f. 519.
[2] Fourth Part of the Institutes, edn. of 1669, p. 199.
[3] Staunford, f. 40.   [4] Second Part of the Institutes, edn. of 1669, p. 693.
[5] Details in this paragraph are mainly based on the account given in W. R.'s treatise, B.M. Harleian MS. 1323, ff. 204-7.
[6] N.N.B., pp. 633-4; Constable, pp. 63-4.

CHAP. IV]   ADMINISTRATION   79

upon record of the livery, the Exchequer proceeded to sue out summons for the payment of relief at the rate of 5 *l.* per knight's fee and proportionately.[1] Remembering that at all stages in the suing out of livery there were heavy fees to be paid to officials,[2] it will be realized that the path was hard by which a man entered on property lawfully descended to him.

If the sole royal tenure found in the inquisition was by socage in chief, livery need only be sued of the crown of the lands so held of it.[3] If, on the other hand, any of the lands descending to the heir were held by knight service in chief, the livery had to include the whole of the ancestor's property even though it was held of other lords by common tenures.[4] This distinction was reflected, moreover, in the position of the minor heir. Where only a socage tenure was involved, the *prochein amy*[5] might have livery and mean rates to the heir's use;[6] where the tenure was by knight service in chief, no livery (with the exceptions that have been noted above) could be obtained until the heir came of age.[7]

Thus it came about that, if a tenant by knight service died, leaving his heir a minor, the lands and body of the child passed into the king's wardship. A small piece of property, a reversion,[8] or even a right,[9] held by this tenure, were each sufficient to draw all the lands descending into the royal control. The king as lord paramount over-rode the rights of the *mesne* lords, and, so long as the heir's lands were in his hand, they might not distrain for services due on those parts of the property held of them,[10] though they did have a statutory right to payment by the king's officers of any actual rents that might be due.[11] The theoretical basis of wardship was that, for the defence of the kingdom, the king must have military service from his tenant or, when the tenant was too young to give it, the means of securing it elsewhere. This explains why a female heir came out of wardship, so far as her body was concerned, at fourteen, seven years before the male, since at that time she was capable of having a husband, who could do service for her lands; if, indeed, she had a husband at that time, her lands too were out

---

[1] Ley, *Learned Treatise*, p. 48.   [2] See Appendix III.
[3] Ley, *Learned Treatise*, p. 53; Dyer, *A.N.C.*, f. 213; Brooke, *A.N.C.*, p. 42.
[4] Ley, *Learned Treatise*, p. 52.   [5] I.e. the next relative unable to inherit.
[6] Bod. MS. Carte 124, ff. 518-19.   [7] Ley, *Learned Treatise*, p. 54.
[8] Ley, *Reports*, pp. 18-19.   [9] Ley, *Learned Treatise*, p. 21.
[10] *N.N.B.*, p. 385.
[11] Staunford, f. 9; 2 Edward VI c. 8.

80 COURT OF WARDS AND LIVERIES [CHAP. IV

of wardship.[1] It also explains why, if an heir had been knighted within the lifetime of his ancestor, he was not in ward either for lands or body, since knighthood was an admission of his ability to serve.[2] Wardship of the body carried with it the right of determining whom the heir should marry, on the basis that his marriage might otherwise be such as would prejudice the king's service. In practice, of course, it would have been impossible to retain all the wards in the king's hand—for one thing, an administrative machine large enough to deal with them could never have been created; for another, it was only by sharing the proceeds of wardship over a pretty wide class of the community that the crown was able to maintain this anachronistic imposition so long. Administrative convenience and realistic policy alike dictated the sale of wards' bodies and the lease of their lands. Of the objections to this practice on ethical grounds, and of the abuses to which it gave rise, something will be said in a later chapter.[3] Here it is enough to note the procedure followed.

The process of obtaining a grant of a ward was normally begun by petition to the master and council of the Court, which included a request for a writ directing the taking of an inquisition, if none had previously been found. There are dozens of files of such petitions amongst the records of the Court, each petition bearing a note over the master's signature as to what action was to be taken on it[4]—'Lett the peticioner have a writt and retourne the office with a Schedule and Confession of thestate the fowerth sitting upon Composicions in Michaelmas terme next,' and similar *formulae*.[5] It was then the clerk's duty to enter the petition, which he must do without charge, and, again, there survive many of the resultant entry books.[6]

---

[1] Ley, *Learned Treatise*, p. 15. If she had no husband, the lands remained in ward until she was sixteen.

[2] Ley, *Learned Treatise*, p. 23. Nor did the king, or other lord, have his marriage. For the effect of knighting during the father's lifetime upon subsequent wardship see Plowden, *Les Commentaries*, 1578, f. 267, Radclife's case; Coke, Reports, vol. IV, p. 483, Constable's case; B.M. Lansdowne MS. 608, f. 13, Earle's case. If knighted during wardship, i.e. after his father's death, the king, or other lord, did have the heir's marriage: see Coke, vol. III, p. 402, Drew Drury's case. According to Ley, *loc. cit.*, in these circumstances the heir was out of wardship for his body, but not for his lands. See, however, Hobart, *Reports*, edn. of 1724, p. 46, Sir Thomas Pickering's case.

[3] See below, pp. 114-19.

[4] Many files of petitions in various bundles of P.R.O. Wards 10.

[5] P.R.O. in Wards 10/27, petitions. [6] P.R.O. Wards 9/214-20.

CHAP. IV]　　　　ADMINISTRATION　　　　81

The petition granted, and the inquisition taken, a copy of the latter had to be deposited in the office of the Court, where a schedule of the value of the ward's property, corresponding with the inquisition, was drawn up. The schedule came before the Court when the grant was considered and the fine for the wardship fixed. Special sittings were held for this purpose, known as compositions for wardships or, less formally, as the beating of the bargain. At them the feodary's certificate and the petitioner's own confession of value were available for comparison with the schedule, and it was the clerk of the wards' responsibility to see that no schedule should pass without being checked either by separate inquisitions from all the counties where the ward's lands lay or, failing them, supplementary surveys by the feodary;[1] he also had to certify whether any inquisition remained of record in the Court giving a better value than the present.[2]

When agreement was reached, details of the grantee's name, the fine and its terms of payment, and sometimes of the exhibition to be allowed for the maintenance of the ward, were added at the foot of the schedule, which was then signed by the master and the attorney.[3] The clerk of the Court then issued a contract, and, upon sight of schedule and contract, one of the auditors made out the indentures of grant, the grantee putting forward two sureties for the payment of the fine. Thereupon a bill for receiving the exhibition was granted under the royal sign manual. The grant then had to pass the signet and the privy seal before the great seal was obtained,[4] and it had to be enrolled by the auditor.[5] The procedure seems unduly complex—there is evidence that, on the king's side, the piles of bills waiting to be signed proved an embarrassment;[6] on the subject's, the expense of time and money was considerable. One contemporary estimate of fees paid to officers in obtaining a grant of wardship suggests 7 *l.* 14*s.* 0*d.* as the total paid out in this way,[7] and Thomas Powell's detailed estimate amounts to a similar sum.[8]

Perhaps because of the difficulty and expense of obtaining a

---

[1] P.R.O. Wards 14/6/11, orders of 28 June 1599.
[2] P.R.O. Wards 14/6/11, orders of 5 May 1606.
[3] There are many schedules in P.R.O. Wards 5. They are paper documents, bearing every trace of being worked on in the way described.
[4] *C.S.P. Dom. 1595-7*, p. 338.
[5] Powell, p. 215.　　　　　　　　　　[6] H.M.C., *Salisbury*, vol. VII, p. 294.
[7] B.M. Harleian MS. 1938, no. 14.　　　　　　　　　　[8] Powell, pp. 215-16.

82   COURT OF WARDS AND LIVERIES   [CHAP. IV

wardship, there was some danger that a petitioner would have second thoughts and fail to pursue the grant. The Court had to guard against this happening, and it did so at every stage of the progress of suing out a grant. When the petitioner received his writ for the holding of an inquisition, he had to take out a bond either to find an office or to return the writ into court at a stated date. What must have been one of the last orders that John Hare drafted before his death provided that, in case of failure by the petitioner to do this, the appropriate feodary was to have a commission and the wardship to be sold to a third party;[1] and the *Instructions* of 1622 also specified that a petitioner who did not attend at the appointed day should lose the benefit of his petition.[2] Similarly, at later stages in the process of securing a grant, the would-be recipient had to be prevented from changing his mind. Hare's order, already quoted, threatened an addition of two shillings in the pound on the sum agreed in the contract, if the grantee did not keep to the time-limit fixed by the Court.[3] Again, on obtaining the schedule he had to bind himself to prosecute the wardship under seal or to return it to the clerk.[4]

There is good evidence among the records of the Court of all the stages in obtaining a grant of wardship that have been outlined; but there is no doubt that, on occasion, the process was short-circuited. This was especially the case where it was desired to reward some servant of the crown. Mary, for instance, wrote to her master of wards, Francis Englefield, that she had granted the wardship and marriage of a youth named Prideaux to Thomas Stukeley;[5] Elizabeth's instructions were, on occasion, even more specific—'It hath pleased her Majestie', Hare was told, 'to grant the Wardship of John Creswell . . . unto one Richard Ryce her highnes servaunt. Wherefore I pray you take notice hereof and enter the same in your offyce, so as her Majesties said servant be not by anie other prevented. . . .'[6] Sometimes the royal intentions were conveyed more formally by warrant under the sign manual: a surviving file of special and immediate warrants[7] includes directions for grants

---

[1] P.R.O. in Wards 1/22, order of 11 Feb. 10 Jas. I.
[2] *Foedera*, vol. XVII, p. 401.
[3] P.R.O. in Wards 1/22, order of 11 Feb. 10 Jas. I.
[4] B.M. Harleian MS. 1323, f. 303.
[5] *C.S.P. Dom. 1547-80*, p. 106.
[6] P.R.O. in Wards 10/43, instructions to Hare, 1598.
[7] P.R.O. Wards 6/1/5, file of special warrants, 1-6 Eliz.

CHAP. IV] ADMINISTRATION 83

of wardships, and there is also a little entry book, entitled *Special and ymmediate warrants and bills assigned directed to the Mr and councell of this courte from kings and Quenes of this realm for passing of things.*[1] This includes four warrants for wardships by Edward VI, four by Mary, and eight by Elizabeth; nor is there any reason to imagine that it is inclusive. Whatever may have been the extent of these direct grants in the earlier days of the Court, there can be no doubt that royal interference was frequent under James I, and, in dddition, semi-private, informal requests for wardships were addressed to the master by individuals. The *Collections* of 1617 hinted broadly that private petitions caused considerable losses, and asserted that all suits for wardship should come before the council of the Court[2]—a demand that subsequent *Instructions* sought to satisfy.[3] In 1617, too, Wallingford begged that the king would not grant any wardship against the instructions of the Court, as otherwise its revenues would decay.[4] The loss in public revenues apart, the officers would naturally disapprove of direct grants, which cut at the root of their fees.

When the heir came of age, he passed out of wardship, but even then he could not enter upon his inheritance until he had sued out his livery. Before he was able to do this, moreover, he had to prove his age, since until that time the inquisition in which he had been found a minor was not superseded. A writ *de aetate probanda* was necessary in order to establish that he had really reached full age. In the old days this had been done by bringing *proves*, all of them forty-two years old at least,[5] to affirm the date of his birth. This they did by stating that it had occurred in the year of some memorable event, such as a great tempest or visitation of plague,[6] or sometimes by recalling its proximity to some happening of personal significance—like that Northumbrian, William de Schaftow, who recollected the birth of John, son and heir of Roger de Wyderington, because he had got drunk in celebrating it and fallen down and broken his leg.[7] Examining a number of fifteenth-century

[1] P.R.O. in Wards 10/2.
[2] B.M. Hargrave MS. 358, f. 14; for an interesting attempt at interference, see *C.S.P. Dom. 1623-5*, pp. 2-3.
[3] *Foedera*, vol. XVII, pp. 61, 67, 402.
[4] *C.S.P. Dom. 1611-18*, p. 466.   [5] Bod. MS. Carte 124, f. 521.
[6] Fitzherbert, *La Graunde Abridgement*, edn. of 1577, Second Part, f. 61.
[7] *Archaeologia Aeliana*, Series I, vol. IV, pp. 326-30. The proof quoted is of date 16 Richard II.

84 COURT OF WARDS AND LIVERIES [CHAP. IV

proofs of this kind, the late Mr R. C. Fowler found them suspiciously repetitive, with a series of remarkably coincidental deaths of daughters, broken legs at football, falls from hay-carts, and other means whereby the birth was alleged to have been fixed in the memory of the witness; and it was his conclusion that the particulars sworn to were fictitious—'the particulars had to be supplied, and a conventional pattern was provided for the purpose'.[1] But in the time of the Court proof of age became, with the increasingly systematic preservation of records, at once easier for the genuine claimant and more difficult for the impostor. At the beginning of James I's reign there was even a scheme to levy 12 d. a year from each parish for the cost of keeping a register of marriages, christenings and burials, since negligently-kept local registers led to inconvenience in matters of wardship.[2] A further modification of procedure was wholly in the heir's favour. He obtained a statutory right to prosecute the writ *de aetate probanda* when he reached full age, even if by the findings of the inquisition post mortem he was still a minor;[3] moreover, once the *de aetata probanda* was found in his favour, even though falsely, it cancelled the inquisition, and the king could not refuse livery.[4]

Where it was definitely proved that land had been taken into the king's hand wrongfully, it was clearly unnecessary for the heir to sue livery, though, since no man might enter upon the king's possession, seisin could not be recovered without an *ouster le maine*; and from Edward I's reign onwards this had been granted *cum exitibus*, that is to say that the king should take no mean rates, although tender for livery had never been made.[5] In the days when the escheator was accustomed to seize lands before the taking of an inquisition, the *ouster le maine* was especially necessary; and though it was established long before the sixteenth century that seizure should not precede office, the *amoveas manum* still issued when the king's title was disproved upon traverse, *monstrance de droit*, or petition. The most obvious case in which it was used was when, although lands had been seized by the king, there proved to be no tenure by knight service in chief, involving prerogative wardship, but only a tenure in common knight service as of some manor, honor or castle;[6] but Ley[7] indicates various other occasions on

[1] *E.H.R.*, vol. XXII, pp. 101-3.   [2] H.M.C., *Salisbury*, vol. XVI, p. 460.
[3] 2 Edward VI c. 8.   [4] Dyer, *A.N.C.*, f. 156.
[5] 28 Edward I c. 19; 29 Edward I.   [6] Brooke, *A.N.C.*, pp. 42, 52.
[7] Ley, *Learned Treatise*, p. 64.

CHAP. IV]　　　　ADMINISTRATION　　　　85

which it might be sought and granted. It is scarcely necessary to add that, if new matter of record subsequently appeared in favour of the king's title he could re-seize the lands; but if the *ouster le maine* had been secured by due process, then a *scire facias* had to issue on the crown's behalf before reseisir took place.[1]

One further matter should be mentioned. The procedure so far discussed may be said to have arisen from the peculiar relationship that existed between the king and those who inherited property held of him; but the widows, no less than the heirs, of tenants in chief were subject to royal restriction. From medieval times the widow had normally received as dower a life interest in one-third of her late husband's lands.[2] This was only granted after the inquisition post mortem was returned and when the widow, appearing either in Chancery or before the escheator, agreed not to marry without the king's licence,[3] which was obtained for a fine that bore reference to the value of her dower.[4] Should she break this agreement and re-marry without licence, she was more heavily mulcted, and to secure what she owed the king might, if he found it necessary, seize her lands.[5] The Court of Wards was naturally responsible for this side of prerogative administration, issuing warrants for the writ *de dote assignanda*,[6] fixing compositions for licences to marry,[7] collecting the fines for marriages without licence, and generally taking charge of the king's widows.

Much of the law that governed the processes that have been examined in this chapter was not at all the creation of the sixteenth and seventeenth centuries, but a part of the medieval land law, grown ever more complex with the passing years, so that when Staunford or Dyer came to expound it they had sometimes to confess uncertainty in phrases like *Quaere* and *Enquire and Learn.* So long as the Court of Wards and Liveries existed, these matters were not merely of academic interest; some knowledge of them was the stock-in-trade of the practical lawyer. What the Tudor and Stuart periods created was the mass of convention which, almost

---

[1] Staunford, f. 80.
[2] F. Pollock and F. W. Maitland, *History of English Law*, vol. II, pp. 418-22.
[3] *N.N.B.*, p. 652; Ley, *Reports*, p. 38.
[4] *C.S.P. Dom. Addenda 1547-65*, p. 310.
[5] *N.N.B.*, p. 431. If the widow never demanded dower of the lands held in chief, she might marry as she pleased without licence (Staunford, f. 18).
[6] Ley, *Reports*, p. 38.　　　　　　　　　　　[7] 32 Henry VIII c. 46 (xxv).

86   COURT OF WARDS AND LIVERIES   [CHAP. IV

as much as the statute and common law, determined the details of procedure, and in the shaping of this body of convention the Court was of paramount importance. Of the administrative practice that resulted from this blending of old and new the main features have perhaps been indicated; but much remains undescribed, and more has been sketched in outline only. The last word, therefore, must be to re-echo—with how much added humility!—Staunford's charming disclaimer—'The rest woulde require so longe a serche that oneles I had gathered and noted them alredie (as I have not done in dede) I should be faine to peruse the hole bodie of ye comon Lawes for the knowleg therof wherunto time seruethe mee not, wherefore at this time myne intent is not to medle with them.'[1]

[1] Staunford, f. 85.

CHAPTER V

JUDICIAL BUSINESS OF THE COURT

THERE is a mass of source material for the history of the Court in its judicial aspect.

In this connexion the central record series is the great class of written pleadings that formed so essential a characteristic of procedure in the Court. From a valuable contemporary list of these,[1] it appears that just under half of the original files of pleadings have survived.[2] Considering the state of other series, and the vicissitudes of the Court's records as a whole, this is a reasonably high proportion. Unfortunately, however, survivals are not evenly distributed chronologically, and there are few pleadings for the first twenty years of the Court's existence.[3] Down to 1638 a system of terminal filing was maintained, but the term in which a particular set of pleadings was filed seems to have little special significance. Many pleadings bear a date, which pretty clearly indicates when they were delivered into Court, and between this and the file date there is a varying time-lag, sometimes of several years. It is likely that the pleadings were treated as current documents, and kept on hand in the clerk's office until such time as a suit was completed, when they were filed. Moreover, from the end of Elizabeth's reign the terminal titles of the files have even less relation to the date of pleadings than previously. No doubt there was by that time a considerable back-log of unfiled pleadings, and it was decided to take a leaf from the Chancery's book[4] and arrange these alphabetically—by the initial letter of the plaintiff's name or, where an answer for debt was concerned, of the name of the person whose

[1] P.R.O. Ind. 10218-10221, list of pleadings, 27 Henry VIII—14 Charles I.
[2] These are mainly in P.R.O. Wards 13, pleadings, with some strays (usually loose pleadings) in P.R.O. Wards 14, pleadings miscellaneous, and P.R.O. Wards 15, pleadings supplementary.
[3] The earliest complete file that I have noticed is P.R.O. Wards 14/4/2, Easter 2 Edward VI; but there are loose pleadings in P.R.O. Wards 14/5/7 and Wards 15/1.
[4] M.S. Giuseppi, *A Guide to the Manuscripts preserved in the Public Record Office*, vol. I, p. 48.

87

88 COURT OF WARDS AND LIVERIES [CHAP. V

lands were charged.[1] Till the last decade of the Court's life this new system was masked by the persistence of terminal titles for each file. Finally, however, it was recognized that such titles were without meaning, and the last files of pleadings in the Court are on a purely alphabetical basis.[2]

Pleadings aside, the Court's entry books are important evidence for its procedure and functions as a court of law. Two series of these entry books are especially valuable—the books of orders, running in a good, though not unbroken, succession from the beginning of Edward VI's reign to the time of the Court's abolition, provide a detailed account of its judicial business;[3] the larger and more formal entry books of decrees, almost complete from 1572 to 1645, are not only evidence for judgments in the Court but often give an outline account of the intermediate stages of process too.[4] Besides these principal series, there are also entry books of affidavits, injunctions and commissions, though most of these cover only the latter half of the Court's history.[5] Moreover, behind the entry books lies the great bulk of original and draft orders, decrees and depositions.[6] It might be argued that, at least where entry books survive, originals of this kind may safely be left aside as being likely to add little to our knowledge of the Court's working. Yet this is not wholly true: drafts and working copies have a value all their own—it is the scribbled note from counsel to his attorney, or the instruction from the attorney of the Court to the clerk of wards, that is often most revealing as to how the judicial machinery really functioned. Certainly it is in material of this sort that the human interest is strongest. It is here that we meet the defendant with his sly request that the Court will be as careful in examining his witnesses as it has been in conducting his own examination—'and then I am sure the businesse wyll be carefullye handled';[7] or the

---

[1] Thus from P.R.O. Ind. 10220 it is clear that the file for Mich. 42-3 Eliz., when the new system started, included those with the initial B; Hil. 43 Eliz. B-C; Easter 43 Eliz. F-G-H; Trin. 43 Eliz. C-A-D-E-F. Mich. 43-4 Eliz. was apparently mixed initials.

[2] P.R.O. Wards 13/145-74.

[3] They are listed in P.R.O. *Wards Guide*, pp. 60-1.

[4] P.R.O. Wards 9/84-102A.

[5] P.R.O. *Wards Guide*, pp. 57, 66.

[6] P.R.O. Wards 1, Proceedings—Decrees; P.R.O. Wards 3, Proceedings—Depositions; and many in P.R.O. Wards 10, miscellaneous records in bundles.

[7] P.R.O. in Wards 3/62, letter of Sir Francis Burnham, 1613.

CHAP. V]   JUDICIAL BUSINESS OF COURT   89

attorney who writes succinctly 'Yf it please you S^r I understand that the defendant's solicitor is in prison.'[1]

To draw attention to what is most significant in this accumulation of the Court's records is not easy. To some extent, however, inquiries may be directed by the best possible mentors—lawyers who, either as counsel or on occasion even as officers, knew the Court and its working inside out. The Court flourished, indeed, in the golden age of the reporters; and though the main interest of most of them lay in the common law courts, it is notable that several included Court of Wards cases in their collections. For the Tudor period there are more than fifty cases in the Court reported by Dyer,[2] and Coke with some thirty odd carries our information into James I's reign.[3] Amongst the other reporters, too, Plowden, Anderson, Moore, Hobart[4] and Croke include a number of Court of Wards cases—though naturally with some overlapping. Curiously enough it was only when the Court had been dissolved for some fourteen years that there appeared a volume specifically devoted to its cases. The anonymous editor of Ley's *Reports*, published in 1659,[5] remarked somewhat naively that 'there lies a trivial Objection against it, that these are Court of Wards Cases, and that Court being now down are therefore useless.'[6] Contemporaries may well have been doubtful as to the triviality of the objection; but however that may be, for the history of the Court Ley's book is of the greatest interest. Attorney for over a dozen years (1608-21) at a crucial period of the Court's existence, Ley's knowledge of the law of wardship and livery was unrivalled, his reporting concise and clear. The seventy-five Court of Wards cases that he describes, all of them dating from James I's reign, form a useful corollary to his *Learned Treatise*.[7]

[1] P.R.O. in Wards 10/23, on bill of costs in Orders etc., Trin. 10 Jas. I. The remark was later crossed out.

[2] *Cy ensuont ascuns nouel cases Collectes per le iades tresreuerend Judge, Monsieur Iasques Dyer, chiefe Iustice del common banke, Ore primierment publies & imprimies*, R. Tottell, 1585; cited here as Dyer, *A.N.C.* Citations have been made from this edition, but in some ways the translation by John Vaillant, 1793, is easier and more satisfactory to use.

[3] *Reports of Sir Edward Coke*, edn. of 1826.

[4] Attorney of the Court 1605-8, but these cases seem mainly to date from the period when he was chief justice of the Common Pleas, as such acting as a judge assistant to the Court.

[5] Sir James Ley, *Reports of Divers Resolutions in Law Arising upon Cases in the Court of Wards etc.*, 1659; cited here as Ley, *Reports*.

[6] *Ibid*. To the Readers.   [7] See above, p. 68.

G

90   COURT OF WARDS AND LIVERIES   [CHAP. V

In addition to the printed reports, there are various manuscript collections of cases in the Court. One such is the selection of decrees from 1553 to 1581, made by John Hare when he was one of the common attorneys of the Court—of particular value since it covers a period for which the official entry books of decrees seem to be lacking. Although not printed, Hare's book nevertheless probably enjoyed some measure of circulation amongst pleaders in the Court: at least six copies of it are still in existence.[1] Another little compilation, sometimes found in association with Hare's decrees[2] and sometimes by itself,[3] probably also circulated. This is a notebook of cases drawn from the third, and from the seventh to tenth, years of James I. It contains a number of cases reported by Ley, but its main interest lies in the inclusion of matters of ordinary, day-to-day judicial business, disregarded by the printed reports, which naturally concentrated on the greater questions of principle. Then again there is the most useful collection of judgments made by Thomas Cole, who had a minor position in the Court in its later days: he reports many earlier cases from records or notes to which he had access, but his real importance is for his reports from late in James I's and on into Charles I's reigns.[4] Besides these three, some other minor collections of cases exist.[5]

Finally, one further type of contemporary compilation offers some guidance. In 1618 William West added to his great precedent book, the *Symboleography*, some examples of pleadings in the Court of Wards.[6] Thomas Cole's manuscript collection, already noted,

---

[1] *Ci ensuit un briefe Collection de toutes tiels decrees fait in le Court de gards queux decidunt ascune doubte in ley ou autrement expresse ou explaine ascun matter necessary pur ester conus daver lexperience de mesme le court, Les queux decrees remaine encorde et enter in les livers appell les liuers de decrees del dit court hors de queux liuers est fait cet collection Et cest coppie e escriete hors del mesme collection, que fuit escriet par l'author, John Hare que fuit escriet par sa maine proprie* 12° *Julij* 1581. Incipiunt Termino Trin. Anno R. Regis Edwardi VI 7.

Copies are B.M. Harleian MS. 1727, Lansdowne MSS. 606 and 607; C.U. MSS. Dd. 3. 9, Hh. 3. 1, Ii. 5. 17. C.U. MS. Hh. 3. 1, gives the fullest title, as above; other citations here are from B.M. Harleian MS. 1727.

[2] B.M. Harleian MS. 1727; C.U. MSS. Dd. 3. 9. and Ii. 5. 17.

[3] C.U. MSS. Dd. 13. 28 and Gg. 3. 26; Dd. 13. 28 cited here.

[4] B.M. Lansdowne MS. 608.

[5] C.U. MS. Gg. 3. 2 is much the same as Ley, *Reports*, but includes additional cases; B.M. Harleian MS. 1588 includes Court of Wards cases, but very briefly reported. B.M. Lansdowne MS. 607 includes, besides Hare's Decrees, cases reported by Coke and Ley and many, temp. Charles I, not reported elsewhere. See also *Winthrop Papers* (Massachusetts Hist. Soc.), vol. II, pp. 1-48.

[6] William West, *Second Part of Symboleography*, edn. of 1641, cited here.

CHAP. V]   JUDICIAL BUSINESS OF COURT   91

includes besides judgments a few precedents after the manner of West.[1] The usefulness of collections of this kind is that they help to distinguish the normal from the exceptional amongst the records.

In its general outlines the Court's procedure was similar to that of the Chancery and the conciliar courts, Star Chamber and the Court of Requests.[2] More specifically, especially in its early days, the Court was modelled on the Duchy Chamber of Lancaster.[3] Duchy Chamber and Court had, indeed, an almost identical blend of judicial and administrative functions, and there was statutory authority for the latter to imitate the procedure of the former.[4] But what characterised all these courts alike was their adoption of a system of written pleadings in the English language.

A case in the Court of Wards began by the delivery into court of a bill or information engrossed in parchment and signed in the bottom righthand corner by counsel acting for the plaintiff. Theoretically there was a distinction between bill and information, the bill being appropriate where a private individual was the aggrieved party, the information where some wrong done to the crown was alleged. In practice, no doubt, a rigid distinction of the kind was not always maintained—what is called *billa* in the contemporary list turns up as an information on the file, and so on. But that some differentiation continued to be made is proved by the ruling of 1610 that a committee, wishing to complain of trespass on his ward's lands, must do so by information and not by bill, since the initiation of suits where a ward's interests were involved lay with the attorney of the Court.[5] In fact, of course, the interest of committee, ward and king often all three demanded the bringing of a case, and any difficulty that might have been expected to arise from the attorney's monopoly of action where a ward was concerned was overcome by the practice whereby he laid his information at the relation of a committee or other aggrieved party. From the attorneyship of Richard Kingsmill (1572-89) onwards, the proportion of suits technically initiated by the attorney increased;[6] but it would be wrong to imagine that this implied neglect of private suitors' grievances. Indeed, the notable latitude that, on occasion,

[1] B.M. Lansdowne MS. 608.
[2] Holdsworth, vol. v, pp. 178-88; *Select Cases in the Court of Requests*, Selden, Soc., pp. xx-xxii.   [3] *T.R.H.S.*, 4th Series, vol. XXIII, pp. 175-7.
[4] 32 Henry VIII c. 46.   [5] C.U. MS. Dd. 13. 28, f. 18
[6] The lists in P.R.O. Ind. 10218-10221 make this clear.

92 COURT OF WARDS AND LIVERIES [CHAP. V

the Court allowed to imperfect bills may well have been a reflection of the essential identity of interest between crown and private plaintiff. Perhaps when a suitor was allowed to put more into his bill,[1] or when by the Court's order a bill was amended,[2] or a plaintiff permitted to take his bill away and put in a new one,[3] the Court acted thus generously because it was in the royal interest that the suits concerned should go forward.

Generally speaking, the bill or information, having alleged a wrong committed, in its conclusion sought a privy seal requiring the defendant to appear and make answer. If this request were granted by the Court, the attorney would fix a day for appearance and answer, sometimes noting on the bill itself the phrase *fiat processus*. In a case brought solely on the king's behalf, process was no doubt served on the defendant either by the Court's messenger or by its pursuivant. When the plaintiff was a private individual, however, he often seems to have had the responsibility of arranging delivery of the writ himself, and one of his servants frequently deposed to having personally delivered it.[4] This was not always so easy as it may sound, moreover, for defendants were apt to be elusive. A typical story was related in Thomas Melior's deposition of 25 January 1603. Describing his attempt to serve a privy seal on William Kinge of Wotton, he told how Mrs Kinge had said that her husband was ill and how he had found the door locked against him; thereupon, calling that he had a privy seal, he had pushed it through a hole in the door.[5] This probably constituted an adequate serving of process, for in the same year it was held that to fix a copy of a privy seal on the party's door was sufficient, provided this were done in the presence of credible witnesses.[6]

A defendant who disobeyed process of the Court ran heavy risks. If he did not appear on the appointed day, he was liable to be condemned in costs;[7] if he refused to answer, or his answer were reckoned insufficient, he might be fined or his body attached;[8] if his disobedience was adjudged to amount to contempt, he might be committed to the Fleet.[9] Moreover, by an invidious custom the

[1] C.U. MS. Dd. 13. 28, f. 4.
[2] P.R.O. Wards 13/74, bill of Wase, put in 23 Nov. 1605.
[3] P.R.O. Wards 9/278, f. 139.
[4] A good example is the deposition of Richard Wilson, servant of Sir Francys Godolphyn, amongst depositions Mich. 20. Jas. I, in P.R.O. Wards 1/22.
[5] P.R.O. Wards 9/527, 25 Jan. 45 Eliz.
[6] C.U. MS. Dd. 13. 28, f. 1.   [7] *Ibid.* f. 4.   [8] *Ibid.* f. 9.   [9] *Ibid.* f. 22.

CHAP. V]   JUDICIAL BUSINESS OF COURT   93

plaintiff seems to have been expected to take a share in the execution of some of these disciplinary measures, just as he had in the original serving of process. Such a system was obviously open to abuse: it is difficult, for example, not to sympathize with that John Roberts who swore, in 1622, that he had never been served with process at the suit of Sir Edward Grevill until he was arrested by the sheriff and handed over to one of Grevill's servants.[1] Even if a defendant made appearance on the appointed day and the content of his answer passed muster, he might still find it rejected for some seemingly trivial reason, such as that it left no room for the officer's hand before whom it had to be sworn.[2]

That some mitigation of the rigours of this procedure did take place is true. As might be expected, where a nobleman was defendant, he was treated with greater consideration than a commoner: there is an almost apologetic note in Burghley's letters in which he acquaints Elizabeth Countess of Rutland[3] and Anne Countess of Warwick[4] of bills exhibited against them. Sickness and old age, moreover, were always accepted as reasons for non-appearance in Court, and in these circumstances arrangements were made for answers to be taken by commission. Again, when Sir Ralph Delaval was defendant in a suit, the Court, bearing in mind the importance of his duties as deputy lieutenant of Northumberland and special commissioner for matters concerning the Border, granted a *dedimus potestatem* to take his answer in Newcastle-upon-Tyne.[5] An answer, taken in this way before a commission, was delivered into court by one of the commissioners.

Before he was in a position to answer the bill or information, the defendant had to have an opportunity of studying it. It was, of course, his own responsibility to see that he got this. In the very early days of the Court he perhaps only saw the allegations against him at such time as he made his appearance. At any rate a bill filed in the Court's first year is listed as having the 'aunswer in the back syde'[6]—which certainly suggests no great formality. More business-like methods developed, however, and in the second half

---

[1] P.R.O. Wards 1/22, depositions, Mich. 20 Jas. I,

[2] P.R.O. Wards 2/194/1.   [3] H.M.C., *Rutland*, vol. I, p. 260.

[4] H.M.C., *Salisbury*, vol. XIII, p. 478; cf. West, *Second Part*, f. 334. If disregarded, the letter was followed by normal process—B.M. Lansdowne MS. 608, f. 52.

[5] Newcastle-upon-Tyne Public Library, Delaval papers, box 29/F.

[6] P.R.O. Ind. 10218, under Trin. 32 Henry VIII.

94   COURT OF WARDS AND LIVERIES   [CHAP. V

of Elizabeth's reign it became usual for the bill or information to have a note inscribed on it that it had been copied for the defendant: this might ultimately be important for the calculation of costs. Another factor making for formality was that the Court used the Star Chamber device of the sworn answer. It was ruled under James I that even a baron must deliver his answer on oath.[1]

The defendant's answer, when he made it, was usually framed in one of two ways. On the one hand, he might put forward what was really a demurrer, claiming that the plaintiff's case was not pleadable in the Court of Wards, and that he should seek remedy, if at all, at the common law or in some other court. If the defendant elected to take this line, it was important that his demurrer should include a statement of all the reasons for making it, since any that were left out could not afterwards be alleged on the day given to maintain it.[2] On the other hand, if there was no hope of a demurrer succeeding, the defendant's answer consisted of a general rebuttal to the effect that there was no case to meet, a specific reply to the allegations made, and finally a request for the case to be dismissed with costs in his favour.

If a defendant were replying to an information (yet another distinction between that and the bill[3]), he was liable to examination upon interrogatories drawn up by the plaintiff. These were, of course, framed in the light of the answer he had made; and yet the plaintiff had to waste no time about the business, for if the interrogatories were not put into court within four days of the delivery of the answer, the defendant was licensed to depart and was discharged of any obligation to be examined upon interrogatories in that suit.[4] If he were examined within the four days, however, the defendant's replies to interrogatories, since they expounded his answer, were valid evidence against him.[5] The plaintiff, too, might carry his case further with a replication, which the defendant might meet with a rejoinder, and so on. It is difficult to assess the importance of these later stages of the written pleading: it may be

---

[1] P.R.O. Wards 9/533, orders of Easter 10 Jas. I.

[2] C.U. MS. Dd. 13. 28, f. 20.

[3] B.M. Lansdowne MS. 608, f. 22, a defendant discharged of being examined upon interrogatories, for the plaintiff should have exhibited a bill and not an information; defendant to a bill was not examined upon interrogatories, *ibid.* f. 59.

[4] *Ibid.* f. 27.

[5] C.U. MS. Dd. 13. 28, f. 23.

CHAP. V]   JUDICIAL BUSINESS OF COURT   95

that in the Court of Wards, as in Chancery and Star Chamber, they became mere matters of form.[1]

Probably more important than this statement and restatement by the parties was the gradual process by which both sides built up the evidence for their case. In this an important part was played by the testimony of witnesses given in reply to interrogatories framed by one or other of the parties. Many hundreds of such depositions upon interrogatories survive,[2] and they are the measure of the effort that was made to place detailed evidence before the Court. Indeed it may have been that some of their detail was excessive and irrelevant. Walter Cary made this allegation against interrogatories in the prerogative courts as a whole, asserting that often they had no effect save to add to costs.[3] But the Court continued to put great faith in interrogatories as a means of establishing fact; and though no additional interrogatories were permitted after the commencement of examination, and second examinations upon the same matter were suppressed, yet new matters that cropped up in the course of pleading were held to justify new interrogatories.[4]

It was neither desirable, nor indeed possible, for the whole business of examination of witnesses to take place in court, and many examinations were in fact made in the country. A surviving calendar, listing those in court and those before commissions, suggests that there was a high proportion of the latter.[5] Commissioners for this purpose were appointed on the basis of nominations agreed by the attorneys of both parties to a suit;[6] they might include counsel for one of the parties, provided the other did not object to his presence on the commission.[7] The commission constituted, it had to give fourteen days warning to those who were to give evidence before it.[8] Perhaps the most striking feature of these commissions is the burden that they laid upon the country

---

[1] Holdsworth, vol. v, p. 181.

[2] Sometimes filed with pleadings in P.R.O. Wards 13, sometimes in P.R.O. Wards 3 and strays in P.R.O. Wards 10.

[3] *The Present State of England*, 1627, p. 20.   [4] B.M. Lansdowne MS. 608, f. 16.

[5] P.R.O. Wards 9/296, calendar of commissions, depositions and examinations. For three sample years the figures are—37 Eliz., 170 examinations in court, 99 by commission; 7 Jas. I, 183 and 185; 1 Charles I, 101 and 79.

[6] Notes of their names, over the signatures of the attorneys for the two parties, were kept on the files of warrants for privy seals and commissions, P.R.O. in Wards 10/64, 67-76, 78.

[7] C.U. MS. Dd. 13. 28, f. 39.   [8] *Ibid.* f. 8.

96   COURT OF WARDS AND LIVERIES   [CHAP. V

gentlemen nominated to serve on them—many of them already heavily involved in judicial and administrative work as justices of the peace or as members of other *ad hoc* royal commissions. It is small wonder if sometimes a clash of duties occurred, such as in 1611 prevented Robert Holmes from being present at the execution of a Court of Wards commission since he was engaged at Quarter Sessions.[1] More pathetic was the excuse of William Oxenbregge some years later, when attempting to extricate himself from membership of a commission. 'I can not heare their answeres', he wrote, 'nor the other commissioners examinations without such lowd speaking as is unfitt for such a buysenes'.[2] There was much sense in the proposal, made in Charles I's reign, for the establishment of an examiner in each county to take depositions in cases depending in this, and other, courts.[3]

Aside from the testimony of witnesses, private deeds and other muniments formed important evidence in suits. The significance of records of this kind is indicated by the long wrangle over the Rutland evidences that succeeded the death of the third earl in 1587.[4] Or again, the mass of private documents still to be found amongst the records of the Court is another proof of the energy with which it sought to bring this kind of evidence under consideration.[5]

To follow a particular case in the Court through all its stages is very difficult indeed. Of its outline a fair account was usually given in the ultimate decree, but for the details of successive motions by counsel before the suit was brought to an issue, and for interim procedure, reference has to be made to the entry books of orders and injunctions, and to the rough notebooks of what was done in court each day.[6] These sources do much to counteract the impression, perhaps left uppermost in the mind if study is simply concentrated upon pleadings, that the Court was merely passive until such time as issue was formally joined. Especially in the issue of injunctions of a temporary character, until the suit was settled, it was in fact extremely active. Injunctions to stay a defendant from waste, to make him avoid from possession of a ward's body or lands or, of more permanent significance, against

[1] P.R.O. in Wards 10/30, correspondence.
[2] B.M. Add. MS. 35124, f. 20.   [3] *C.S.P. Dom. 1637-8*, pp. 78-9.
[4] H.M.C., *Rutland*, vol. I, pp. 261-84; *Salisbury*, vol. V, p. 187.
[5] P.R.O. Wards 2; see below, pp. 176-7.   [6] P.R.O. *Wards Guide*, p. 65.

CHAP. V]   JUDICIAL BUSINESS OF COURT   97

the prosecution of suits in other courts, were frequent.[1] These had
the full weight of the Court's authority behind them, and upon
affidavit of a breach of an injunction an attachment was awarded.[2]
Sometimes, it seems, the injunction may well have operated unjustly, as in the case of John Thurbarne early in James I's reign,
against whom the attorney, at the relation of a certain Francis
Bussey, obtained an injunction preventing a suit at common law,
before ever Thurbarne had been served with process or made
answer; and content with his injunction, Bussey did not trouble to
call Thurbarne into court.[3]

The pleadings completed (and, if they had grown bulky, breviates
supplied[4]), the next step was the publication in the Court of the
depositions of witnesses. Further examination of witnesses after
publication could only be made in exceptional circumstances,[5] and
normally the case was at this stage ready for hearing. The usual
course of the Court, in fact, was that at the order for publication
a day for hearing was set down; and though a more complicated,
and more expensive, procedure was for a time substituted by
Cranfield, Naunton returned to something like the earlier practice.[6]
Either way, in the fixing of a day for hearing there was negotiation,
and often agreement, between the attorneys of the parties, as
appears from a letter written by one of his clients to John Hare,
when he was one of the common attorneys of the Court—'Good
Mr Hare', wrote Robert Cholmeley, defendant in a suit in which
Richard Corry was plaintiff in 1587, 'I pray you agree with Mr
Pickeringe that the hearinge of the cause betwene Mr Corry and
me bee set downe to be the xj[th]. of Novembre next for my replye.
Harry Cholmeley and Richard Corry did agre the last terme before
Mr Pickeringe that if those matters were not ordered in the
Cuntrie, they would desire this terme to have a day set downe for
heringe therof the next terme.' The other common attorney (who,
incidentally, was Pickarell, and not Pickeringe as Cholmeley had it)
signified at the foot of the note that the plaintiff had agreed to this.[7]

At least during the second half of its existence, the Court had
separate sittings for hearings and for routine matters. As early as

[1] West, *Second Part*, ff. 318, 331-3, and see opening ff. of P.R.O. Wards 9/298,
entry book of injunctions.
[2] C.U. MS. Dd. 13. 28, f. 2.   [3] P.R.O. Wards 13/67.
[4] C.U. MS. Dd. 13. 28, f. 7; P.R.O. Wards 9/514, Audley *v.* Harrys, orders of
Easter 7 Edward VI.
[5] B.M. Lansdowne MS. 608, f. 45.   [6] *Ibid,* f. 24.   [7] P.R.O. in Wards 1/10.

98   COURT OF WARDS AND LIVERIES   [CHAP. V

1599, Richard Perceval wrote to Salisbury, desiring his presence at the hearing of certain causes, and, since Salisbury apparently could not attend on the Tuesday, promised to try to reserve these cases to the day following, even though Wednesday was normally a day for motions and matters of revenue.[1] This distinction was subsequently maintained. Some fragments of a notebook of motions and hearings, dating from the latter part of James I's reign, show that Monday, Tuesday, Thursday and Saturday were ordinarily reserved for hearings, Wednesday and Friday for the more routine business of motions.[2] There was a similar arrangement up to the very eve of the civil war.[3]

When a case came up for hearing, the written pleadings, depositions and documentary evidence were available for the Court's consideration, and these formed the centre around which the arguments of counsel turned. The master and council of the Court —that is, its principal officers—decided a proportion of cases on their own initiative. So far as these were concerned, the influence of the attorney of the wards, as the Court's chief legal officer, was paramount: on occasion, indeed, Ley describes a decision as 'resolved by the Attorney and Court'.[4] Where the precedents were not clear, however, and doubtful legal issues raised, reference was made to the law officers—the attorney-general and solicitor-general—to individual serjeants and to the common law judges. Their fees figure in the receiver-general's accounts from the Court's earliest days, at first among miscellaneous expenses, and later under the heading Fees and Diets. For a long time these payments settled down at annual sums of 10 l. each to the lord chief justice and to the chief justice of the Common Pleas, and 4 l. to the attorney-general.[5] In 1604, however, increased business led to the fees of the two chief justices being doubled, and to a similar fee of 20 l. yearly also being allocated to the lord chief baron of the Exchequer.[6]

The character of the assistance rendered by these men to the Court varied from case to case. Sometimes it was quite informal —'The Attorney of the Wards asked another Question by word of

[1] H.M.C., *Salisbury*, vol. VIII, p. 541, where dated 1598.
[2] P.R.O. in Wards 10/30, fragments of notebook of motions, hearings etc., 13 and 15 Jas. I.
[3] P.R.O. in Wards 10/51, miscellanea.
[4] Ley, *Reports*, p. 20.   [5] P.R.O. Wards 9/387, f. 278.
[6] P.R.O. Wards 9/88, f. 461, decree of Mich. 2. Jas. I.

CHAP. V] JUDICIAL BUSINESS OF COURT 99

Mouth', Hobart reported in his account of Pickering's case.[1] Sometimes a case was drawn up and submitted to them by the attorney,[2] often with the agreement of counsel on both sides, who set their hands to it.[3] There is good evidence of the care with which the judges assistant, as they came to be called, set about their task. On one occasion in Mary's reign, having heard counsel's arguments, they deferred their decree until they were further advised;[4] and half a century later, in the Earl of Cumberland's case, though at the initial hearing their views were pretty clear, 'yet because it was but their opinions as they conceived the case, Prima facie' they arranged to hear further argument.[5] These hearings were by no means always in court. Dyer reports a decision from early in Elizabeth's reign that was arrived at after consideration by an assembly of all the justices at Serjeants' Inn and a subsequent debate of four and a half hours' duration at Burghley's house in the Savoy;[6] Sammes' case of 1610 was another that was argued at Serjeants' Inn.[7] In circumstances of this sort the judges assistant delivered their opinion in writing to the attorney of the wards, who brought it into Court.[8] From time to time, on the other hand, they were actually requested to sit in the Court itself, and then trial was conducted at the bar.[9] In an Elizabethan picture of the Court the two chief justices are shown on either side of the master.[10]

It can scarcely be doubted that the influence of the judges assistant was for the good. At times the principles of the common law and the practice of the Court were contradictory, and the views of judges and officers pulled in opposite directions. In a case reported by Dyer, he, Saunders and the serjeants held that, if a man were found falsely to be of age upon a *de aetate probanda*, the king had no remedy—a decision opposed by the master and by Keilwey, the surveyor of the liveries;[11] or again, in another case, he reports the officers' point of view but adds bluntly 'quod non credo'.[12] It was perhaps due to the judges assistant that decisions were by no means unreservedly in favour of the crown, and that

---

[1] Henry Hobart, *Reports*, edn. of 1724, p. 46.
[2] P.R.O. Wards 9/103, f. 33, decree in Lutterell's case.
[3] P.R.O. Wards 9/84, f. 498, decree in Wroughton's case.
[4] P.R.O. Wards 9/516, f. 312, Duncombe v. Pattenham.
[5] Ley, *Reports*, p. 4.   [6] Dyer, *A.N.C.*, f. 286.   [7] Ley, *Reports*, p. 12.
[8] Sackville MSS. 7701-2, an example of a judges assistants' opinion.
[9] P.R.O. Wards 9/344, Probert's case, 26 May 1627.
[10] See below, p. 168.   [11] Dyer, *A.N.C.*, f. 156.   [12] *Ibid.* f. 260.

100 COURT OF WARDS AND LIVERIES [CHAP. V

the Court escaped the worst evils that might result from a too close connection between executive and judicature, where judge and counsel for the crown tended to be merged in the same personality.

Despite the importance that certainly attaches to the judges assistant, it must not be imagined that every case involved their decision, or even indeed that it was necessarily given a detailed hearing in court at all. Many matters, especially where questions of fact rather than law were at issue, were settled arbitrarily. Often —perhaps most often—such arbitrations were by one or more officers of the Court, as in the case of the coheirs of Benjamin Gonson at the end of Elizabeth's reign, when the attorney arbitrated;[1] or, two or three years later, in Wellar v. Carrill, where the suit was remitted first to the clerk and auditor and then to the surveyor, clerk and auditor for settlement;[2] or again, in Hollyday v. Ferrers et al., in 1629, where it was submitted to the surveyor, receiver-general and auditor.[3] Occasionally, too, counsel of the two parties were nominated to arbitrate between them.[4] Most interesting of all, moreover, a case was sometimes completely turned over to commissioners in the country. Such was, for instance, the procedure in the taking of the account of a certain Marie Doylie, widow, in 1620, when Norfolk commissioners were appointed to proceed from day to day until they had determined the cause summarily.[5]

In any event, whether judgment was given upon the opinion of the judges assistant, upon the decision of the master and council, or upon the finding of a commission with arbitrary powers, it was normally embodied in a formal decree of the Court.

There remained the question of costs. A ruling about these, in general terms, was usually included in the decree. The party to whom costs were granted thereupon made a detailed demand, which was put forward by his counsel; and on receipt of this demand, the attorney of the wards then sought the other party's exceptions to it. With both these statements before him, he assessed the costs to be allowed, sometimes working through the costs claimed item by item, allowing some and disallowing others, some-

---

[1] P.R.O. Wards 9/88, f. 294.   [2] P.R.O. Wards 9/88, f. 451.
[3] P.R.O. in Wards 10/53, auditors' certificates.
[4] C.U. MS. Dd. 13. 28, f. 1.
[5] P.R.O. in Wards 1/99, commission to take account of Marie Doylie.

CHAP. V]   JUDICIAL BUSINESS OF COURT   101

times only stating an over-all figure without any explanation of how he had reached it. In either event the amount allowed was nearly always considerably less than the amount claimed.[1]

Collection of costs was authorized by privy seal.[2] Amongst the depositions for Michaelmas term 1622 is a vivid account of the difficulties the successful litigant might, on occasion, meet when he presented this and claimed his due from his adversary. Henry Carter deposed that, going through Lincoln's Inn Fields, he was unexpectedly overtaken by John Elliot, with whom he had apparently been at issue in the Court. Elliot wasted no time in beginning to revile his former opponent, 'calling him base dog base slave and suche like, sayeing that it were a good deed to cut this deponents throat', and, suiting the action to the words, putting his sword point at Carter's face. At this not very appropriate moment, Carter produced the Court's privy seal for payment by Elliot of 4 l. 10s. costs and, when Elliot refused to take it, cast it on the ground before him. At this Elliot went his way, but not before he had made it clear that 'he cared not for three or foure poundes costes and that this deponent was no officer of the court', nor before he had repeated his former abuse.[3]

This sort of incident serves as a reminder that, though the Court of Wards was not primarily a penal court, and though it was mainly concerned with civil cases, yet it needed penal powers, both to enforce respect for its own process and to punish those defendants who had committed wrongs amounting to crime. There is evidence that it had, and used, such powers. Litigants were sometimes, for instance, committed to the custody of the usher,[4] and upon proved contempt might be imprisoned in the Fleet;[5] a false information was punished by committal to the Counter and a fine.[6] To the Fleet, too, was committed a defendant proved guilty of waste— though that decree was afterwards respited;[7] another defendant, who to waste had added an illicit claim to plead *in forma pauperis*, was bound over before the justices of the peace of his home county;[8]

[1] There are many bills of costs on files of orders in P.R.O. Wards 1; others in P.R.O. Wards 10.
[2] A specimen privy seal for this purpose in P.R.O. Wards 10/27, formulary book.
[3] P.R.O. in Wards 1/22.
[4] P.R.O. Wards 9/241, 19 May 2 Jas. I.   [5] C.U. MS. Dd. 13. 28, f. 22.
[6] B.M. Lansdowne MS. 608, f. 44.
[7] P.R.O. Wards 9/516, f. 341, Swyft's case.
[8] P.R.O. Wards 9/88, f. 475, Newton v. Batman.

102   COURT OF WARDS AND LIVERIES   [CHAP. V

ravishment of ward was punished by fine.[1] Upon a woman who had contracted marriage with a known idiot, and had afterwards had the rashness to seek maintenance in the Court, there was passed a suspended sentence of whipping—to take effect if she should trouble Court or committee again.[2] Moreover, behind penal powers of this kind exercised by the Court stood those of Star Chamber. There was punished by fine of 500 *l.*, damages, costs, imprisonment, bond for good behaviour, and confession at the Assizes a defendant who had resisted the serving of process out of the Court of Wards.[3] The Star Chamber had also jurisdiction in cases of perjury committed in the Court.[4]

Something must be said about counsel practising in the Court, for in all stages of the procedure outlined they were active, and on counsel's conduct of a case turned much of the success that a litigant might hope to enjoy. The Court of Wards was another sphere of activity for the common lawyer. By royal proclamation of 1546 no one might plead there without previously reading in one of the Inns of Court, unless specially appointed by the chancellor and the two chief justices with the advice of the benchers of the Inns.[5] Otherwise no particular qualification was required. The inclusion of Court of Wards cases in the collections of the common law reporters suggests that any counsel might expect to find himself appearing, at some time or other, before the Court; on the other hand, the lack of printed collections of cases or tracts specifically relating to the Court's business, until the publication of Ley's *Learned Treatise* in 1642, is an argument against very much specialization. No doubt if a list of pleaders in the Court were constructed (and, since counsel signed pleadings, there is evidence for such a list), it would be found that some names recur more frequently than others, like Ralph Bossevile, who seems to have practised extensively in the Court before becoming clerk of the wards,[6] or Sherfield, who was a popular counsel under James I.[7] But there is no appearance of pleading being confined to a small

[1] B.M. Lansdowne MS. 608, ff. 50, 53, 56.
[2] *Ibid.* f. 38.
[3] *Les Reportes del Cases in Camera Stellata,* ed. W. P. Baildon, p. 167.
[4] *Ibid.* pp. 1-2.   [5] Holdsworth, vol. IV, p. 271.
[6] P.R.O. Wards 9/516 for his appearances in Court.
[7] See, however, *Journal of Ralph Assheton,* Chetham Soc., 1848, pp. 114-16, 125-6, for a litigant who was dissatisfied with Sherfield.

CHAP. V]   JUDICIAL BUSINESS OF COURT   103

class, enjoying a particular expertise in matters of wardship and livery. Nor did the Court concern itself unduly with the counsel who appeared in it. In 1603 it limited the fees that they might take,[1] and Carew, on becoming master, put before them the two great aims of modesty in manner and pertinency in matter.[2] Beyond this, however, there is no evidence of interference, and indeed with the appointment of common attorneys, who as minor officials of the Court could be held responsible for the observance of due procedure, there was no need to assert direct discipline over counsel.[3]

If we turn from matters of procedure to the type of judicial business transacted, one thing is at once apparent, and that is the very close inter-relationship between the administrative and judicial functions of the Court. Indeed to treat separately of the two, as has been done in the previous and present chapters, can only be justified on grounds of convenience, for no such distinction would have been recognized by contemporaries. The point may be made again that the principal administrative officers of the Court ranked as judges, not merely carrying out certain judicial duties individually but also taking their places at the council table when cases came up for hearing. These cases, moreover, had a double connexion with the administrative business of livery and wardship. On the one hand, most of them arose directly from problems cropping up in the normal course of administration; on the other, once judgment was given it became a precedent which helped to determine future administrative practice—a fact that gave the Court's decisions particular significance. 'If the rules and maxims of law in the first raising of tenures *in capite* be weakened', Bacon asserted, 'this nips the flower in the bud, and may do more hurt by a resolution in law, than the losses, which the King's tenures do daily receive by oblivion or suppression, or the neglect of officers, or the iniquity of jurors, or other like blasts, whereby they are continually shaken'.[4] In 1601 the officers went so far as to assert that the whole making or marring of the Court's proceedings depended upon a particular case then under consideration.[5]

---

[1] P.R.O. Wards 14/3/20, draft orders of 11 May 1 Jas. I.
[2] P.R.O. S.P. 14/69, no. 69, discourse to the Court.
[3] See above, pp. 30-1.
[4] Bacon, vol. VII, p. 547.   [5] H.M.C., *Salisbury*, vol. XI, p. 438.

104　　COURT OF WARDS AND LIVERIES　　[CHAP. V

Directly or indirectly all cases were revenue matters, and a great proportion of them quite simply concerned the levy or discharge of debt to the crown. This was, in fact, the historical origin of the Court's jurisdiction. In the days before its statutory foundation those summoned to appear before the master were predominantly defaulting accountants and other debtors,[1] and at the Court's erection its jurisdiction in these matters was confirmed,[2] the Exchequer losing such part of it as it had previously exercised.[3] Process for debt was, and remained, a principal preoccupation of the Court: sometimes a whole file of pleadings consisted of answers to debts,[4] and in the entry books of decrees discharge of arrears forms the largest single item. Much of this business was no doubt technical in character and referred to the auditor, on the basis of whose certificate the Court would reach its decision and frame its decree.[5] Occasionally, however, legal issues were raised, sometimes so complex that a case was submitted to the judges assistant for their opinion.[6] From time to time such cases of debt involved consequential action, as where leases were declared forfeit for non-payment of rent.[7] Yet it would not be just to represent the Court in its judicial capacity as operating always and solely in the king's financial interest: in several cases where, for some reason or other, a committee did not enjoy the wardship granted to him, or a lessee the lands, the bonds they had given for payment were cancelled.[8]

In matters other than debt the Court's administrative and judicial business were similarly connected. As a court of law one of its principal functions was to combat concealments of tenures in chief and punish the heir who thus attempted to escape his feudal obligations. Proceedings against wards entering their lands before livery sued were authorized by the statute that erected the Court,[9] and against heirs guilty of such intrusion the attorney of the wards laid information, seeking a privy seal that should direct their appearance and a *ducens secum* for the bringing in of evidences.[10] In much the same way, an heir who refused the marriage tendered

---

[1] See above, p. 12.　　　[2] 32 Henry VIII c. 46 (xiii).　　　[3] *Ibid.* (xxii).
[4] An example is P.R.O. Wards 13/11, pleadings, Easter 15 Jas. I; the list of pleadings shows others.
[5] *C.S.P. Dom. 1638-9*, p. 609.　　　[6] B.M. Harleian MS. 1727, ff. 4-5.
[7] B.M. Lansdowne MS. 608, f. 26.
[8] B.M. Harleian MS. 1727, ff. 20, 31, 38.　　　[9] 32 Henry VIII c. 46 (xxxi).
[10] West, *Second Part*, f. 325.

CHAP. V] JUDICIAL BUSINESS OF COURT 105

to him by the king's committee, and who would not pay the recognized fine for such refusal, was dealt with by the Court, which simply addressed a *caveat* to the clerk of the liveries, ordering him to make stay of livery until such time as the heir came into line.[1]

Again, the inquisition post mortem, which has been seen above to have been basic to the whole administration of livery and wardship, frequently came under consideration by the Court as a judicial body. It was inevitable that, amongst the great mass of inquisitions taken, returns should vary in accuracy and precision, and, since so much turned on the inquisition, it was important for king and subject alike that there should be means of remedying its imperfections. By a series of judgments the Court established three separate categories of imperfect inquisitions, and provided for each category a different remedy.

First, there were some inquisitions so incomplete that the Court adjudged them void outright. This seems always to have been its decision where the inquisition failed to make clear the county in which the lands held by the deceased lay. Such was the omission in the inquisition on Roger Raysing early in Elizabeth's reign,[2] and on John Bailie some half century later.[3] Both were declared void by the Court, and so, contemporary with the second, was an office that described lands as *in vel prope* Dorchester, that too being reckoned to lack certainty of either town or county.[4] Another sort of inadequacy led to the voiding of an inquisition in Dakin's case; it failed to show by virtue of what writ it had been taken, and there was no writ or commission attached to the return.[5] Most obvious of all imperfections, the inquisition on John Jon was self-contradictory, and inevitably ruled void for its repugnancy.[6] In circumstances of this kind it was established by the Court that a *mandamus* should issue for the taking of a new office, without any regard whatever for the findings previously made.

The second category of imperfect offices was intermediate between those void outright and those that the Court adjudged good. In this group were reckoned inquisitions where the jurors had expressed doubt or ignorance as to lord or services in phrases like *de quo tenetur Juratores ignorant* or *sed per que servicia Juratores*

---

[1] C.U. MS. Dd. 13. 28, ff. 2, 7.
[2] Dyer, *A.N.C.*, f. 209.
[3] Coke, *Reports*, vol. VI, p. 456. [4] Ley, *Reports*, p. 24.
[5] *Ibid.* p. 31. [6] Hobart, *Reports*, edn. of 1724, p. 38.

H

106 COURT OF WARDS AND LIVERIES [CHAP. V

ignorant,[1] or even where they had let an unguarded *prout patet,* suggesting lack of absolute certainty, slip into their return.[2] The Court dealt with uncertain offices of this kind in accordance with a statute of Edward VI's reign,[3] not declaring them void but merely insufficient and to be completed by a *melius inquirendum,* ordering a second inquisition. As distinct from the inquisition upon a *mandamus,* however, that upon a *melius inquirendum* was merely supplementary to the first office and had no independent existence of its own;[4] thus if the first inquisition and that on the *melius inquirendum* were found in separate counties, the latter was void,[5] or, again, should the first office later be voided, that upon the *melius inquirendum* was automatically void too.[6]

Finally, there was a large class of offices which, though technically perfect and therefore neither void nor insufficient, were yet felt by the subject to be untrue findings, which would operate to his harm. For an inquisition of this kind his remedy lay in the traverse, and though, as has been seen, the traverse was arduous,[7] the decree books made it clear that it accounted for a very considerable proportion of the Court's judicial business.

A further category of cases was that concerned with the interpretation of the Henrician statutes of Uses and Wills.

Most of the cases relating to uses were complex and do not readily lend themselves to short description. Mention must be made, however, of the famous decision in Tyrrel's case that made void a use upon a use,[8] and a further case is worth describing, not merely because it concerned no less a person than Oliver Cromwell, but also because it is in many ways typical of a kind of suit that was frequently before the Court. Sir Henry Cromwell was seised of the Augustinian friary in Huntingdon, held of the crown by knight service in chief, as was so much of what had formerly been ecclesiastical property. He suffered a common recovery of it to the use of himself and his wife for their lives, with remainders to his second son, Robert, to Robert's heirs male, and to his own right heirs. Robert Cromwell, who was of course Oliver's father, obtained the power to limit the use to his wife for her life for a jointure, a power that he exercised after his mother had died and

[1] Dyer, *A.N.C.,* ff. 155, 292, 306.
[2] Coke, *Reports,* vol. VI, p. 495.
[3] 2 Edward VI c. 8.
[4] Hobart, *Reports,* edn. of 1724, p. 50.
[5] B.M. Lansdowne MS. 608, f. 9.
[6] Ley, *Reports,* pp. 22-4.
[7] See above, p. 76.
[8] Holdsworth, vol. IV, p. 469.

CHAP. V]   JUDICIAL BUSINESS OF COURT   107

his father had surrendered his estate for life. When Sir Henry died, his eldest son succeeded and sued livery of his lands; when Robert died, the other lands of which he was seised being held in socage, the question arose as to whether or not Oliver should be in ward during the lifetime of his mother. Since she held for life all the *capite* lands, and only a remainder descended, Oliver was adjudged out of wardship so long as she lived.[1]

The statutes of Wills had permitted a tenant in chief by knight service to devise, or by act executed in his lifetime to grant, two parts of his land for the advancement of his wife, preferment of his children or paying of his debts, the third part being left to the king's wardship or primer seisin.[2] These enactments produced a good deal of judicial business in the Court. In a straightforward case, it is true, the division of the lands for the taking of the king's share, might be a simple administrative action, carried out by the auditors on the basis of a survey made by the feodary concerned. But where a third did not descend for the king's rights, there was a problem for the Court to settle as to whence it should be taken.[3] Further, if the statutes had given the subject a limited freedom to devise, they had also given the king certain wardships and primer seisins, where he would have had none before—that is, on one third of land conveyed during life for the purposes mentioned in the statute. Thus the statutes and the common law were to some extent contradictory, and much learning was displayed in argument as to whether or not, in a particular case, an heir was in ward or should sue livery.[4]

For the rest, a very wide range of business came within the purview of the Court. Sometimes it is to be seen dealing with the worst complexities of the medieval land law, sometimes with a simple intrusion upon a ward's lands. Questions of fact as well as law might perplex it, as, for instance, when it was faced with the problem of whether the child born thirty-nine weeks after the death of a woman's first husband, and thirty-eight weeks after her marriage to a second husband, was the child of the first or the second.[5] And to some queries raised the answer could only be

[1] Ley, *Reports*, p. 60.   [2] 32 Henry VIII c. 1; 34, 35 Henry VIII c. 5.
[3] Examples are Coke, *Reports*, vol. IV, p. 484, Parker's case; Ley, *Reports*, p. 42, Price's case.
[4] Dyer, *A.N.C.*, f. 181, Mody's case; f. 313, Gray's case; f. 345, Thornton's case; Ley, *Reports*, 51, Menfield's case.
[5] B.M. Lansdowne MS. 608, f. 54.

108   COURT OF WARDS AND LIVERIES   [CHAP. V

found in applied commonsense, like the Court's sensible decision that a committee who sowed corn before his ward's minority ended might reap it after the young man had reached full age.[1]

Such were the main types of case that came before the Court. It would, of course, be possible to classify its judicial business in another way, distinguishing between those suits that were undertaken on the crown's behalf, those in protection of the rights of wards, and those at the instance of committees or tenants of the king. If such a classification were adopted, it would be found that, of the three, the king's business naturally loomed largest. There was statutory authority for preferring his suits before all others,[2] and the chief task of the Court was to see that he was not defrauded of his rights. In fact, this motive was often present even when a case appears to fall into the second or third category, and was nominally brought in the ward's or committee's interest.[3]

Yet despite the preponderance of what may be termed royal pleadings examples can easily be found, over the whole field of livery and wardship, where the Court gave rulings that told against the crown. Thus, when it was laid down in Digby's case that the king should never have wardship or primer seisin except where there was an heir general or special, the Court was setting definitive bounds to its own administrative competence;[4] so it was in a case reported by Cole, where it ruled that, a wardship vesting legally in a common person before the king's title, the king should be barred of it.[5] Nor, in a long series of judgments, did it hesitate to uphold the principle that tenure of the king as of some manor, honor or lordship was not *in capite*, unless the manor etc. had been anciently annexed to the crown.[6] It showed a similar independence in its judgment in the case of Browne and Coke that, if wardship of the body and land were severed, the land might not be retained after the heir's full age for the value of a marriage that he had refused,[7] and in Hale's case where the king's interest was held to be determined by tender of livery, so that the heir having bargained and sold his lands during the continuance of his livery, and then died, the bargainee was not answerable for the mean profits.[8]

---

[1] B.M. Lansdowne MS. 608, f. 20.
[3] See below, p. 113.
[5] B.M. Lansdowne MS. 608, f. 12.
[7] Dyer, *A.N.C.*, f. 260.

[2] 33 Henry VIII c. 39 (li.).
[4] Coke, *Reports*, vol. IV, p. 470.
[6] See above, p. 75.
[8] Coke, *Reports*, vol. IV, p. 481.

CHAP. V]   JUDICIAL BUSINESS OF COURT   109

Again, in connexion with the king's rights over idiots, the Court ruled in Tourson's case that though all mean acts done by an idiot from birth were void, the crown was only entitled to the profits of his lands from the date at which his idiocy was established by inquisition.[1]

As has been hinted above, much of the Court's independence it owed to the judges assistant; but the extensive use made of their help is symptomatic of an even more fundamental influence in the Court. Crompton put the matter succinctly when he wrote, 'En cel court choses couient estre trettes solonq' le common ley.'[2] The Court showed all the common lawyer's respect for precedents. In his collection of decrees, Hare noted that an entry book had previously been kept of all cases considered by the judges assistant; though even in his time this had apparently gone astray, it is interesting that he should have desired the keeping of a similar volume—'car est bon service et necessary pur future temps.'[3] It has been seen that sometimes, with the consent of the parties and to cut a long case short, the Court would proceed arbitrarily; on occasion, too, it gave relief in equity, even at the instigation of the judges assistant themselves.[4] But for the most part it acted in accordance with precedent and, except where there had been modification by statute, its judgments were based on the common law of medieval times.

No institution exists in a vacuum, and in Tudor and Stuart times there was a good deal of overlapping of functions and jurisdictions. The Court of Wards had contacts of varying kinds with many other bodies, both judicial and administrative, of its day.

The simplest of these was where a plaintiff, for any reason, had brought a suit that could be shown to be outside the Court's jurisdiction. If the defendant's demurrer made out a *prima facie* case that this was so, plaintiff's counsel would be ordered to prove that the suit did lie in the Court,[5] and, should he fail to do that, then pleadings would be in abeyance and the matter possibly remitted for trial in the appropriate court. Examples are plentiful enough of cases turned over to the common law courts,[6] and in

[1] Coke, *Reports*, vol. IV, p. 478.
[2] *L'Authoritie et Iurisdiction des Courts*, edn. of 1594, f. 112.
[3] B.M. Harleian MS. 1727, f. 8.   [4] Ley, *Reports*, pp. 26-7; 35-6.
[5] P.R.O. Wards 9/514, order of 2 May 7 Edward VI.
[6] C.U. MS. Dd. 13. 28, f. 8; B.M. Harleian MS. 1727, f. 32.

110   COURT OF WARDS AND LIVERIES   [CHAP. V

1587 Burghley referred to the chancellor of the Duchy of Lancaster a suit between a ward and another regarding lands in the duchy.[1] Sometimes proceedings went on contemporaneously in the Court and elsewhere, and the Court's action was conditional upon the outcome of a case within another jurisdiction: there is, for instance, a deposition of Leonard Purley in 1622 that by bringing a successful action of trespass at the Lincoln assizes against George Forster, he has terminated a Court of Wards injunction, giving Forster possession of the manor of Welby until it should be recovered by the deponent by due course of law.[2] Now and then, too, there is a hint of unofficial pressure to remove a suit from the Court, as in a letter from Buckingham to Cranfield, where the duke begged the master to dismiss a case, 'wherein you shall do a favour to a special friend of mine'.[3]

On the other hand, the Court jealously guarded its jurisdiction, where a case really belonged to it. Injunctions restraining suits at common law were very frequent indeed,[4] and cases in the Marshalsea and Verge were also stayed.[5] More than once the Court came into contact with Chancery: Cole reports an occasion where it protected its usher against one of the Chancery officers,[6] but the most famous instance of the overlapping jurisdictions of the two courts was the case of Fuller v. Hall.[7] A decree in very strong terms was made against the questioning of matters determined in the Court by either the Court of Orphans of the City of London or the ecclesiastical courts,[8] and indeed in 1626 it was held that decrees and acts of the Court were not to be questioned in any other court.[9] Such action, it may well be argued, was defensive, and it may be supposed that the more frequently the Court fulminated against interference, the more effectively that kind of interference was taking place. But the Court's policy in regard to its relationship with other courts had its positive side too, as the recorder and chamberlain of London found when they received an order to appear in the Court, with the city's ledger book that was required as evidence in a suit.[10]

---

[1] C.S.P. Dom. 1581-90, p. 419.
[2] P.R.O. Wards 1/22, depositions, Mich. 20 Jas. I.   [3] Sackville MS. 8719.
[4] P.R.O. Wards 9/297-303, entry books of injunctions, for examples.
[5] B.M. Lansdowne MS. 608, f. 17.
[6] Ibid. f. 11; B.M. Lansdowne MS. 607, f. 80.
[7] See below, p. 135.   [8] B.M. Lansdowne MS. 608, f. 63.
[9] Ibid. f. 51.   [10] P.R.O. Wards 9/85, f. 3.

CHAP. V]   JUDICIAL BUSINESS OF COURT   111

With the various courts, then, the Court of Wards perhaps rather more than held its own. From other quarters, however, came spasmodic interference that it was more difficult to resist effectively. Thus there was occasionally royal intervention in a case pending before the Court, as when Mary issued a direct warrant forbidding further proceeding in the suit Duncombe v. Pattenham.[1] The Council, too, sometimes restrained the Court's action,[2] and in James I's reign the development of procedure by petition to the House of Lords meant a still further check.[3] Throughout the Court's history, wherever members of Parliament were involved in its suits, difficult questions of privilege arose and prevented, or at least delayed, proceedings.[4] Parliamentary privilege extended to members' servants, and on one occasion the Speaker's servant was discharged from the Court by authority of a letter from his master.[5] In any account of the Court it is well to remember these limitations to its authority.

[1] P.R.O. in Wards 10/2, special and immediate warrants, Henry VIII-Eliz. The case of Duncombe v. Pattenham is very interesting. A decree in the latter's favour had been drawn up when Mary issued this stay of proceedings. Upon her death the Court made a decree granting Pattenham costs, in which it was alleged that Mary's intervention had been procured 'per sinister meanes encontre tout bon order, et equitie.' (B.M. Harleian MS. 1727, f. 19.)

[2] *A.P.C. 1556-8*, p. 335; *C.S.P. Dom. 1625-6*, p. 442.

[3] See below, p. 135.

[4] H.M.C., *Report*, vol. IV, p. 46; vol. V, p. 13.

[5] Notestein, Relf and Simpson, *Commons Debates 1621*, vol. VI, p. 185.

CHAPTER VI

THE WELFARE OF WARDS AND IDIOTS

BY a rather charming touch, the seal of the Court of Wards in successive reigns included, beneath the royal arms, the figures of two young children with a scroll bearing the words *Pupillis Orphanis et Viduis Adiutor* or a similar expression.[1] Some clerk in the Court of James I's time, making a pen-trial on the cover of one of its books, hit upon an even more grandiloquent variant—*Curia Wardorum et Liberacionum Imperatoris maximi Caesaris Augusti Jacobi Pupillis orphanis et viduis Adiutrix*;[2] and if a suspicion remains that he was scribbling with his tongue in his cheek, the same reign saw a public pronouncement by Sir George Carew that the king's purpose was 'to imitate and approach as neere as may be, the offices and duties of a naturall father'.[3] Turns of phrase of this sort serve as reminders that the king's guardianship implied duties as well as rights. It is pertinent to inquire how far such duties were fulfilled.

In one respect the Court seems certainly to have provided effective protection for the ward—in all matters of litigation it did a great deal to safeguard his interests, at least against third parties if not always against the crown.

The positive side of this protective policy appears in almost any file of pleadings in the Court, a high proportion of which, as has appeared in the last chapter, are found to have been initiated by the attorney on the ward's behalf. It was the attorney, indeed, who had the primary responsibility for seeking redress if a ward's lands were intruded upon, his woods cut down, or any other wrong done to him. It was even held that, since the minor heir had 'no other protector but the Attorney of the Court of Wards', a committee wishing to complain of trespass on his ward's lands might only do

---

[1] *Archaeologia*, vol. LXXXV, p. 306. For a similar children *motif*, under the circumstances natural enough, see *Archivio di Stato* Florence, *Magistrato dei pupilli*, vol. 246, miniature at head of Statutes of 1384.

[2] P.R.O. Wards 9/396, f. 325.

[3] P.R.O. S.P. 14/69, no. 69, discourse to the Court.

112

CHAP. VI]   WELFARE OF WARDS   113

so by information and not by bill;[1] again, even though an heir was of age, until such time as he had sued out his livery, only the attorney could make complaint on his behalf.[2] The impression left by the pleadings is that, especially in the Court's later days, the attorney was usually active in discharging this sort of obligation. The fact was that he had a particular reason for being so, since every wrong done to a ward was, directly or indirectly, a wrong done to the king. Hesketh, attorney at the end of Elizabeth's reign and in the opening years of James I, put this dual motive for bringing a case quite frankly when he informed against a group that had wrongfully entered on a ward's lands in Wales; he spoke of the 'great preiudice of his Maiestie, and disinherison of his Maiesties Ward' that had resulted.[3] One of Ley's informations provided another example of its being in the royal interest to protect the ward. During a visitation of his province Norroy king of arms had pulled down and defaced from their proud position in York minster the coat armour, crests and so on of one of the royal wards, presumably on the ground that they were wrongfully borne. Ley countered by seeking a privy seal causing him to answer and show cause why they should not be set up again. The case had its amusing side, for it was alleged that, at the time of the funeral of the ward's father, Norroy himself had received the sum of 100 l. for publishing ensigns of armoury, tricking them, and setting them up in the place where they lawfully stood; but its importance is that it shows a coincidence of interest of crown and ward. Had the aspersion on the ward's gentility passed unchallenged, the value of his marriage would have decreased, since he might not be married to a gentlewoman unless he were himself of gentle birth.[4]

Scarcely less important was the negative aspect of the Court's endeavour to protect the heir. The principle was established that only in the Court of Wards could a ward be sued, where the attorney would advise and act for him—a most important development of the medieval common law practice whereby, if an infant were sued, one of the court's officers appeared in his defence. One curious effect of the application of this principle, scarcely predictable, was

[1] C.U. MS. Dd. 13. 28, f. 18.
[2] Ibid. f. 16.
[3] West, Second Part, f. 323.
[4] Ibid. f. 334. It is clear from B.M. Lansdowne MS. 607, f. 66, that suits might also be undertaken on behalf of the younger brothers and sisters of the ward, since the ward's own estate was reckoned to be affected by these matters.

114   COURT OF WARDS AND LIVERIES   [CHAP. VI

described by Lord Sheffield to Robert Cecil in 1601. Sheffield, writing in furtherance of a suit, the parties to which are unfortunately not named, told how one of them 'out of a cunning humour holds himself as a ward in the Court for want of paying his livery, and thereby holds this gentleman his adversary with delays, so that he cannot have further trial of the laws of this realm for the recovery of his own. The case is extraordinary, for this ward is so young that he is grey headed with age, and yet under this pretext, debars him that sues him of all lawful proceedings'.[1] The incident suggests that the ward's immunity from suits elsewhere than in the Court itself was regarded as a valuable privilege.

But if royal responsibilities were fulfilled to this extent, that the ward's interests were safeguarded in suits at law, over the wider field of wardship administration the protective took second place to the profit-making. In particular, the practice of selling wardship and marriage made effective protection difficult of realization. Sales of this kind, it is true, involved no new principle: the legality of such transference of the guardian's rights had been recognized from medieval times—for instance, the grantee, or as he was often termed committee, was entitled to the writ of ravishment of ward in the same way as the original guardian.[2] What was new, however, was the high degree of organization which the Court brought to the whole business of sale.[3] As has been seen above, sales of wardships and marriages became the principal item of the Court's income, and during the century's working there was something like a thirty-one-fold increase in this source of revenue.[4] One, though not the chief, cause of that increase was the growing number of wards revealed and sold. In Edward VI's reign sales averaged thirty-five a year, under Mary forty-nine, and in the first ten years of Elizabeth sixty-four; by 1610-13 they stood at an average of one hundred and twenty-three, and early in Charles I's reign (1628-30) at one hundred and thirteen.[5] The importance of these figures is

[1] H.M.C., *Salisbury*, vol. XI, p. 242.
[2] *N.N.B.*, p. 342.
[3] 32 Henry VIII c. 46 (ix) gave the master, receiver-general, auditors, or three of them of whom the master was to be one, authority to make sales.
[4] See above, pp. 57-8.
[5] The figures for the reigns of Edward VI and Mary are calculated from grants enrolled on the patent roll, and calendared in *C.P.R.* They include what were, in effect, retrospective grants, where, having previously entered into indentures of wardship, the committee had for some reason omitted to obtain a patent and

CHAP. VI] WELFARE OF WARDS 115

easily apparent. The social significance of a system that involved such great numbers was clearly very considerable, and it will be well to determine how it affected them.

The most striking feature of the practice of sale was its inherent possibility for evil. Prospective purchasers were on the spot with amazing rapidity. Officially, suit for a wardship began with a petition seeking a writ for the holding of an inquisition post mortem; but on occasion anxious buyers anticipated this, and even the tenant's death, by an informal approach to the master. In requests of this sort it seems to have been thought sufficient to allege reasonable probability of the tenant's decease in the more or less immediate future—he is 'likely to die',[1] 'now given over by his physicians',[2] 'said to lie desperate sick',[3] or 'not like to live long'.[4] Nor were all suitors as apologetic for this kind of anticipation as Sir Edward Stafford, who, writing to Robert Cecil in 1604 for the wardship of a nephew of his cousin, Sir Reade Stafford, had the grace to add, 'I know it is not the custom to grant anything of any man's afore he be dead, so am I not so unmannerly to demand it, but that it will please you if such a thing happen to have me in remembrance'.[5] It appears likely that, at any rate until the *Instructions* of 1610, there were many cases where a committee was virtually chosen before the heir was technically in wardship at all. Nor did this practice stop at the sort of informal arrangement so far considered; there is also evidence for conditional grants of wardship—'if he be under age at his father's death'—passing under the great seal.[6]

It is fair to add that a proportion of these suits for prospective wardship originated from the heir's relations, anxious no doubt to avoid his custody falling into the hands of a stranger. The likelihood of the young heir being snatched away from his kinsfolk was, indeed, one of the most obnoxious corollaries of the Court's policy of sales, especially during the first half of its existence. The table

now remedied the deficiency. The figure for 1-10 Eliz. is calculated from P.R.O. Wards 11/4/19, that for 1610-13 from P.R.O. Wards 9/150 B, and that for 1628-30 from P.R.O. Wards 9/163.

[1] *C.S.P. Dom. 1603-10*, p. 302.
[2] H.M.C., *Salisbury*, vol. XI, p. 375.
[3] *Ibid.* vol. X, p. 121.   [4] *Ibid.* vol. XII, p. 36.
[5] *Ibid.* vol. XVI, p. 264. For other examples see *ibid.* vol. X, p. 123; vol. XI, p. 193; vol. XIV, pp. 108, 242; vol. XVIII, p. 457; and *C.S.P. Dom. 1581-90*, pp. 235, 551, 558; and *C.S.P. Dom. 1603-10*, p. 609.
[6] *Ibid.* p. 181.

116   COURT OF WARDS AND LIVERIES   [CHAP. VI

at note[1] indicates clearly enough that, until Robert Cecil's mastership, little preference was shown to the mother or other relations when grants of wardship and marriage were made. In Edward VI's reign only one ward out of every five was sold to his mother, to a kinsman, to his own use, or to trustees appointed by his father; the rest appear to have gone to strangers. Under Mary the proportion was higher, approaching one in three, but in the opening years of Elizabeth's reign it had sunk to one in four. Nor did Burghley—despite the boast of his biographer that he 'preferred natural mothers, before all others'[2]—in fact show marked favour to the ward's family. The figures for a period of three years in the latter part of his administration (1587-90) give a proportion of only one grant to mother, relation, or ward himself in every three made. The effects of this disregard of family feeling were apparent in the agitation against wardship that arose at the beginning of the seventeenth century. There must certainly have been hard cases to produce the bitter criticisms levelled at the whole system by James I's first Parliament, and amongst the calamities alleged to result from wardship prominence was given to the removal of children from their relations.[3] The main demand of the critics, that wardship should go to the nearest of blood, was of ancient origin. In Edward III's reign Parliament had desired this solution;[4] and though the ruling of the common law was not quite clear, Bacon, quoting *naturae vis maxima et suus cuique discretus sanguis*, asserted that it preferred a natural to a civil protection.[5] There was also to hand the example of the *prochein amy* guardian of socage tenure—the nearest relative unable himself to inherit.

[1] Grants of Wards in select groups of years:

Date	Total granted	To mother, kin or ward himself	Calculated from
reign of Edward VI	232	46	C.P.R. Edward VI
reign of Mary	258	83	C.P.R. Mary
1558-63	365	88	C.P.R. Elizabeth
1587-90	225	73	P.R.O. Wards 9/150 B
1611-14	368	168	ibid.
1628-30	222	128	P.R.O. Wards 9/163

This table gives only a rough indication of the proportion of wards granted to members of their own families, column 3 including only those grants where the records used *either* state that the grant is to mother, kin or ward *or* show a coincidence of surname between ward and grantee. It is possible, therefore, that some grants to mothers who had remarried, and appeared under their new names, are not included.   [2] Peck, vol. I, p. 20.

[3] P.R.O. S.P. 14/52, no. 88, observations on an intended petition.

[4] *Reports . . . touching the Dignity of a Peer*, vol. I, p. 309.   [5] *P.D. 1610*, p. 26.

CHAP. VI] WELFARE OF WARDS 117

It was apparently in the light of current criticisms of this kind that Robert Cecil decided to modify the sales policy of the court. In 1603 he generalized what had previously been the jealously guarded privilege of a few faithful servants whom the crown wished to reward,[1] and permitted tenants in chief to buy, during their own lifetimes, the wardship of their heirs and vest it in trustees.[2] More important, his *Instructions* of 1610 allowed the ward's family one month's pre-emption in which to purchase his custody, and laid it down that near friends nominated by the ancestor were to enjoy preference in obtaining a grant of wardship.[3] Despite their efforts to increase the Court's productivity, Cecil's successors did not go back on his guarantee of 1610, and in the *Instructions* of 1618 and 1622 this concession was retained.[4] It followed that the proportion of wards committed to relations increased: in 1611-14 it stood at a little under one-half of the total grants, in 1628-30 at well over one-half.[5] Of course, the effect of this reform must not be exaggerated. Many families either through bad advice, or through indifference, or quite simply because they lacked the necessary cash, failed to purchase the wardships of their young relations. In this later phase of the Court's existence, Sir Henry Spelman was still able to accuse it of leaving the mother doubly bereaved, 'equally lamenting the death of her husband and the captivity of her child'.[6]

Yet, in this last connexion, as an apologist of the Court pointed out, the mother's guardianship was not always an unmixed blessing, since she might decide to marry again, carrying with her the children's estate, 'as a Sawce to the hungry enough appetite of a Father in Law . . . as good a guardian to the Children, as the *Woolf* or *Fox* is to the *Lambs*'.[7] Two cases, chosen at random from those heard in the Court, give point to the accusation. Towards the end of Elizabeth's reign, the attorney exhibited a bill that the mother and stepfather of a certain Bridgett Molineux concealed the child's wardship, cornered evidences, arranged to marry her in disparagement, and neglected her—'by which negligence the same warde of late fell into a cole pitt a verie greate depth and by that fall was so grievouslye brused that thereby she was in verie greate perill of her

---

[1] William Petre and Nicholas Bacon are examples, *C.P.R. Edward VI*, vol. III, p. 302 and *C.P.R. Philip and Mary*, 1553-4, p. 2.
[2] See below, pp. 136-7.
[3] P.R.O. S.P. 14/61, no. 6, pp. 2 and 7.
[4] *Foedera*, vol. XVII, pp. 66-7, 401.   [5] See above, p. 116, note 1.
[6] *History and Fate of Sacrilege*, edn. of 1846, p. 176.   [7] *T.N.T.*, p. 158.

118   COURT OF WARDS AND LIVERIES   [CHAP. VI

life.'[1] Or again, some thirty years later, a fellow of Magdalen College, Edward Drope, deposed that a young ward named Richard Rogers, whose tutor he was, became ill on a visit to his mother, the wife of a Northamptonshire gentleman, Sir Robert Banister. On this occasion, Drope alleged, the stepfather behaved with great inhumanity, refusing to let anyone sit up with the ward, turning his horse from the stable and his tutor from the house. When the boy was subsequently lodged with a local justice of the peace, Banister threatened this benefactor with fines and pursuivants out of the Court.[2] Nor did all tenants in chief trust their wives: when Gilbert Lord Gerard, for instance, was setting out on a voyage of exploration, he requested that, in the event of his death, his son's wardship might be committed to a cousin and brother, since he feared the malice of the boy's mother.[3] These examples suggest that it is possible to criticize the Court too hardly for its choice of committees: at least the stranger who obtained a wardship had not a monopoly of inhumanity.

Moreover, it may be that there is another factor to be considered. Amongst the answers to criticisms of the Court made in 1604, it was asserted that, even where a ward was granted to someone other than his mother, the child was not physically removed from her presence until it was of age to be put to school.[4] Of its nature, this is an extremely hard statement either to prove or disprove, but there is some evidence that the Court was on occasion moved by tender feelings, as it certainly was when, early in Charles I's reign, it left two sickly little girl wards, Mary and Anne Copley, seven and six years old, with their mother and did not hand them over to the committee; the mother herself was in a consumption, so that perhaps the Court's kindliness in this connexion was, from a medical point of view, ill-advised.[5] How far the Court went in this sort of effort to prevent the separation of infants from their mothers can only be estimated after much more intensive work on its proceedings than has so far proved possible; but meanwhile the possibility that particular cases were considered on their merits should be borne in mind as something that may have done a little to mitigate the harshness of the policy of sales.

[1] P.R.O. Wards 13/50, pleadings, Easter 40 Eliz.
[2] P.R.O. in Wards 10/63, bundle of depositions, 1628.
[3] *C.S.P. Dom. 1619-23*, p. 205.
[4] P.R.O. S.P. 14/52, no. 88, observations on an intended petition.
[5] P.R.O. Wards 1/118, order of 20 June 4 Charles I.

CHAP. VI]   WELFARE OF WARDS   119

Yet even so, when all is said, the sale of wardships was an odious practice. There is something singularly revolting about the way in which the royal wards were bartered for, 'bought and sold like horses', as the critics of 1604 put it.[1] Nor was the resulting interruption in the child's way of life and background necessarily limited to the occasion on which he was transferred to his original committee. Wardship might be granted in survivorship,[2] in which case the heir might be passed successively from guardian to guardian; or again, the original committee might obtain a licence to assign the wardship to a third party,[3] these re-sales often being made at greatly increased prices.[4] It is difficult to resist the impression that, in these circumstances, the ward was simply regarded as a commodity on which the king and successive committees sought to make what profit they could, and that little interest can have been directed towards his welfare. Particularly sad must have been the position of the heir who, through ill health, looked like being a bad speculation, as did the ward, obtained from Robert Cecil on a kind of hire purchase in 1594, whose buyer asked for remission of half the price for two years anyhow and, if the ward should die, altogether.[5] But, exceptionally unhappy cases of this sort apart, sale and re-sale made it almost impossible for the Court to exercise effective control over committees: Carew is known to have planned an inspection of them in each county, but there is no evidence that his plan materialized, and it was certainly never put into regular operation.[6] It was this lack of direct control which, more than anything else, made impossible a comprehensive system of education of the royal wards.

During the middle ages what may be termed the educative aspect of wardship had been very prominent; indeed, it is not going too far to say that the whole institution was based on the premise that the lord, both by right and duty, must bring up the minor heir in such a way as befitted his station in life. The crown's function in this connexion had been particularly stressed, and Fortescue's description of the royal court as 'the supreme academy for the nobles of the realm, and a school of vigour, probity, and manners' typified

[1] P.R.O. S.P. 14/52, no. 88, observations on an intended petition.
[2] *C.P.R. Elizabeth, 1558-60*, p. 33.
[3] C.U. MS. Dd. 13. 28, f. 3.   [4] *T.R.H.S.*, 4th Series, vol. XXXI, p. 107.
[5] H.M.C., *Salisbury*, vol. IV, p. 522.
[6] P.R.O. S.P. 14/69, no. 69, discourse to the Court.

120 COURT OF WARDS AND LIVERIES [CHAP. VI

the point of view of these times.[1] So pervasive was the belief in the value of the training that the young ward received that many children were placed in the houses of the great in an exactly similar way, even though their father were still alive and they were not in wardship at all. Nor is there any need to explain the popularity of the practice by suggesting, as did a cynical foreign observer, that men were better served by strangers than they would be by their own children.[2] Rather it represented an effort to secure education in those virtues that the age most admired.

As a result of this tradition, it was felt in Tudor and Stuart times that the crown was responsible for the education of its wards. The Court of Wards had not been in existence for ten years before Latimer raised the objection to a policy that regarded only revenues at the expense of education. 'The Kynge hath a great meanye of wardes', he said forthrightly in one of his sermons, 'and I trowe there is a courte of wardes, why is there not a schole for the wardes, as well as there is a courte for their landes? Whye are they not set in scholes, where they maye learne? Or why are they not sent to the vniuersities, that they may be able to serue the kyng when they come to age?'[3] Almost contemporaneously, Starkey, in the *Dialogue*,[4] put similar sentiments into the mouth of Cardinal Pole: 'And euer they wych have the nobylyte in ward must be bounden to make a rekenyng and count before a iuge appoyntid therto, not only of al his intrate, rentys, and reuenewys, but much more of the orderyng and institutyon of hys ward both in vertue and lernyng.' Demands of this kind produced two separate plans for the education of the royal wards, both worthy of attention in themselves, though it is extremely unlikely that either was given a trial.

The first of these, entitled *Articles devised for the bringinge up in vertue and lerninge of the Queenes Majesties wardes beinge heires Males*, was framed by Sir Nicholas Bacon, when he was attorney of the Court, and sent by him to Burghley soon after the latter became master in 1561. The plan was to apply only to those wards whose lands were of at least 100 *marks* value yearly. It is remarkable for the suggestion, cutting at the root of the trouble, that no wardship was to be sold or granted away before the heir was married

---

[1] Fortescue, *De Laudibus Legum Anglie*, ed. and trans. by S. B. Chrimes, p. 111.
[2] *A Relation of the Island of England*, Camden Soc. 1847, p. 25.
[3] *Fourth Sermon*, 1549.
[4] Early English Text Soc. Extra Series, vol. xxxii, p. 186.

CHAP. VI] WELFARE OF WARDS 121

by the queen's appointment. For the rest, it is interesting from the point of view of the history of education for the modernity of many of its suggestions. Heirs male of nine years and over were to live together in houses chosen for the purpose—one in the town and one in the country (a plan dictated, no doubt, by the frequent outbreaks of plague and other infectious sickness in London). There the youths were to be subject to a regular routine and discipline, under a 'graue man' as chief governor, and five school-masters—'The first to read a lecture of the temporall or Cyvill Lawe, & one other de disciplina militari. The second to teach the Latyne and greeke tounge to whom for assistaunce an usher would by ioyned able to teach them to write fayer. The third the frenche and other Languages. The iiij[th] musicke and qualities thereuppon dependinge. The vth to ryde, to vawlte, to handle Weapon and such other thinges as therto belongeth.' There was provision for a steward and various other servants, and also for a chaplain, while a surgeon and a physician were 'to be of Councell with this howse'. The governor and steward were to account to the master and council of the Court. Time-tables were appended, and the whole had distinct points of similarity to a modern public school.[1]

The second plan was drafted in 1570 by the explorer, Sir Humphrey Gilbert. Its basis was in one way a little wider than the earlier project, since it was to extend to anyone who could spend 13 $l.$ 6$s.$ 8$d.$; on the other hand, it only included wards of over twelve years of age, whereas Bacon intended that they should be taken at nine. The scope of the plan was a great deal more ambitious than that previously put forward. The staff included schoolmasters to teach Latin and Greek grammar, Hebrew, Logic, French, Italian, Spanish, High Dutch and music; nine ushers to assist in the various subjects; readers in moral philosophy, natural philosophy, civil law and divinity; two mathematicians and a doctor of physic; teachers of horsemanship, soldiery, map-plotting, swordsmanship and dancing; a lawyer to 'teache exquisitely the office of a Iustice of peace and Sheriffe', a herald of arms, a librarian, a treasurer, and a rector—the duty of the last-named being to see that the wards were able to follow their own bent. The fees of each were specified, and over them all was to be the master of the wards, as chief governor, with a yearly allowance of 200 $l.$ for the

[1] B.M. Add. MS. 32379. The plan is discussed in *Archaeologia*, vol. xxxvi, p. 343.

I

122 COURT OF WARDS AND LIVERIES [CHAP. VI

work entailed. The earlier device was compared above to a public school; an enthusiastic editor of this later plan has compared it to the University of London! Certainly the proposed institution is rather akin to a university than to a school—some research work was expected from certain of the staff and it was suggested that printers should be compelled to deliver to the library a copy of each new book published. The translating of the dream into reality was another matter. Elizabeth herself was by no means unenlightened; but it is not likely that she would look with any favour upon a scheme that, by its author's own admission, entailed a yearly expense of 2,966 *l.* 13*s.* 4*d.* in wages and commons for the staff, as well as some initial expenditure.[1]

Moreover, besides the cost of erection and upkeep of schools such as were envisaged in these plans, both schemes involved a more fundamental difficulty. On the one hand, neither could be grafted on to a system in which sale of wardship was central to the policy pursued; on the other, the financial position of the monarchy was not strong enough to make possible the abandonment of that policy. So it was that these plans remained in the realm of theory, and the continuance of the practice of selling wardship meant that the responsibility for education of the minor heirs was turned over to the class of grantees and purchasers.

The Court, it is true, made some attempt to see that the committee fulfilled this obligation. It generally gave him the wherewithal to do so, by granting, along with wardship of the body, an annuity or exhibition out of the ward's lands, which was intended to be spent on the heir's maintenance and education. In the later days of the Court the exhibition had settled down to an average of one tenth of the yearly value of the lands, but earlier it was more generous,[2] and there was even, on occasion, an effort to set it on a sliding scale, with an increase when the ward reached twelve years old for his bringing up 'in good discipline and exercises worthy of his estate and for an ornament of the common wealth'.[3] Further than this, the Court endeavoured to maintain at least a loose control over the committee, developing the covenants of the indenture of wardship with this end in view. These always bound the committee, in general terms, to bring up his ward 'in good

[1] *Queen Elizabethes Achademy*, ed. by F. J. Furnivall, Early English Text Soc. Extra Series, vol. VIII, pp. 1-12.
[2] See above, pp. 57-8.   [3] *C.P.R. Philip and Mary, 1557-8*, p. 62.

CHAP. VI] WELFARE OF WARDS 123

erudition, vertues, and decent qualities',[1] and sometimes provided more specifically that, every fourth year after he reached ten years of age, the boy should be brought before the master and council so that his manners, education and learning might be examined.[2] Again, there were certain well-understood principles—sometimes negative, sometimes positive in their application—that the Court usually enforced. The committee, for instance, was not allowed to put a ward to be apprentice without its licence;[3] or, on the other hand, contempt in conveying a ward from his committee was dissolved if he had been put to the university for his learning.[4]

Yet, inevitably, the education a ward obtained depended on the person into whose hands he had fallen, and in whose household he dwelt. A possible saving factor here was that, since men purchased wards either to marry them to their own children or to sell them again at a profit, it did not pay wholly to neglect their education, and indeed money spent on it might be regarded as being in the nature of an investment. Even this factor, however, sometimes operated in an opposite, and less desirable way if we are to believe contemporaries. Gilbert asserted that wards were deliberately kept uneducated, not merely because education was expensive but also because, with the qualifications it gave, they might disdain to marry their purchasers' daughters,[5] Thomas Smith that study was discouraged lest the ward should, as a result of it, become sick and die before the benefit of his marriage was enjoyed.[6] Still more significant than the criticisms of these publicists, since it was a casual comment, made by a man who had no axe to grind, was Gervase Holles' explanation of the deficiencies in his grandfather's education as something that 'comonly young wardes have who are left to their owne will.'[7] On the balance, it is probable that the youth who fell into wardship was less likely to obtain a good education than he who escaped coming into the king's hand.

It seems likely that to the education of only two categories of royal wards was more careful attention quite often given—to those

[1] West, *First Part*, section 330.
[2] P.R.O. in Wards 10/27, formulary book; and H.M.C., *Various Collections*, vol. II, p. 250.
[3] C.U. MS. Dd. 13. 28, f. 40; B.M. Harleian MS. 1727, f. 32.
[4] C.U. MS. Dd. 13. 28, f. 2.
[5] *Queene Elizabethes Achademy*, Early English Text Soc. Extra Series, vol. VIII, p. 1.
[6] *De Republica Anglorum*, ed. L. Alston, 1906, p. 121.
[7] *Memoirs of the Holles Family*, Camden Soc., p. 215.

124 COURT OF WARDS AND LIVERIES [CHAP. VI

who were members of the nobility, and to those of recusant families.

So far as the first group is concerned, it must be admitted that the position of the nobleman left a minor is obscure. It was categorically stated in 1604 that he paid a fine only, the wardship being granted to his own use.[1] But this claim is not substantiated by the records of the Court, which show that such wardships were frequently granted to third parties,[2] and the even more curious point has been brought out by Mr Hurstfield that, for some of the most important noblemen's wardships falling during Burghley's mastership, there is no record of a grant either to the ward himself or to another.[3] But whatever may have been the theoretical position of the noble ward, there is little doubt that, in practice, he was placed in the household of some great man, and in this way something of the real intentions of medieval wardship was fulfilled. Wolsey, for instance, was an enlightened guardian, possessing, although he lived before the erection of the Court, his own instructor of wards.[4] There is ample proof, too, of the care that Burghley, for all his public duties, spent upon the young men in his charge—notably a draft, corrected in his hand, for a timetable of exercises and studies for the young Earl of Oxford: the young man was to have an active and varied day, with tuition in dancing, French, Latin, writing and drawing in the mornings, cosmography, more Latin, French and penmanship in the afternoons.[5] Again, as may be imagined, this was an aspect of wardship that James I found attractive, and on occasion he delivered a lecture to Robert Cecil on this theme.[6]

As for the recusants, here, where education impinged most obviously on state security, the Court seems to have acted with some energy. It was a cardinal point of its policy that all committees should be men 'sownde in religion',[7] but where Catholic wards were concerned especial care was taken. Fabian Philipps

[1] P.R.O. S.P. 14/52, no. 88, observations on an intended petition.
[2] E.g. George Lord Dacre to the Duke of Norfolk, 9 Eliz.; the Earl of Cumberland to the Earl of Bedford, 13 Eliz.; Lord Zouch to Thomas Cecil, 17 Eliz. P.R.O. Wards 9/150 B., ff. 312, 304, 295.
[3] *T.R.H.S.*, 4th Series, vol. XXXI, pp. 104-5.
[4] George Cavendish, *Life and Death of Thomas Wolsey*, Dent 1899, pp. 25-6.
[5] P.R.O. S.P. 12/26, no. 50, exercises and studies of Edward de Vere; and see Hurstfield, *op. cit.*, p. 106.
[6] Transcripts of Salisbury MSS. 214/66.
[7] P.R.O. S.P. 14/69, no. 69, discourse to the Court.

CHAP. VI] WELFARE OF WARDS 125

states that these were placed under Anglican bishops for tuition,[1] and there is some evidence of that practice. Salisbury was ordered by James I to deliver the young Lord Mordant to Abbot, then Bishop of London, although the boy's wardship had apparently been committed to his uncle, Lord Compton.[2] Sometimes the ward resented, and resisted, this episcopal control, like that Walter Henningam who, the Bishop of Coventry and Lichfield complained in 1629, 'doth utterly decline me';[3] sometimes his friends attempted to hide him away, or made excuses that he was too sick to travel.[4] But the policy was maintained, and the Court's attitude even reflected by individual committees, such as the Earl of Northampton, who, in its later days, set his ward, Lord Petre, to study with a Protestant tutor at Oxford.[5] There were, too, other manifestations of the same policy—on occasion livery was stayed until a ward should conform;[6] again, the Court extended its care to the younger brothers and sisters of the ward, sometimes removing them from their recusant mother.[7]

The practice of selling wardship of the body of the minor heir has thus been seen to have had deleterious effects on his welfare. Moreover, sale of wardship was only half the story. Not only the wardship of the minor holding by knight service, but also his marriage, was within his overlord's jurisdiction; and where any part of the lands inherited was held in chief of the crown, the king's right to the marriage was paramount over the claims of those lords of whom the rest was held.[8] So it came about that the crown was able to accompany grant of wardship by grant of marriage; and indeed, from the purchaser's point of view, it was the latter, with the prospect it offered of providing for daughters or other dependants, that proved so infinitely attractive. It was the sale of marriages, however, that constituted the most spectacular evil of the whole system administered by the Court of Wards.

At best the committee's marriage rights imposed a crippling burden on the ward's estate. Only by paying him a heavy fine could the ward compound for his marriage and obtain freedom of choice as to whom he would marry, failure to compound resulting

---

[1] *T.N.T.*, p. 71.   [2] Transcripts of Salisbury MSS. 214/66.
[3] *C.S.P. Dom. Addenda 1625-49*, p. 730.
[4] *C.S.P. Dom. 1619-23*, p. 113.   [5] H.M.C., *Report*, vol. v, p. 111.
[6] B.M. Lansdowne MS. 608, f. 16.   [7] *Ibid.* f. 24.   [8] Staunford, f. 10.

126 COURT OF WARDS AND LIVERIES [CHAP. VI

in a stay of his livery and right to enter upon his lands.[1] Especially in the first half of the Court's existence, such fines appear to have been arbitrary. The allegation, made by a Venetian during Mary's reign, that the crown deliberately proposed unsuitable marriages so that the wards had no alternative but to pay the fine for refusing them,[2] is inherently improbable. But while the crown was scarcely guilty of this abuse, it is reasonable enough to assume that committees sometimes were. At any rate it was admitted in the *Instructions* of 1610 that they had exacted greater fines than in reason or equity they should have done.[3] Even at the recognized rates, fines to compound were severe, being assessed for male wards at two years' value of lands held in possession, and one and a half, one and a quarter, or one, of those held in reversion, and for females at three years' for lands in possession, and two years', or one and a half, for lands in reversion.[4] Remembering the other expenses that the heir had to meet in connexion with suing out of his livery, a fine of this magnitude must have acted as a substantial discouragement from marrying otherwise than as the committee elected.

So, to a great extent, a system of forced marriages obtained, checked by the Court only in so far as it applied medieval legislation against disparagement,[5] and on occasion, where there was gross impropriety in the marriage proposed, might take equitable action against the committee—perhaps it was in this way that it came to consider, early in James I's reign, the scandal of a ward committed for education to a schoolmaster, who 'did marry him, being but 14 years, to his daughter, a harlot of 28 years'.[6] The pleadings of the Court, it must be admitted, leave an impression in the mind that there was some activity along these lines, but inevitably it was spasmodic and did little to remedy a great social evil.

The objection to these forced marriages was increased by the youth of the contracting parties, this being especially the case where female heirs were concerned, for if unmarried at sixteen the girl might recover her heritage without anything given either for ward or marriage.[7] Contemporaries alleged that the effects of marriage at so early an age were disastrous—Brinklow, for instance,

---

[1] C.U. MS. Dd. 13. 28, ff. 2 and 7.
[2] E. G. Salter, *Tudor England through Venetian Eyes*, p. 103.
[3] P.R.O. S.P. 14/61, no. 6, p. 2.　　　　[4] *C.S.P. Dom. 1640-1*, p. 483.
[5] T. F. T. Plucknett, *Legislation of Edward I*, p. 117.
[6] C.U. MS. Dd. 13. 28, f. 24.　　　　　　　　　[7] Staunford, f. 21.

CHAP. VI]   WELFARE OF WARDS   127

asserted that the parties never favoured one another after reaching the age of discretion, 'to the great encreasing of the abhomynable vyce of adultery, and of dyuelyssh dyuorcement;'[1] Sir Thomas Smith expressed the same complaint,[2] and later still the parliamentary critics of 1604 re-echoed it.[3] It has been suggested that early marriages were brought about in another way, by the father marrying his children during his lifetime so as to prevent them from falling into wardship when he died.[4] This, however, can only have been the case to a limited extent—though it avoided wardship to the *mesne* lord it did not avoid royal wardship.[5] It is possible, however, that the whole practice of selling wards did give rise to another danger: the Venetian ambassador, Barbaro, hinted darkly at an undue intimacy between young wards of opposite sexes committed to the same guardian.[6]

Having regard to the abuses consequent on the sale of wardships and marriages, it is easy to condemn the crown for persisting in a policy that looked mainly to revenues and so little to welfare. Yet in fairness it must be admitted that there were other reasons, besides the purely financial, for the practice of selling wardship of the body and marriage. To retain all wards under the direct guardianship of the crown, and to arrange their marriages, would have implied a centralized, royal control quite out of spirit with Tudor England. The practice actually followed, whatever social evils it brought in its train, was nevertheless typical of that partnership between the monarchy and the most influential sections of the community that accounted for so much of the success of the Tudor dynasty. Sale of wardships and marriages was comparable to sale of the monastic lands in so far as both gave to wide classes a vested interest in a system that it was in the royal interest to maintain. This is perhaps the supreme paradox in the history of the Court of Wards—that the feature of its policy most obnoxious to thinking contemporaries and to ourselves was, in a certain way, the *raison d'être* for its continuance. What was hateful to men as

[1] *Complaynt of Roderick Mors*, Early English Text Soc. Extra Series, vol. XXII, p. 18.   [2] *De Republica Anglorum*, ed. L. Alston, p. 121.
[3] P.R.O. S.P. 14/52, no. 88, observations on an intended petition.
[4] By F. J. Furnivall in *Child Marriages, Divorces and Ratifications*, Early English Text Soc. Original Series, vol. CVIII, p. xli.
[5] Constable, p. 126; Coke, *Reports*, vol. III, p. 300.
[6] *C.S.P. Ven.*, vol. V, p. 356.

128 COURT OF WARDS AND LIVERIES [CHAP. VI

tenants in chief was profitable and attractive to them as royal committees.

Amongst the offices vested in the Court at the time of its erection was that formerly exercised by the governor of the king's idiots and naturals. Since the time of Edward I the crown had claimed the wardship of all born fools, and the claim had received recognition in the *Prerogativa Regis*.[1] Writs to inquire concerning alleged idiocies had been directed to both escheator and sheriff,[2] and a regular system of examination instituted. If a man knew his own age and the names of his father and mother, and could tell up to 20*d*. he was adjudged no idiot;[3] by a statute of Edward III the power to beget children became another qualification or proof of sanity.[4] Moreover, even if idiocy were established by these tests, the chancellor was still supposed to summon the fool before him and make his own examination.[5] Such safeguards were necessary, for the idiot was automatically deprived of all control of his property. All transferences made by him, even previous to the proof of his insanity, were void;[6] profits of his land, once he had been found an idiot, went to the crown except for the bare minimum that was needed for his own necessities;[7] if the king wasted his lands, he could only obtain remedy by petition.[8] Though he subsequently became sane, his property remained in the king's hands throughout his lifetime, unless he sued out a writ directing his re-examination or ordering that he should be brought before the Council; if he were then found no idiot, the office that found him insane was void and needed no traverse.[9] After his decease an *ouster le maine* had to be sued by his right heirs to secure the return of his property.[10]

---

[1] Staunford, f. 33. [2] *N.N.B.*, pp. 581-3. [3] *Ibid.* p. 583.

[4] 31 Edward III. For a good definition of idiocy cf. *Les Termes de la Ley*, edn. of 1671, p. 419—

'Ideot is he that is a natural fool from his birth, and knows not how to Count twenty pence or name his Father or Mother, nor tell his own age, or such like easie and common matters, so that it appears he hath no manner of Understanding, reason or government of himself. But if he can read, or learn to read by instruction and information of others, or can measure an Ell of Cloth, or name the Days of the week, or beget a Child, or such like, whereby it may appear he hath some light of Reason; such a one is no Ideot naturally.'

[5] C.U. MS. Hh. 4. 7, f. 47. [6] Staunford, f. 34; Coke, *Reports*, vol. IV, p. 478.

[7] C.U. MS. Hh. 4. 7, f. 50. [8] *Ibid.* f. 49. [9] *N.N.B.*, p. 582.

[10] West, *First Part*, sect. 368 (wrongly entitled 'a grant of the keeping of an Ideot'); P.R.O. in Wards 10/1, the case of William Gifford late Ideot, 6 Eliz., is an interesting account of a suit for an *ouster le maine*.

CHAP. VI]   WELFARE OF WARDS   129

In the person of a lunatic, that is, someone merely temporarily insane, the king had no certain interest, but only the duty of exercising a sort of trusteeship over his lands.[1] The position of the lunatic was thus distinct from that of the idiot. Any alienations that he had made previous to his lunacy remained valid;[2] the king had to provide for his household as well as his personal needs from the profits of his property and, if the lunacy ended, render any surplus profit that might have accrued.[3]

Such was the background of the law in the early years of the Court of Wards and Liveries, with a clearly marked distinction between idiot and lunatic. This distinction was initially reflected in the terms in which the two were committed. Where an idiot was concerned, the king could grant custody of the body and of the lands, with issues to be expended at the discretion of the committee.[4] In the case of a lunatic it was different. Custody of the body was, technically, not the king's to give away, and it had been laid down in Frances' case that he might not grant the lunatic's lands to another to take the profits *a son oeps demesne*.[5] At first, then, royal grants of lunatics seem to have avoided formal transference of custody, and to have included a covenant by the committee that he would answer such surplusage as remained after his own maintenance and that of the lunatic and his family had been paid for.[6] This surplus was to be restored to the lunatic if he recovered his sanity,[7] and if the committee's expenses claimed were unreasonable, action of account lay against him.[8]

Actually it appears that the distinction between idiot and lunatic, originally so definitive, was not long maintained. On the one hand, so far as the body of the fool was concerned the question was mainly one of terminology, and gradually the word custody crept into grants of lunatics. Certainly by the early seventeenth century these were sued for and obtained in much the same fashion as the wardship of heirs. The *Instructions to begge a Warde*, quoted in a previous chapter, are immediately preceded by a set of similar *Instructions to sue for a Lunatick*.[9] A commission for the holding

[1] Staunford, f. 37; and see Beverley's case in Coke, *Reports*, vol. II, p. 568.
[2] C.U. MS. Hh. 4. 7, f. 48.   [3] *Ibid.*   [4] *C.P.R. Edward VI*, vol. III, p. 301.
[5] *English Reports*, vol. LXXII (Moore), p. 399.
[6] P.R.O. S.P. 12/1, no. 18, Englefield to Cecil on the laws respecting the possessions and custody of lunatics.
[7] *C.P.R. Edward VI*, vol. IV, p. 230.   [8] C.U. MS. Hh. 4. 7, f. 50.
[9] B.M. Harleian MS. 1938, ff. 28-9; a similar set of instructions is printed in Powell, pp. 209-12.

130   COURT OF WARDS AND LIVERIES   [CHAP. VI

of an office of lunacy had to be obtained,[1] and when this was returned into the Court, the clerk or the auditor would make out a schedule which, when the master had signed it, became the basis for the indentures of grant. Two sureties had to be found that the committee would account yearly to the auditor for the commodity and stock of the lunatic,[2] and finally the grant had to be enrolled in the auditor's office. Moreover, if in some ways the terms of the grant of a lunatic were approaching those of the grant of an idiot, in one important way the conditions upon which a committee obtained an idiot approximated to those originally binding the grantee of a lunatic—namely that he should account for any surplus of the rents and profits.[3]

Methods of dealing with idiots and lunatics were thus gradually assimilated to each other. A formulary book of the Court, dating from the second half of its existence, still gives, it is true, separate instruments for the indentures of grant of the two categories of madman; but their differences are minute and scarcely significant.[4] West prints one indenture, which he entitles impartially *Grant of Idiot or Lunatick*;[5] and Powell, after describing how the grant of a lunatic is obtained, adds 'For the Ideot, I had almost forgot him. Howsoeuer the matter is not great: For it is but a foolish business when all is done. You haue a faire example of a Lunaticke before your eyes'.[6]

This part of royal wardship was not open to quite the same abuses as the wardship of minor heirs, for the large questions of education and marriage did not arise. More important perhaps, it is pretty clear that no great effort was made by the crown to turn it to profit; nor was the committee allowed to do so. At any rate from the *Instructions* of 1610, it was not the practice to take any composition for lunatics, but to commit them to their best and nearest friends[7]—an arrangement repeated in 1618 and 1622.[8] This rule seems to have been kept fairly rigidly in the subsequent period: when the Earl of Pembroke died in 1630, Lord Arundel, claiming that the countess was insane, begged her custody because his son was her heir apparent, but his suit was rejected.[9] Nor do surviving accounts

---

[1] For such an inquisition see West, *Second Part*, ff. 311-12.

[2] The auditor took a fee of 4*s*., and his clerk of 10*s*. and more for declaring these accounts.   [3] P.R.O. in Wards 10/27, formulary book.   [4] *Ibid*.

[5] West, *First Part*, sect. 365.   [6] Powell, pp. 216-17.

[7] P.R.O. S.P. 14/61, no. 6, p. 9.   [8] *Foedera*, vol. XVII, pp. 68, 404.

[9] T. Birch, *Court and Times of Charles the First*, vol. II, p. 74.

CHAP. VI] WELFARE OF WARDS 131

of those who held idiots and lunatics suggest that they were more profitable to the committee than to the king.[1] A typical entry reads 'they haue defraied out more than they haue receyued by xlvij *li*. xvj *s*. vij *d*. ob. qua. So that it appeareth that thear is nothinge left to mayntayne the said lunatyke withall but that the charge and burden of his lyving and sustentacion will depende onlie upon the said Richard Hille one of these accomptantes and father of the same lunatike.'[2] It is pretty clear, too, from what Thomas Powell had to say that an idiot was equally unprofitable. 'Be assured', he warned, 'that your selfe is somewhat the wiser man, before you goe about to beg him, or else neuer medle with him at all, lest you chance to play at *handy dandy*, which is the Gardian, or which is the foole? and the case alter *e Converso ad Conversum*.'[3]

There were no doubt dark places in the treatment of the insane, and individual keepers were not always all they should have been. In 1609, for instance, the deputy feodary of Somerset described in grim terms the condition of a lunatic whom he had visited. He found him in an under-room, chained and ironed on a straw bed 'after the fashion of Bedlam', and ill clad, although he said that he had sufficient food and, when cold, wrapped himself in his bed-clothes; his keeper had let some of his land.[4] Or again, the case of Edward Lingen of Stoke Edith in Herefordshire seems hard. After holding the office of sheriff, he was imprisoned by the Council of the Marches for refusing to pay alimony to his wife, who desired to live apart from him; while he was in prison, his adversaries had him found a lunatic at an inquisition at which he was not allowed to be present; he was carried to his own house, where he remained in bondage for ten years until finally the Council appointed referees who restored him to his lands. His wife told the other side of the story; but weighing the arguments of both parties, it is difficult not to sympathize with Lingen.[5] On the other hand, it is true, not only that hard cases make bad law, but that it is the exceptional case that looms largest in the records. It is not without significance that, in the two instances quoted, an effort was made, however tardily, to protect the lunatic's interests. Nor should the mistake be made of expecting from the sixteenth or seventeenth century

[1] P.R.O. Wards 8/50-9, Wards 9/16 & 19.
[2] P.R.O. Wards 9/16, ff. 51-2.   [3] Powell, p. 217.
[4] *C.S.P. Dom. 1623-5 Addenda*, p. 542.
[5] H.M.C., *Report*, vol. XIII, App. IV, p. 271; *C.S.P. Dom. 1634-5*, pp. 60, 74, 87, 90, 373.

132   COURT OF WARDS AND LIVERIES   [CHAP. VI

the same standards and sense of responsibility as exist in our own day.

One thing seems certain. The welfare of the insane must have been very largely dependent on the attitude of the officers of the Court of Wards, necessarily a variable matter about which it is difficult to generalize. As has been seen, however, the lines on which the Court's policy developed were not, so far as the insane were concerned, either selfish or unenlightened. Nor is there lacking evidence of a more detailed character to fortify the impression that the Court, on this side of its activities, fulfilled its responsibilities with energy and fairness. Its decisions as a court of justice on occasion favoured the insane person rather than the royal committee—notably in Blewit's case, where it was held that the committees of a lunatic might not create copyholders within one of his manors, since they had no legal estate in it.[1] Again, to some degree it took over the chancellor's obligation to make a personal examination of anyone found an idiot by inquisition; and several times, finding such a person to be no idiot, discharged the proceedings.[2] It is also worth while to instance in this connexion the examination by Rudyerd, the surveyor, and Fleetwood, the receiver-general, of Katheryne Tothill, an alleged idiot. They began by 'some gentle entrances by way of discourse, that she might not take any apprehension at our coming thither', and then passed on to question her. They discussed her illness, and how she passed the time; she told them she read the Bible, and picked out certain of the Epistles; she understood the meaning of the Communion service and, on more worldly matters, 'knewe a Groate, a Sixpence and a 20s. peece'. Some of the questions asked were, of course, the common form of examinations in lunacy, but the report of the two officers is full of kindness and humanity,[3] and we happen to know from another source that they succeeded in freeing Katheryne from the imputation of idiocy.[4] One should not generalize from a single example, but if Rudyerd and Fleetwood were typical of the Court's officers it may be said to emerge with credit from a difficult, and thankless, part of the business that it was called upon to perform.

[1] Ley, *Reports*, p. 47.
[2] *Ibid*. pp. 25-6; B.M. Lansdowne MS. 608, ff. 65, 73.
[3] P.R.O. in Wards 10/67, examination of Katheryne Tothill, 28 Nov. 1626.
[4] B.M. Lansdowne MS. 608, f. 52.

CHAPTER VII

THE AGITATION AGAINST THE COURT

THE most unpopular feature of the Court of Wards has already appeared. The practice of selling wardships and marriages was medieval in origin, but, as has been seen, the Court's systematic development of such sales into its principal source of revenue was criticized, from its earliest days, on ethical and sociological grounds. It was argued, rightly or wrongly, that too much attention was paid to the crown's profits and too little to the physical and moral welfare of the royal wards. Moreover, the policy of sales apart, there were two further grievances against the Court. On the one hand, the leasing of wards' lands to speculators, out to obtain the last pound profit from them, frequently meant exploitation to the ultimate detriment of the minor and his family.[1] On the other, the judicial process of the Court, in which many found themselves involved, was alleged to be slow, expensive and arbitrary.

Of these additional grievances, the first was perhaps of the oldest standing. Exploitation by the lessee appeared at its worst where, not content with the income from the ward's lands, he realized a portion of their capital value by selling stock or timber without replacing them, or where, to secure maximum short-term profits, he cropped the land till it was exhausted and let farm buildings fall into decay. Actions of this sort constituted what was known as waste, against which a good deal of legislation had been directed in medieval times,[2] and which the Court constantly attempted to check on its own account. A covenant against waste was included in the indentures of lease, and the feodary had the right to survey any ward's lands yearly, no doubt to ensure that none was being committed.[3] Carew, during his short mastership, went further, and put forward a plan, suggested by Bacon, for an examination of

---

[1] Often, of course, the grantee of the ward's body and the lessee of his lands were one and the same person.

[2] Magna Carta c. 4. provided for punishment of waste by loss of wardship of the lands; the Statute of Gloucester c. 5 gave the heir whose lands had been wasted a remedy in damages; the Articuli super Cartas c. 18 gave remedy against an escheator committing waste. [3] *T.N.T.*, p. 48.

133

134 COURT OF WARDS AND LIVERIES [CHAP. VII

wards' property by the principal gentlemen in each county.[1] Yet it may be doubted how effective a check on waste was provided either by the law or by the Court's administrative practice, and losses sustained in this way remained one of the chief objections to wardship. In Edward VI's reign the Venetian ambassador, Barbaro, described how houses were decayed, woods felled, and estates despoiled through the working of wardship.[2] Thomas Smith, too, painted a picture in closely similar terms—

> He, who had a father, which kept a good house, and had all things in order to maintain it, shall come to his owne, after he is out of ward-shippe, woods decayed, houses fallen downe, stocke wasted and gone, land let foorth and plowed to the baren . . . so that not of manie yeres and peradventure never he shall be able to recover, and come to the estate where his father left it.[3]

It is true that Smith is professedly giving both sides of the argument for and against wardship; but comparing his exposition of the two, there is no doubt that he himself thought of it as a social evil. His complaints against waste were echoed many times in the succeeding period, when the agitation against the Court and all it stood for really began.

But indeed, even when the lessee's exploitation of the ward's estates did not amount to waste, the loss of income through the period of a long wardship could have a serious effect on the family fortunes. Where descent of a property was successively to minor heirs, the disaster might well prove irredeemable. Such a case seems to have been that of a ward named Trelawney, who in 1612 obtained an inquiry into the state of his property on the ground that he and his ancestors had been perpetually in wardship for three or four descents.[4] It would be interesting, though not easy, to work out the average incidence of wardship amongst tenants in chief: Fabian Philipps estimated such minority descents at not more than one in three or four.[5] That is a high figure, and the more significant when it is recalled that, as the apologist of the Court, Philipps was was not likely to exaggerate one of the principal causes of its unpopularity.

[1] Bacon, vol. XI, p. 288.
[2] *C.S.P. Ven.*, vol. V, p. 356.
[3] Thomas Smith, *De Republica Anglorum*, ed. L. Alston, p. 121.
[4] C.U. MS. Dd. 13. 28, f. 23. It looks as if the Court was thinking to temper justice with mercy as, by the *Instructions* of 1610, it was entitled to do.
[5] *T.N.T.*, p. 34.

CHAP. VII]   AGITATION AGAINST COURT   135

To the long-standing complaints against the evils resulting from sales of wardships and leases of the minor's lands, there was added in Elizabeth's time, and later, a growing discontent with the Court in its judicial capacity. Its procedure followed the general lines of that of the prerogative courts, and shared their unpopularity at the time when they began to be denounced by the common lawyers. 'What is the Court of Requests but a paper Court, and so is the Chauncerye and the Court of Wardes but paper Courtes', a certain Hitchcock was alleged to have exclaimed in 1584.[1] So long as these courts provided quick and efficient justice, they served their purpose; but when suits became long, and costs increased, unpopularity was bound to follow. In 1621 the House of Commons set up a committee for complaints against the courts, and some of the surviving indications of its business give an idea of the abuses in the Court of Wards. There was, for instance, the case of Fuller v. Hall, in which confusion of jurisdictions led to the plaintiff being attached by the chancellor and the defendant being committed by the master of wards,[2] or again it was asserted at this time that an order in the Court cost 3s. as opposed to 4d. in the King's Bench or Common Pleas.[3] About the same period, the growth of procedure by petition to the House of Lords provided yet further examples of alleged wrongs. The petitioner sometimes sought that his case should be removed from the Court for trial at the common law;[4] sometimes he asked that a specific injunction or decree of the Court should be reversed;[5] sometimes he simply complained of his treatment there, and in general terms sought redress.[6] Some of the cases were undoubtedly hard, especially so that of John Purdye, driven by his persecutions in the Court to leave his native land and, in his old age, seek service with the Prince of Orange; his wife had previously died of grief at the many unjust suits brought against them.[7] Most significant of all, however, is the instance of the petitioners who said quite naively that they were 'tied up in the Court of Wards' and too impoverished to defend themselves.[8]

---

[1] P.R.O. in Wards 10/50, deposition of John Birche in a bundle of depositions of various dates.

[2] Notestein, Relf and Simpson, *Commons Debates 1621*, vol. IV, p. 117.

[3] *Ibid.* vol. V, p. 532.   [4] H.M.C., *Report*, vol. IV, pp. 33, 41, 72.

[5] *Ibid.* vol. XIII, App. VII, p. 33; vol. IV, pp. 20, 42, 69.

[6] *Ibid.* vol. IV, pp. 16, 39, 46, 70, 112.

[7] *Ibid.* vol. IV, p. 70.   [8] *Ibid.* vol. IV, p. 87.

136   COURT OF WARDS AND LIVERIES   [CHAP. VII

Contemporary with general discontents of this kind against the Court's judicial practice there is also a hint of a more specific grievance against favouritism and near-corruption, which might turn the Court into an instrument of private vengeance. A memorandum, probably dating from 1632, asserted that Chancery, Court of Wards, Court of Requests, Duchy Court and Exchequer Chamber all granted *subpoenas* too easily, without security or the exhibition of a formal bill of complaint; and this, it was alleged, 'begetts many long and tedious sutes to the great impouerishing and vexation of the People which are the Defendants and is a great meanes for diuers contentious persons to reuenge themselves of their Aduersaries and to wrack their mallice uppon them: the plaintiff being *amicus curiae* and commonly paying little or smale Costes to the party grieued.'[1] The case of Harcourt *v.* Roberts in the Court suggests that there was, indeed, substance to this complaint, for the defendant, Roberts, claimed that officers had behaved with great partiality. The attorney, at that time Sir Walter Pye, had suppressed examinations of Roberts' witnesses and, later, refused to hear one of the principal of them; Chamberlain, the clerk, had erased the verdict of the original jury, Pye had ordered a new one and made it abundantly clear how they were to find. Amid all this dishonest practice, the master was said to have maintained silence.[2] This last allegation is the most interesting of all, for it implies that Naunton was ineffectual in presiding over the conduct of judicial business, which is indeed borne out by a private letter of 1633, where the writer maintained that, under Naunton, the attorney did whatever he pleased.[3]

Such were the strongly felt grievances against the practice of the Court on both administrative and judicial sides of its activity. Robert Cecil, it must be admitted, did make some attempt to meet current criticism, at least on the matters of sales of wardships and leases of lands. Within a few months of James I's accession, a revolutionary change in the procedure of sales was made, when it was decided to allow tenants in chief to purchase during their own lifetime—as it were in advance—the wardships and marriages of their heirs. In the autumn of 1603, commissions were appointed

[1] P.R.O. S.P. 16/230, no. 18, grievances worthy of reformation in the Courts.
[2] *C.S.P. Dom. Addenda 1625-49*, p. 496.
[3] T. Birch, *The Court and Times of Charles I*, vol. II, p. 229.

CHAP. VII]   AGITATION AGAINST COURT   137

on a county basis to effect such bargains,[1] and the feodaries (generally members of the commission for their county) had the responsibility of arranging that this new facility should be advertised —the feodary of Cornwall and his fellow commissioners, for instance, published it at the sessions at Bodmin and Truro, and arranged for it to be made known in every parish.[2] The following February a similar commission was granted to the master, surveyor, attorney, receiver and auditors, along with Sir John Popham, chief justice of the King's Bench, authorizing them to make compositions in much the same way.[3] Salisbury's *Instructions* of 1610 modified the old practice of sales even further by giving the heir's friends one month's pre-emption of the wardship, which meant that, if money were available, the wardship and marriage might be retained in the family, even if the father had not had the foresight to purchase it during his own lifetime.[4] The *Instructions* of 1610 also allowed, at the Court's discretion, mitigation of fines or rents where estates were encumbered or there were large numbers of children to provide for.[5]

In all this, Robert Cecil's policy had about it a touch of his father's wise moderation, but his successors seem to have done little to remove the causes of unpopularity. The *Instructions* of 1618 and 1622 alike repeated the preamble of Salisbury's *Instructions*, with its tender solicitude for the ward's welfare, and both continued the practice of giving first refusal of the wardship to the heir's near friends.[6] So far as other grievances were concerned, Cranfield as master offered in the House of Commons to make satisfaction for them in his person or estate or both.[7] But despite declarations of this sort, the Court was in fact so committed to a policy of high revenues that the removal of grievances became impossible.

In any case, the agitation against specific practices had long since grown into a demand for the abolition alike of the Court and of the feudal tenures that it administered. As early as 1598, when proceedings on Burghley's death were held up for want of a master,

[1] H.M.C., *Salisbury*, vol. xv, pp. 266, 276.   [2] *Ibid.* p. 264.
[3] P.R.O. Wards 9/110, f. 32. B.M. Lansdowne MS. 608, f. 28 lists thirteen wardships bought during lifetime down to 6 July 1604.
[4] P.R.O. S.P. 14/61, no. 6, p. 5.   [5] *Ibid.* p. 13.
[6] *Foedera*, vol. xvii, pp. 66, 400-1.
[7] Notestein, Relf and Simpson, *Commons Debates 1621*, vol. ii, p. 44.

K

138   COURT OF WARDS AND LIVERIES   [CHAP. VII

there was some discussion as to the possibility of abolishing the Court, and of substituting in place of its revenues a fixed yearly payment to the crown.[1] The matter came to nothing, but it is interesting that, in the last year of Elizabeth's reign, a project for restoring Catholicism on her death included a proposal to get rid of the Court.[2]

James' first Parliament, which no one could accuse of Catholic leanings, showed the same desire to be rid of wardship, which was included amongst the grievances brought forward by Sir Robert Wroth on 23 March 1603-4.[3] A committee was then appointed to consider Wroth's matters—this was particularly strong from the point of view of wardship, for it included John Hare, the clerk of the wards, and Edward Lewknor, who practiced a good deal in the Court.[4] Three days later the House resolved to proceed by way of petition to the king to give them leave to treat, and the Lords were asked for a conference with a view to their joining the petition.[5] Initially they seem to have agreed to a joint petition readily enough, and indeed suggested that it should also include the question of respite of homage. In addition they expressed the desire, however—which was a very different matter—that Goodwin's case should also be considered and, the Commons being unwilling to allow this, the proposal for a joint petition was for the time being dropped.[6] Not until 16 May, as the result of an effective speech by Sir Maurice Berkley, was it taken up again.[7] Nor did the second negotiation have a better fate than the first. The Lords agreed on 21 May to a conference,[8] but within a week Wroth made it clear that he did not like the way things were going,[9] and the reply from the Lords, delivered on 1 June, justified his forebodings, for they refused to join in the petition.[10] James had made his dislike of the whole proceedings apparent, and the Commons were left with no alternative but to explain what they had done in the *Apology* of 20 June, and leave it at that.[11] They returned to the point at issue in their third session when, in the course of a debate on scutage, a member said that its removal tended to the taking away of wards— 'Yea said some I wold it myght be tomorrowe y^t wards myght be

---

[1] *C.S.P. Dom. 1598-1601*, p. 110.   [2] *C.S.P. Dom. 1601-3*, pp. 281-2.
[3] *H.C.J.*, 23 March 1603-4.   [4] *Ibid.*
[5] *H.C.J.*, 26 March 1604; H.M.C., *Salisbury*, vol. XVI, p. 141.
[6] *H.C.J.*, 27 March 1604.   [7] *H.C.J.*, *Diarium*, 16 May 1604.
[8] *H.C.J.*, 21 May 1604.   [9] *H.C.J.*, *Diarium*, 26 May 1604.
[10] *H.C.J.*, 1 June 1604.   [11] *H.C.J.*, 20 June 1604.

CHAP. VII]   AGITATION AGAINST COURT   139

taken away, yea answered others to morrow to moroe in. . . .'[1] The writer's enthusiasm has played havoc with his spelling and calligraphy alike.

These negotiations of 1604 leave no doubt of the bitterness that was felt against wardship. The old complaints of children being seized from their kinsfolk and sold to strangers appeared again, together with the accusation that wards' lands were spoiled and wasted. The ingenious theory was advanced that, since the origin of wardship was for serving the king in his wars against Scotland, it was no longer necessary after the union of both kingdoms under one monarch; but, on the other hand, a possible danger was foreseen in case a Scot should become master of the wards.[2] Despite this strength of feeling, however, the legality of wardship was admitted: it was represented as a grief and no wrong, and the king was to be asked to abolish it as of grace and not as of justice.[3] For the rest, it was the Commons' intention to put forward again the proposal of 1598, the substitution of an annual composition for wardship and kindred royal rights. Throughout, their proceedings were careful and moderate, and they showed a clear understanding of practical difficulties—the vested interests of officers of the Court, of *mesne* lords, and the problem of how the annual composition was to be levied.[4]

The agitation against the Court of Wards, and in a wider sense against all the incidents of tenure in chief, came to a head in the fourth session of the first Parliament, in the spring of 1609-10. Even then, however, the Commons did not abandon their offer of an annual composition in return for the income that they were proposing to take from the king. Indeed, from the moment when, on 19 February, the question of abolition was again mooted, the proposal to be rid of wardship was accompanied by a suggestion for a yearly payment to the crown in its stead.[5] According to an entry in Walter Yonge's diary, this was to be 100,000 *l.* per annum, with a further 20,000 *l.* for Salisbury to compensate his loss of the mastership and 10,000 *l.* for the rest of the officers as compensation

---

[1] P.R.O. S.P. 14/24, no. 13, arguments used in House of Commons concerning scutage.

[2] P.R.O. S.P. 14/52, no. 88, observations on an intended petition (wrongly dated in *C.S.P. Dom. 1603-10*, p. 589, as 1610).

[3] *H.C.J.*, 27 March 1604.

[4] *H.C.J.*, 26 May 1604.

[5] *P.D. 1610*, p. 11.

140 COURT OF WARDS AND LIVERIES [CHAP. VII

during their lifetimes.[1] The whole sum was to be raised from lands held in chief, so that those who were to enjoy the advantage of abolition were themselves to pay for it.[2]

As a first move the Commons had to obtain the king's leave to treat, and this they did through the Lords, who appointed a committee on 26 February to approach James.[3] Two days later he answered the Lords, reserving the right to grant, or not to grant, the petition as he might choose.[4] On 2 March Salisbury delivered the royal reply to the Commons in characteristic language, careful 'neither to blowe us up with hope, nor drowne us in despayre.' James professed himself interested in wardship chiefly as the protector of the young heirs; its financial utility to the crown was a secondary consideration. Nevertheless, his answer contained the shrewd hint that composition would have to be not only on the basis of present profits, but of potential revenues.[5] On 5 March there was a debate on the matter in the Commons, followed three days afterwards by further conference with the Lords.[6] On 11 March the Commons' request for a speedy answer was delivered to the king, and on 13 March leave to treat was granted.[7] The fact was that James could not give an absolute refusal to their approaches. 'Parliament', wrote Sir Thomas Edmondes just at this time, 'doth strongly insist that the Court of Wards be dissolved, and will treat of no other matter till that is done'.[8] In that kind of negative power lay the Commons' strength.

Once leave to treat was given, the centre of discussion in the resultant negotiations was the amount to be granted as annual composition and the extent of the concessions expected from the crown in return.[9] Directly after obtaining permission to petition, the House of Commons went into committee and decided to offer 100,000 *l.* yearly in lieu of all that the crown received from feudal tenures except for aids, informing the Lords of this decision on 26 March.[10] The Lords postponed their answer until after Easter and, in the upshot, till they had had an opportunity of consulting the king, who, it was rumoured in the meantime, desired to raise

---

[1] *Diary of Walter Yonge, Esq.*, Camden Soc., p. 19.
[2] *Ibid.* and *P.D. 1610*, p. 11.   [3] *Ibid.* p. 19.   [4] *Ibid.*
[5] *Ibid.* pp. 20-2.   [6] *Ibid.* p. 22.   [7] *Ibid.* p. 27.
[8] H.M.C., *Downshire*, vol. II, p. 257.
[9] For the development of the Commons' demands in the way of concessions from 26 March to 18 July, see the Memorial in *H.L.J.*, vol. II, pp. 660-2.
[10] *P.D. 1610*, pp. 29-30; *H.L.J.*, vol. II, p. 660.

CHAP. VII] AGITATION AGAINST COURT 141

the Commons to 300,000 *l.*[1] Roughly speaking, that estimate of his demands was accurate, for on 26 April the Commons were told that he would not accept less than 200,000 *l.* in addition to a sum equal to that which he would lose by his concessions. Moreover, though he was prepared, on these terms, to sacrifice the incidents of the feudal tenures, the tenures themselves were to be maintained.[2] This latter reservation was as important in practice as the excessively high annual payment that he demanded, for the Commons felt that wardship was so much a prerogative matter that it could not be extinguished unless the whole basis of the feudal tenures was destroyed too.[3] On 4 May they informed the Lords that they would not offer more than 100,000 *l.*, which was really to break off negotiations.[4] Salisbury made an effort to keep the question open, with a strong plea for moderation—'What tempest is come amongst us that we can not cleare our meanings by conference?'[5] —and the reminder that another opportunity to get rid of wardship might not present itself.[6] He had, indeed, received a pretty broad hint from Sir Thomas Lake that James' figure was simply intended as a basis for discussion.[7] But, as things stood, the divergence between the Commons' offer and the king's demands was too wide to encourage the Commons, and in any case the question of impositions was now occupying much of their time and attention.

Thus the initiative for renewing discussions had to come from the Lords. It was they who sought a further conference on 26 May,[8] and on 8 June they pressed the Commons to expedite their deliberations.[9] Meantime, the Commons had hit upon an effective retort to the king's excessively high demand for annual composition. From the start of June they had under consideration the concessions to be demanded from the crown,[10] and on 18 June their message to the Lords asked guidance, not merely as to the lowest price required, but significantly enough as to whether anything would be yielded beyond their original ten points of 26 March.[11] Though James, fixing his figure at 140,000 *l.* a year, made it clear that this sum was

[1] H.M.C., *Downshire*, vol. II p. 271.
[2] *P.D. 1610*, p. 30, and *ibid.* Appendix A.
[3] Ralph Winwood, *Memorials of Affairs of State*, 1725, vol. III, p. 145.
[4] *P.D. 1610*, p. 31.
[5] P.R.O. S.P. 14/55, no. 58, collections out of divers speeches.
[6] Ralph Winwood, *Memorials of Affairs of State*, 1725, vol. III, p. 160.
[7] Transcripts of Salisbury MSS. 128/118.
[8] *H.C.J.*, 26 May 1610. [9] *H.C.J.*, 11 June 1610.
[10] *H.C.J.*, 1 June 1610. [11] *H.L.J.*, 18 June 1610.

142   COURT OF WARDS AND LIVERIES   [CHAP. VII

not intended to cover more than the original ten concessions,[1] the Commons went ahead with additions on 26 June, 16 July and 18 July.[2] The final stages of the agreement were as rapid as its original discussion had been slow. No doubt because they were by then including the abolition of purveyance amongst their demands, on 13 July the lower house offered 180,000 *l.* as annual composition,[3] and four days later went up to 200,000 *l.*[4] Their definitive terms were stated in the Memorial of 21 July, which was accepted by the Lords.[5]

When James prorogued Parliament, therefore, it seemed as if the great contract for the abolition of feudal tenures was as good as in being. That this was not the case, however, appeared very rapidly when the new session commenced in the autumn. The Lords lost no time in attempting to bring the negotiation to a conclusion, seeking a conference on 23 October.[6] But it is clear that the Commons were unenthusiastic, and just over a week later James asked them sharply for a decision as to whether they would proceed with the contract or not.[7] While their answer to this was still under discussion, moreover, he intervened again, sending a message to the House on 5 November that it was never his intention to proceed finally with the contract unless first, and quite apart from the agreed annual composition, he might be granted supply.[8] The debates consequent on this message concluded with an answer to the king that the Commons could not proceed with the contract.[9] For this seemingly sudden collapse of the agreement there were various reasons—first, at the time of the July negotiation the vital, and difficult, question of how the annual composition was to be levied had been left unsettled; again, the Commons had come back to Westminster unwilling to go further with the business unless some satisfactory answer were given to their grievances; and, most important of all, James' raising of the issue of supply and his insistence that the yearly compensation should be 200,000 *l. clear* killed whatever chance might be left of the great contract being implemented.

Thus the one sustained effort ever made to abolish wardship by mutual agreement failed. Viewing the negotiations for the great

---

[1] *P.D. 1610*, p. 121.
[2] *H.L.J.*, vol. II, pp. 660-2.
[3] *H.C.J.*, 13 July 1610.
[4] *H.C.J.*, 17 July 1610.
[5] *H.L.J.*, vol. II, p. 662.
[6] *P.D. 1610*, p. 126.
[7] *Ibid.*
[8] *Ibid.* p. 128.
[9] *Ibid.* p. 131.

CHAP. VII]   AGITATION AGAINST COURT   143

contract as a whole, something may be said of the attitude and conduct of the parties to them.

Once again, as in 1604, it is the moderation of the Commons' position that is striking. Since that date the growing financial difficulties of the king, and his need of supply, had strengthened their hand, and in the spring of 1609-10 they were better able than before to insist on consideration of their grievances. Yet, at least so far as reported debates go, their proceedings were tactful and courteous: as late as July, Bacon begged on their behalf that the sound of their grievances should not be harsh in the king's ears— 'it is but *gemitus columbae*, the mourning of a dove'.[1] Their original offer of 100,000 *l.* yearly payment as compensation was not wholly unreasonable, and in July they put it up steeply to meet the king's demands, though they also increased the list of concessions that they expected in return. Throughout they seem to have been guided by two elements in the situation—that wardship was a prerogative of the king, which he had the full right to enjoy, and that, if it was to be abolished along with other burdensome incidents, substantial revenues must be provided in its place. It was only when they became suspicious of James, as the other party to the agreement, that the contract broke down.

About James' attitude it is difficult to be so categorical: he seems, indeed, to have been in two minds about the negotiation. Certainly at the end of April he endeavoured to keep it open,[2] and as late as 21 November he asserted his willingness to consider a clear offer for wards and marriages.[3] But the wider plan, involving not merely abolition of the Court but of the whole system of military tenures, the king pretty clearly disliked, and it seems probable that he only considered it on Salisbury's strong advice. It is clear that the master of the Court acted as a go-between from Commons to king and king to Commons, and he is said to have lost favour with James for the part that he played. The story is told that the Earl of Dunbar carried to the king the advice of a dying peer not to lose the Court of Wards, and that James was so pleased with the advice that he wished he were 10,000 *l.* in debt to save the peer's life—'and ever after the Earl of Salisbury, who had been a great striver in that business, and was the man aimed at, began to

---

[1] Bacon, vol. XI, p. 203.
[2] Transcripts of Salisbury MSS. 128/118.
[3] *C.S.P. Dom. 1603-10*, p. 644.

144 COURT OF WARDS AND LIVERIES [CHAP. VII

decline'.[1] Certainly James was critical of Salisbury's speeches about the contract, and it appears that Lake, who was close to the king, made trouble between them.[2]

Salisbury's own relationship to the whole business of the contract is exceedingly interesting. If, on the one hand, he was distrusted by James for having advised negotiation with the Commons, equally, on the other, he was suspect by those who were pressing for the abolition of the Court. A libel of the times, for instance, implies that it was he who was deliberately responsible for the failure of the great contract.[3] The plain fact was that Salisbury had so much to lose by abolition that it was difficult to believe him in earnest about it. 'No Subject offers to his country as I have offered', he himself said, 'for in thus relinquishing the Court of Wards I am robb'd of my right Arm, and of the greatest Strength I have to merit the Love of many'.[4] Contemporaries found it scarcely credible that such renunciation was sincere, and even those who accepted his zeal for the contract sought a mercenary motive to explain his actions. Thus Yonge had the story that the Prince of Wales was, in any case, about to claim the mastership of the wards, and that Salisbury thought it well to accept abolition and a substantial pension rather than lose his office without compensation.[5] Or again, Taverner repeated the rumour that, having intended to quit the mastership and receive 5,000 *l* pension for it, Cecil had changed his mind and no longer favoured abolition.[6] In fact, neither assessment was quite just to Salisbury. As far back as 1603, he was reported to have spoken in favour of turning wardship into a fixed annual rent,[7] and his whole policy showed an awareness of the unpopularity of wardship and a sincere desire to minimize oppression. His conduct in 1609-10 was not out of character.

Finally, something may be said of two groups that, though in no sense parties to the contract, would have been greatly affected had it materialized—the *mesne* lords, whose right to wardships would have been swept away, and the officers who would have lost their valuable positions in the Court. For the former the chances of compensation seemed poor. Some years before the negotiation for

[1] Goodman, quoted in Bacon, vol. XI, p. 223.
[2] Transcripts of Salisbury MSS. 134/43.   [3] *Ibid.* 128/78.
[4] Ralph Winwood, *Memorials of Affairs of State*, 1725, vol. III, p. 194.
[5] *Diary of Walter Yonge, Esq.*, Camden Soc., p. 19.
[6] H.M.C., *Downshire*, vol. II, p. 86.   [7] *Camden Miscellany*, vol. X, p. 63.

CHAP. VII] AGITATION AGAINST COURT 145

the contract, Coke had made light of their significance.[1] Provision for their compensation was made in one draft act that survives,[2] but a second, and fuller, proposed measure, apparently in John Hare's hand, makes no mention of it,[3] and in a related document consisting of answers to objections to his draft Hare dismissed the matter cavalierly—'the subiecte hath litle use of his tenure by knight service'.[4] Nor do the *mesne* lords seem to have been considered in the debates on the contract. Rather more attention was paid to the officers. In the early stages of the negotiation, as has been mentioned, pensions on a generous scale were proposed for them. Their recompense for loss of position was provided for in a paper on the proposed changes, which was corrected by Salisbury.[5] Naturally enough, too, they were provided for in Hare's draft act, which imposed an additional rate upon all freehold land for the four years following so that they might be compensated.[6] Yet, in the upshot, they too seemed unlikely to receive substantial compensation. The Commons, it is true, remembered them, but only to ask the king that he would make suitable provision;[7] the king tried to make their pensions a responsibility of the Commons, and something not to be paid for out of the yearly composition of 200,000 *l*.[8] The local officials were totally disregarded. When, in July, the contract was agreed and Parliament prorogued, James set out on progress towards Northamptonshire, and as he went he was looked after anxiously by the escheators, feodaries and other officers because, as a contemporary letter-writer put it, 'there is no proviso in the agreement that cares for them, who (*pro facto*) are blown up. Amen.'[9]

Though no comparable attempt to reach an agreed basis for the abolition of wardship was afterwards made, king and Parliament alike remembered the negotiations of 1610 and both, at different times, made tentative moves to re-open them. James seems to have raised the question of abolition in 1614,[10] and again in 1621.[11] In

[1] P.R.O. S.P. 14/24, no. 62, project by Coke, 1606 (?).
[2] P.R.O. S.P. 14/55, no. 56, project for composition, 1610.
[3] P.R.O. S.P. 14/55, no. 60, draft act, 1610.
[4] P.R.O. S.P. 14/55, no. 57, note of objections, 1610.
[5] P.R.O. S.P. 14/52, no. 87, note of profits peculiar to the king's tenures, 1610.
[6] P.R.O. S.P. 14/55, no. 60.   [7] *H.L.J.*, vol. II, p. 661.
[8] *P.D. 1610*, p. 128.   [9] H.M.C., *Downshire*, vol. II, p. 328.
[10] *C.S.P. Dom. 1611-18*, p. 231.
[11] Coke, *Fourth Institute*, edn. of 1669, pp. 202-3.

146   COURT OF WARDS AND LIVERIES   [CHAP. VII

the latter year Parliament was prepared to give him a yearly rent in exchange, provided that thirteen conditions, listed by them, were observed;[1] but, if we are to believe Fabian Philipps, the judges then advised against the putting down of the Court as being prejudicial to the subject.[2] It is perhaps more likely that, once again, James put his demands for compensation too high, or that he could not, after all, tolerate the loss of prestige entailed: he is reported to have told Charles that, though the alternative revenue might make him a rich prince, it would never make him a great one.[3] At least, nothing resulted; and though, five years later, in Charles I's second Parliament, a committee of the House of Commons was appointed to consider a way of petitioning the king on the same matter, the attempt was not more than half-hearted.[4]

Meantime, the continued unpopularity in which the Court stood was revealed by a warm debate in the House of Commons of 1614 on the second reading of the bill against continuance of liveries, which was a government measure. Its detailed provisions are not known, but it met with opposition on various grounds, among them the suggestion that its end was to remove certain fees from the Petty Bag to the Court itself, 'as one like to drown, that will catch his Fellow, and drown him with him'. In this debate Fuller brought up the grievance—as old as the Court itself, and older—of denial of the subject's right of traverse.[5] Seven years later, the debates of the 1621 Parliament brought out other grievances—against prosecutors for wardships,[6] secret inquisitions, and high fees.[7] Cranfield himself, then master, propounded eight matters concerning the Court that he considered in need of redress.[8] At the beginning of the next reign Sir Edward Coke returned to the topic of traverses, when speaking in favour of a bill against secret inquisitions; the course of the Court of Wards only allowed traverse by bill, which was in his judgment a restraint of the common law.[9]

It is at first sight odd that further questions of principle relating to livery and wardship were not raised in the Parliaments of this period, and Fabian Philipps took this for evidence that they did not constitute a serious grievance.[10] But the argument from silence

---

[1] Coke, *Fourth Institute*, edn. of 1669, pp. 202-3.   [2] *T.N.T.*, p. 147.
[3] *Ibid.*   [4] *H.C.J.*, 4 May 1626.   [5] *H.C.J.*, 14 May 1614.
[6] Notestein, Relf and Simpson, *Commons Debates 1621*, vol. II, p. 44.
[7] *Ibid.* vol. IV, p. 51.   [8] *Ibid.* vol. IV, p. 117.
[9] *Commons Debates in 1625*, Camden Soc., p. 17.
[10] *T.N.T.*, p. 92.

CHAP. VII]   AGITATION AGAINST COURT   147

is dangerous—the fact is that members were fully occupied with other pressing matters: foreign policy, religion, privilege of Parliament, monopolies, tonnage and poundage and forced loans—and, above all, in proceeding against the illegalities of offending individuals.

In this last connexion, however, the impeachment of Cranfield, Earl of Middlesex, provides interesting evidence regarding the Court of which he was master. One of the principal charges in the Commons' indictment against him was, in general terms, 'for procuring the good orders of the court of wards to be altered; for that this was done by his principal procurement, to the deceit of the king, oppression of the subject, and the enriching of his own servants'.[1] Basically, the good orders were Salisbury's *Instructions* of 1610. These, it is true, had been modified in 1618, but the alterations of that year had only been made after reference to the chancellor and chief justices of both benches. Cranfield's *Instructions* of 1622, however, though debated before James[2] and referred to ten lords of the Council, were apparently pushed through without expert legal consideration outside the Court's own officers, whom the master could bully into agreement.[3]

In more detail, Cranfield was accused on four grounds—of doubling certain fees for liveries; of creating a new officer, a secretary, and allowing him to take undue fees for forwarding petitions; of proceeding unjustly for concealments of wards; and of leaving in the secretary's control a signature-stamp, which was placed on even the most important instruments instead of Cranfield's autograph. He was found guilty on the first and fourth count,[4] but so far as the wider issue went it is significant that, even after his impeachment, in May 1624, Coke found it necessary to ask that *of grace* the new *Instructions* might be revoked, and the former amended.[5] Nor, apparently, was the request heeded by James, since, on 4 July 1625, answering the grievances of the last reign, Charles promised to recall the *Instructions*, which must have remained in existence until that time.[6] The whole episode shows a growing impatience with the extortionate fees taken by the officers of the Court, and a strong opposition to the new measures

---

[1] *State Trials*, vol. II, col. 1190.   [2] *Ibid.*
[3] P.R.O. S.P. 14/165, no. 1, objections against Middlesex.
[4] *State Trials*, vol. II, col. 1242.
[5] *H.C.J.*, 19 May 1624.
[6] *Commons Debates in 1625*, Camden Soc., p. 39.

148 COURT OF WARDS AND LIVERIES [CHAP. VII

to increase its public revenues. The agitation was not merely against individual officials, but against the considered policy which it was their duty to administer.

The increasing strength of that agitation through the eleven years' tyranny can, in the absence of Parliaments, only be inferred from references in the letters and other writings of the time. Writing in this period, Spelman thought it worth while to turn aside from his main thesis to make a reasoned attack on wardship.[1] It is of this period, too, the mastership of Lord Cottington, that Clarendon tells how 'all the rich families of noblemen and gentlemen were exceedingly incensed, and even indevoted to the Crown, looking upon what the law had intended for their protection and preservation to be now applied to their destruction; and therefore resolved to take the first opportunity to ravish that jewel out of the royal diadem'.[2] Cottington was himself accused of taking bribes,[3] and it is interesting that in 1641 Whitelock, after noting that various great officers of state resigned, either through a feeling of insecurity or to satisfy others, immediately adds that Cottington was replaced by Saye and Sele.[4]

In February 1640-1 the House of Commons in the Long Parliament appointed a committee to inquire concerning the irregular proceedings of the Court and the abuses of feodaries, escheators and other officers;[5] the committee was empowered to receive petitions, and there is evidence that it was sitting later in the spring of the same year.[6] Its findings are not known, but the *Grand Remonstrance* perhaps incorporated the more serious abuses it had revealed, articles 43-6 relating to wardship. The Court was said to have been grievous in exceeding its jurisdiction; the estate of many families had been weakened, and some ruined, by excessive fines for compositions of wardships, leases of above a hundred years had been illegally made to draw on wardship, and undue proceedings had been used in the finding of inquisitions to make the jury return

---

[1] *History and Fate of Sacrilege*, edn. of 1846, pp. 175-7. He also wrote an erudite paper, 'The Origin, Growth, Propagation and Condition of Feuds and Tenures by Knight-Service in England' (*English Works*, edn. of 1727, p. 1), but it has little bearing on the contemporary situation.

[2] *History of the Rebellion*, ed. Macray, vol. I, p. 199.

[3] N. Wallington, *Historical Notices of the Reign of Charles I*, 1869, vol. I, p. 213.

[4] B. Whitelock, *Memorials of the English Affairs*, edn. of 1853, vol. I, p. 134.

[5] *H.C.J.*, 16 Feb. 1640-41.

[6] Notestein, *Journal of Sir Simonds D'Ewes*, p. 491.

CHAP. VII]   AGITATION AGAINST COURT   149

a verdict favourable to the king.[1] As a final statement of the grievances against the Court, the *Grand Remonstrance* is disappointing—so many of the major objections of the preceding years are unmentioned in it; the truth is that they could not be included within the bounds of a single, general document of protest.

Bearing in mind how many of the Parliament party held lands in chief of the crown, it is not unfair to include the Court as an important subsidiary cause of the Civil War. It was a cardinal blunder of James I not to realize that wardship and livery were anachronisms, and to refuse the Commons' offer of composition in 1604 and 1609-10.

[1] S. R. Gardiner, *Constitutional Documents of the Puritan Revolution*, 2nd edn., p. 213.

CHAPTER VIII

THE FINAL DAYS OF THE COURT

THE history of the Court in the last stormy days of its existence developed in close connexion with the changing political situation. In 1643-5, with the royal and parliamentary forces nicely balanced, there were in effect two rival courts, at Oxford and at Westminster, each denying the validity of the other's jurisdiction. Subsequently, in the winter of 1645-6, an ordinance was passed for the complete abolition of the Court, and the triumph of Parliament during the spring of the next year made it effective. In June Oxford capitulated, and within a month the seal of Charles's Court was brought to Westminster and ceremonially broken; in July the king's agreement to the abolition was made one of the conditions of peace. The ordinances of these years were given statutory confirmation by the first Parliament of the Protectorate. At the Restoration the possibility of reviving the Court was seriously canvassed, but it is significant of the changed terms on which the monarchy was restored that other counsels prevailed and that the dissolution of the Court was once again confirmed.

Such was the outline of events. A more detailed examination of the period may begin with the adjournment of the Court to Oxford, which the king had entered on 29 October 1642 and where, for the next three years, he kept his headquarters. The Court was adjourned there by royal proclamation of 27 December;[1] Parliament petitioned against this transference of business, but the king was adamant that term should be held in Oxford.[2] At once the conflict of allegiances arose, and the problem of the Court's personnel presented the first difficulty. Saye and Seale, the master, sought direction from the House of Lords as to whether he should obey the king's summons, and was ordered not to go to Oxford;[3] in February the king issued two commissions to inquire which officers of the Court had failed to attend,[4] and from a list compiled

[1] Steele, no. 2336.   [2] *H.L.J.*, 18 Jan. 1642-3.   [3] *Ibid.*
[4] W. H. Black, *Docquets of Letters Patent and other Instruments passed under the Great Seal of Charles I at Oxford in 1642-6*, pp. 2, 4. A copy of the second commission is in B.M. Egerton MS. 2978, f. 70.

150

CHAP. VIII]   FINAL DAYS OF THE COURT   151

as a return to the second of these it is clear that the surveyor of the liveries, the attorney, both auditors, the usher and messenger[1] had not appeared.[2] On the other hand, Fleetwood, the receiver-general, and the ancient clerk, Richard Chamberlain, had accompanied Charles, and Cottington, who had previously had seven years' experience as master of the Court, subsequently joined the king at Oxford, and in January 1643-4 the new seal was given into his custody.[3] The three judges assistant were also in Oxford, and available to advise.[4] Meantime, in the summer and autumn of 1643, the king made new appointments to some of the offices: in June, John and Robert Heath, the sons of the lord chief justice, were appointed as auditors in place of Maynard and Tooke;[5] in November, Orlando Bridgeman was created attorney.[6] Even so, the defection of so many of the Court's great officers was no doubt an embarrassment, and as late as September 1645 their absence was the subject of a further commission of inquiry.[7]

Naturally enough, Parliament disliked the removal of the English courts to Oxford. When its petition against the transfer was disregarded, it passed an ordinance against the adjournment.[8] Later, there were further ordinances to prevent the judges from going to Oxford,[9] and a declaration was issued that the continued holding of the Courts there would 'much tend to the Prejudice of the Commonwealth'.[10] On 1 June 1643 more positive action was taken by the Commons: a committee was appointed to consider how to divert the revenue of the Court of Wards from going to Oxford, and how to turn it to the use of the Commonwealth.[11] A month later it was ordered that money paid at Oxford for wardships, since the House had forbidden such payments, was to be re-paid to the Commons; the estates of any who had compounded, or should compound, at Oxford were to be sequestered.[12] In August a further committee of the Commons was to examine Saye and Seale, and discover from him what had happened to the Court's revenue during the past year.[13]

Perhaps as a result of the deliberations of these committees, it

---

[1] Although on 18 Jan. the House of Lords had ordered that he should have a pass to go to Oxford for the term.   [2] B.M. Egerton MS. 2978, f. 70.
[3] Steele, no. 2523.   [4] B.M. Egerton MS. 2978, f. 69.
[5] Black, *op. cit.*, p. 356.   [6] *Ibid.* p. 369.   [7] *Ibid.* p. 274.
[8] *Acts and Ordinances of the Interregnum*, vol. I, p. 65.
[9] *Ibid.* vol. I, pp. 133, 299.   [10] *H.L.J.*, 30 May 1643.
[11] *H.C.J.*, 1 June 1643.   [12] *H.C.J.*, 1 July 1643.   [13] *Ibid.* 1 Aug. 1643.

152   COURT OF WARDS AND LIVERIES [CHAP. VIII

became obvious that, however much Parliament disliked the Court, expediency demanded that it should be continued for the present in Westminster, as an off-set to the Oxford Court; hence the curious paradox of these later years, when the men who had consistently opposed wardship and livery themselves maintained their own Court of Wards and Liveries. A committee of the House of Lords was, therefore, appointed not only to consider means of annulling the new seal, made at Oxford, but also how to establish the master, surveyor, and attorney in their old position.[1] In December the Commons sequestered William Fleetwood, Richard Chamberlain and, though he had initially remained in London, Hugh Audley of their offices.[2] The following spring Charles Fleetwood was appointed to his brother's position, and arrangements made for the Committee of Revenue to appoint other officers in place of those who had deserted the Parliament[3]—one of the new officers was Miles Corbett, made clerk in May 1644.[4] Meanwhile, the Lords had ordered Saye and Seale to sit in his place in the Court to dispatch business there and the clerks to attend in their several places.[5] Officials of the Court, as well as lawyers, attorneys, clerks and solicitors practising there, were among those to whom the commissioners of the great seal were ordered to tender the *Solemn League and Covenant*.[6] The whole policy was entirely opportunist; but it was not to be expected that Parliament, merely because it disapproved of wardship and livery, would leave the revenues from these sources to Charles.

Thus for some three years the Court was duplicated, and it is interesting to try to assess the balance of wardship business and profits as between the royal and parliamentary Courts—though inadequate documentation, especially for the Oxford Court, makes this difficult. Of the royalist Court of Wards it is only possible, indeed, to give an incomplete and uncertain picture. One of its few surviving records includes a list of sixty wardships disposed of by the king between Hilary 1643 and Trinity 1645—ten of them so substantial that the fine for each was rated at 1,000 *l.* or over.[7]

---

[1] *H.L.J.*, 28 Nov. 1643.   [2] *H.C.J.*, 11 Dec. 1643.   [3] *Ibid.* 25 March 1644.
[4] B.M. Add. MS. 34253, f. 30.   [5] *H.L.J.*, 1 Feb. 1643-4.
[6] *Acts and Ordinances of the Interregnum*, vol. I, p. 374.
[7] P.R.O. P.R.O. 30/26/91. They were rated as follows: Francis Lord Brooke—19,130 *l.*; Henry Winchcombe—1,500 *l.*; John Mallett—2,000 *l.*; Nicholas Slaning—1,000 *l.*; William Herbert—2,500 *l.*; Hugh Stewkeley—1,000 *l.*; Sir Edward Stradling's heir—1,500 *l.*; John Banks—1,000 *l.*; Thomas Markham—

CHAP. VIII]   FINAL DAYS OF THE COURT   153

Again, since there exist docquets for grants of at least two wardships that do not figure in this list,[1] it was clearly not quite complete, and the possibility must be borne in mind that for some few of Charles' grants no evidence remains. Even if a substantial allowance is made for this, however, it is clear that the number of wardships at the king's disposal was a great deal smaller than in normal times. Statistics apart, the royal proclamation of 11 November 1643 leaves no doubt that there was very considerable neglect in confessing wardships and suing out livery before the Oxford Court.[2] Nor was this the only way in which the king's feudal income fell. Although a wardship might be revealed, and a grant of the body and lease of the lands made in due form, there was still the question of collection of fines and rents, which as the king's position worsened must have become progressively more difficult. Accompanying the list of wards sold at Oxford are two other accounts—one of actual sums of money received, the other of arrears unpaid. It is significant that the first amounts only to 26,066 l., and the latter to 82,454 l.[3]

The impression is left that the scope of the Oxford Court was limited. There has not yet come to light any evidence of its having transacted that purely judicial business which had been a main function of the Court in earlier times. Even such scraps of evidence as have survived for its activity on the administrative side suggest a rather personal, and not very effective, conduct of business. A petition of Ann Lamb, for instance, seeking a writ after her husband's death, shows that sittings for compositions were still regularly held; but the direction as to action on the petition is over the signature of Charles' secretary of state, Edward Nicholas, who was not, so far as we know, an officer of the Court, and there is the additional rather pathetic note by Chamberlain—'But this was all that was donne in this business because none came about the same afterwards to mee.'[4] The former clerk was still corresponding with Sir Edward Heath about this case in 1650.[5] No doubt the Court,

4,000 l.; Hugh Smyth—2,500 l. In the cases of Slaning, Herbert and Markham the rating was formal only, since their fathers had been killed in the king's service; see below, p. 158.

[1] Black, *op. cit.*, pp. 363 (Edward Trevor) and 407 (Sir Oliver Boteler).
[2] Steele, no. 2508.
[3] P.R.O. P.R.O. 30/26/91. But of these arrears 48,771 l. were a book-keeping matter only, since they related to heirs whose fathers had been killed in the king's service; see below, p. 158.   [4] B.M. Egerton MS. 2978, f. 87.
[5] P.R.O. in Wards 10/1, Chamberlain correspondence.

L

154 COURT OF WARDS AND LIVERIES [CHAP. VIII

especially in the first months after the move to Oxford, was a useful means of supplying the king's war chest: in the sixteen months between November 1642 and March 1644 the receiver-general paid over 7,725 *l.* to the paymaster-general.[1] But it was almost impossible for it to produce a regular and stable income. Apart from its lack of experienced personnel, a further difficulty must have arisen from the absence of records, for the most part left at Westminster. Again—and perhaps this was the most serious limiting factor of all—it had to face the constructive opposition of the parliamentary Court, staffed mainly by men experienced in the administration of wardship and livery, and enjoying advantages that were denied to the Oxford Court.

For the Westminster Court in these years, the records are much fuller,[2] and that fact is in itself suggestive: it is certain that the parliamentary Court had a greater element of administrative continuity than the king's, that the range of its business was wider and more nearly approximating to the earlier functions of the Court of Wards, and that it was financially a good deal more profitable than the Oxford Court. Only in the year 1642-3, before Parliament had made up its mind to continue the Court in opposition to Charles, was there a really serious interruption of business. The evidence already discussed implies that until at least the late autumn of 1643 officers were not sitting regularly for the despatch of their duties, and this interim is clearly marked in the records. From

---

[1] B.M. Egerton MS. 2978, f. 67.

[2] The following have been noted amongst P.R.O. Wards records as including material for this period:

Legal. Wards 9/577, entry books of affidavits; Wards 9/240, memoranda of bills, answers etc.; Wards 9/296, calendar of commissions, depositions and examinations; Wards 9/102A, entry book of decrees; Wards 9/556-8, entry books of orders; Wards 9/182 and 183, short calendars of evidences; Wards 9/291, docquet book of privy seals and commissions; Wards 9/294, entry book of commissions; in Wards 10/51, bundle of depositions; in Wards 10/67, file of warrants for privy seals and commissions, and of writs returned.

Administrative. Wards 9/220, entry book of petitions and compositions for wardship; Wards 9/163, entry book of receipts for sale of wards; Wards 9/202, entry book of money and obligations received; Wards 9/172, docquet book of writs; Wards 9/314, list of transcripts of inquisitions; Wards 9/83, entry book of liveries; Wards 9/274, feodaries' bonds.

Process. Wards 9/699, 11/3/8, 9/339, in 10/55, 9/700, auditors' certificates of debts of collectors; Wards 9/52, 9/53, 11/4/30, portion of 9/334, 11/16/11, books of abstracts of arrears certified; Wards 9/235, staying of process; in Wards 10/60, certificates of arrears of wards whose committees have no privilege of Parliament. For the many sheriffs' books see *Wards Guide*, pp. 47-51.

CHAP. VIII]   FINAL DAYS OF THE COURT   155

9 July 1642 until 28 June 1643 only two hundred and forty-eight writs directing the all-important inquisition post mortem were issued from Westminster, as against a thousand and twenty and seven hundred and twenty-six in the two years previous.[1] The year December 1642–December 1643 seems to have seen the entering of only five particulars for leases.[2] In the same way, depositions entered fell markedly, which implies that litigation was notably diminished.[3] However—and this is very important indeed—the interruption of business did not last long enough for its effects to be felt too disastrously in the financial sphere. In the history of institutions there is frequently to be observed a process not very different from what the economic historian terms geographical inertia. Old habits count for much, and an ancient office can. live for some months at least on the routine established during long years of efficient administration. So it seems to have been with the finances of the Westminster Court in this year 1642-3. Despite the undoubted decline of business, the income now secured from wards' lands totalled 17,369 *l.*, and sales of wardships 13,641 *l.* for the year ending Michaelmas 1643.[4] At first sight both figures are amazingly high, having regard to all the circumstances of the time. But the king's complaint in January 1643-4 that Audley was still receiving revenues at Westminster makes it clear that the parliamentary Court was flourishing.[5] That it was able to do so was because feodaries continued in the ways that they knew.

Of course, the success enjoyed by the Westminster Court must not be exaggerated. The recently discovered view of account just mentioned shows a heavy over-all drop, under most heads of income, from the high figures of the eleven years' tyranny.[6] In particular, the return from wards' lands fell to something like half of what it had previously been, and from sales of wardships to a little over a third. But the appropriate comparison is not with the Court prior to the outbreak of the Civil War, but with the royalist Court at Oxford. Here there is no doubt of Westminster's superiority, which, income aside, is reflected in the wide range of its orderly activities. Once it was decided to maintain the Court and resume its full functions, no time was wasted. In

[1] P.R.O. Wards 9/172, docquet book of writs.
[2] P.R.O. Wards 9/195, particulars for leases.
[3] P.R.O. Wards 9/577 shows only 45 depositions entered for 19 Charles I.
[4] Appendix II.
[5] Steele, no. 2523.   [6] Appendix II.

156   COURT OF WARDS AND LIVERIES [CHAP. VIII

nineteen months from June 1643 to February 1644-5 seven hundred and sixty-eight writs directing inquisitions post mortem went out.[1] On the judicial side also business seems to have been rapidly and effectively resumed: even when it must have become clear that the Court's days were numbered, in the last three full terms of its existence, appearances averaged rather more than fifty a term.[2]

The situation had the elements of absurdity. The overlapping of the two jurisdictions and the confusion that resulted may both be imagined. Record data regarding sale of wards and lease of lands show that in no less than twenty-three counties both Courts were operating.[3] On occasion, a single unhappy ward was sold twice over to separate purchasers, sometimes, though not always, with a wide divergence in the fines fixed. Thus Henry Winchcombe's wardship was granted by the Oxford Court to his mother for a fine of 1,500 l.,[4] and by Westminster to James Fiennes for 500 l.;[5] William Fitzherbert's by Oxford to Lord Newcastle to the ward's own use for 100 l.,[6] and by Westminster to Nathaniel Hollowes for 7 l. 13s. 4d.[7] The fine for Thomas Draper's wardship, on the other hand, was assessed by both Courts at 800 l.,[8] and that for Sir Robert Crane's daughters at 1,700 l. by the royal Court and 1,500 l. by the parliamentary Court.[9] In circumstances of this kind effective guardianship no doubt went to whichever of the grantees could secure the ward's body, and the tragic possibilities for the child's uprooting and abduction were considerable. Some affidavits before the Westminster Court, relating to the wardship of Hester

[1] P.R.O. Wards 9/172, docquet book of writs.
[2] Calculated from P.R.O. Wards 9/557.
[3] P.R.O. P.R.O. 30/26/91 shows the Oxford Court dealing with wards or estates in Anglesey, Berks, Brecknock, Bucks, Cambridge, Carmarthen, Carnarvon, Chester, Cornwall, Cumberland, Denbigh, Derby, Devon, Dorset, Essex, Flint, Glamorgan, Gloucester, Hereford, Hertford, Kent, Leicester, Lincoln, London, Middlesex, Monmouth, Norfolk, Northampton, Nottingham, Oxford, Radnor, Salop, Somerset, Southampton, Stafford, Surrey, Sussex, Warwick, Wilts, Worcester, York. P.R.O. Wards 9/163 shows the Westminster Court similarly in Bedford, Bucks, Chester, Cumberland, Denbigh, Derby, Devon, Dorset, Durham, Essex, Gloucester, Hertford, Huntingdon, Kent, Lancaster, Lincoln, London, Middlesex, Montgomery, Northampton, Northumberland, Oxford, Somerset, Southampton, Stafford, Suffolk, Surrey, Sussex, Warwick, Wilts, York.
[4] P.R.O. P.R.O. 30/26/91, f. 7.   [5] P.R.O. Wards 9/163, f. 125.
[6] P.R.O. P.R.O. 30/26/91, f. 7.   [7] P.R.O. Wards 9/163, f. 125.
[8] P.R.O. P.R.O. 30/26/91, f. 8; Wards 9/163, f. 123.
[9] P.R.O. P.R.O. 30/26/91, f. 9; Wards 9/163, f. 125.

CHAP. VIII]   FINAL DAYS OF THE COURT   157

Quarles, are illuminating in this connexion. A certain Henry Mordant obtained the grant of her wardship from the king, and, coming to claim his prize, told one deponent that 'he had his authority from Oxford where there was as good law to be had as ever was'.[1] In those counties where both Courts attempted to function, each in rivalry with the other, everything must have turned on the sympathies of the feodary. Of this officer during the period disappointingly little is known—no feodaries' accounts for these last years have been discovered. Such evidence as there is, however, suggests that the feodaries as a whole still looked to Westminster rather than Oxford. Two figure in in the list of 1643 as having failed to attend at Oxford, one of them being stigmatised 'an Arch-Rebell',[2] but there is no reason to imagine that that list is complete. The Westminster docquet book of writs and commissions issued from June 1643 till the abolition shows the feodaries of London, Northants, Norfolk, Warwick, Cumberland, Westmorland, Kent, Glamorgan and even Oxford figuring on commissions, which creates a strong presumption of their loyalty to Parliament.[3]

The greater efficiency of the Westminster Court at the centre was thus, in all probability, accompanied by a larger measure of control in the localities. But both Courts must have suffered seriously from the disturbed conditions of a country at war. The whole yield of wardship and livery was dependent on regular returns of inquisitions post mortem and feodaries' surveys, and then upon efficient collection of debts—all matters that were of singular difficulty during the Civil War. As early as September 1642 a correspondent of Tooke, the auditor, wrote him about some money due to be paid—'I would fayne be ridd of my money, for the times are full of doubts'.[4] The troubles of the times were used by the under-sheriffs of Lincoln and Kent in the summer of 1645 to excuse their failure to execute process out of the Westminster Court.[5] Even the crucial inquisition post mortem was affected, if we are to go by the chance example of Toby Barraclough of Halifax, an interested party in an inquisition, who complained that the escheator first postponed it and then, when Barraclough had hidden away his evidences from the Scottish troops in the place

[1] P.R.O. Wards 9/577, p. 368.
[2] B.M. Egerton MS. 2978, f. 76.
[3] P.R.O. Wards 9/172.
[4] P.R.O. in Wards 10/40, correspondence.
[5] P.R.O. in Wards 10/51, bundle of depositions, Easter 1645.

158   COURT OF WARDS AND LIVERIES [CHAP. VIII

and could not get at them, held it without taking them into consideration.[1]

One other curious factor tended to keep down the revenues of both Courts. Each party arranged that there should be special exemptions for the heirs of tenants killed on military service on its behalf. Parliament passed an ordinance that wardships in such cases were to be granted free to the mother or next friend of the ward;[2] the king's practice to grant them to the ward's own use without fine or rent amounted to much the same thing[3]—he had first promised this concession to the heirs of all who died in the campaign of 1640 against the Scots.[4] Actually the notion was not a new one, for a statute of 1523 had provided that the feoffees or executors of any killed in the king's service should have wardship of the heir.[5] But what was new was the strange situation of two opposed parties using the same bribe to bring men to their rival standards.

The artificiality of the whole situation must have been apparent, and the abolition of the Court was Parliament's ultimate object. As early as April 1643 it was within the terms of reference of a Commons' committee to consider how this might be effected;[6] in July of the same year[7] and later, in August 1644,[8] committees were appointed specifically to prepare ordinances for the Court's removal. Apparently it was only the exigencies of the political and military struggle which postponed a measure from going through, until the parliamentary party was strong enough to enforce it on the king and not make it a mere gesture of self-denial. On 20 September 1645 the Commons finally resolved on the abolition of the Court and of tenures in chief;[9] they returned to the proposal of 1609-10 that the king should be granted 100,000 *l.* yearly as compensation, but that sum was to be allocated by Parliament and not expended at his own discretion.[10] It is worth noting that the debate on abolition arose from the discussion of an ordinance for discharging the wardship of the heirs male of Sir Christopher Wray, who had been killed in the Parliament's service; the wider question was raised by

---

[1] Wards 9/577, p. 403.
[2] *H.C.J.*, 24 July 1643.
[3] B.M. Egerton MS. 2978, f. 68.
[4] H.M.C., *Report*, vol. v, p. 331.
[5] 14 and 15 Henry VIII c. 14.
[6] *H.C.J.*, 14 April 1643.
[7] *H.C.J.*, 24 July 1643.
[8] *H.C.J.*, 23 Aug. 1644.
[9] *Acts and Ordinances of the Interregnum*, vol. I, p. 833.
[10] *H.C.J.*, 20 Sept. 1645.

CHAP. VIII]   FINAL DAYS OF THE COURT   159

Selden, Maynard, St John and Whitelock.[1] It was not until four months later, on 24 February, that the Lords agreed with the Commons' vote, and the Court ceased to exit.[2] The symbolic act of abolition was the breaking of the seal of the Oxford Court, which occurred yet another four months later.[3] As Parliament's position improved, it was prepared to concede less in return for the taking away of the Court: in the articles of peace of July 1646 the yearly payment offered was reduced to 50,000 l.[4]

The jurisdiction of the Court might be abolished, but it was naturally some years before its business could be completely terminated. First, there was the problem of securing the payment of outstanding debts. The Commons followed their resolution for the Court's removal by a printed declaration that wardships, liveries, primer seisins and mean rates, falling before it was put down, should be answered to the Commonwealth.[5] In May 1646 an order of the House, also printed, dealt with money due on bonds and rents, owing in like manner from before the abolition, and it empowered the receiver-general to take payments and issue acquittances.[6] There seems to have been some difficulty in bringing in the arrears, for further parliamentary measures were found necessary.[7] The continuance of business of this sort involved a good deal of administrative activity, for when bonds were made void by payment they had to be cancelled or returned. There is evidence that the Revenue Committee undertook some of this work in the summer of 1646, and Hugh Audley, who seems to have found his way back into favour, was involved in it over a period of some years: indeed in June 1648 the House of Lords authorized him, upon a certificate from the receiver-general that a debt was paid, to return the relevant bonds and indentures to the persons concerned.[8] In much the same way, responsibility for the posting of arrears was laid on James Tooke, who, in accordance with successive orders of the Revenue Committee of 23 December 1647, 22 February 1647-8 and 17 May 1649, transmitted into the Exchequer

[1] B. Whitelock, *Memorials of the English Affairs*, edn. of 1853, vol. 1, p. 577.
[2] *H.L.J.*, 24 Feb. 1645-6.
[3] *H.C.J.*, 3 July, 1646.
[4] *Thurloe's State Papers*, vol. 1, p. 79.
[5] P.R.O. E.163/22/3/19, 4 Nov. 1645.
[6] *Ibid.* 2 May 1646.
[7] *H.L.J.*, 21 Sept. 1647 and 27 Nov. 1648; *Acts and Ordinances of the Interregnum*, vol. 1, p. 1013.
[8] *H.L.J.*, 14 June 1648.

160 COURT OF WARDS AND LIVERIES [CHAP. VIII

no less than forty-two schedules of arrears and debts.[1] They were given a memoranda roll to themselves.[2] Some idea of the magnitude of this work is provided by Tooke's petition of 15 February 1650, in which, in seeking remuneration, he claimed that eleven clerks had been concerned in the business of certifying arrears.[3]

Again, it must surely have been necessary in common fairness to do something to safeguard the interests of those who had purchased wards previous to the abolition of the Court. The only measure of this kind that has so far been noted is a bill that went through the House of Lords in April 1647, by which those who had compounded for wards or idiots, but whose grants had not been passed before the Court was put down, were to obtain their patents when their bills had been signed by the Speakers of both Houses. Somewhat curiously the bill is not mentioned in the Commons' journals, and it apparently did not become an ordinance.[4] No doubt, too, there was some outstanding judicial business to be settled, and in October 1646 the Commons named a committee to consider how decrees and proceedings in the Court might be brought to an effectual determination.[5] As late as 1654, legal papers of the Court were requisitioned by the Exchequer.[6]

One question that was not easily settled was the allocation of pensions to the former officers of the Court, or rather to those of them who had adhered to the Parliament—William Fleetwood, Chamberlain, and the other Oxford officials were, of course, automatically disqualified. Regarding the remainder, however, the House of Lords had ordered that competent provision should be made,[7] and the Commons expressed their agreement, with a slight alteration, to which the Lords consented on 4 March 1645-6.[8] Later in the year, therefore, the Commons appointed a committee to report upon suitable compensation for the principal officers, and all other ancient officials holding by patent.[9] This committee seems only to have taken the principal officers into account; it assessed their pensions, in the first instance, on the basis of six years' value

---

[1] P.R.O. E.368/669, L.T.R. Memoranda Roll, *Record' de arrearag' extra nuper Cur' Wardorum et Liberacionum Annis xxiij & xxiiij and* 1649. [2] *Ibid.*

[3] P.R.O. Wards 14/7/15, papers concerning the Court's records under the Commonwealth etc.

[4] H.M.C., *Report*, vol. VI, p. 169. [5] *H.C.J.*, 30 Oct. 1646.

[6] P.R.O. Wards 14/7/15, papers concerning the Court's records under the Commonwealth etc. [7] *H.L.J.*, 27 Dec. 1645.

[8] *A Brief of the Case of the Officers belonging to the Court of Wards and Liveries not yet recompenced* etc., 1654. [9] *H.C.J.*, 24 Nov. 1646.

CHAP. VIII]   FINAL DAYS OF THE COURT   161

and one year's damage, proposing that Saye and Seale, the master, should be granted 10,000 *l.*; Rudyerd, the surveyor, 6,000 *l.*; Wandesford, the attorney, 5,000 *l.*; and Charles Fleetwood, who had succeeded his brother as receiver-general when the two took opposite sides, 3,250 *l.* These sums were to be paid, the committee recommended, out of arrears, fines of delinquents and lands of delinquents.[1] It is worth while commenting, as a contemporary did, that all the beneficiaries, except Wandesford, were themselves members of Parliament.[2]

All the same, it is doubtful if the proposed compensation was ever paid, at any rate in full—Charles Fleetwood, for instance, was later said to have received 2,000 *l.*, only a little more than half the sum suggested by the committee.[3] In any case, the other officers remained unsatisfied—Hanchett, the usher, was, if we are to believe his story, hit particularly hard[4]—and so in 1649 the committee was ordered to take them into account,[5] and various new members were added for this purpose.[6] Compensation was now proposed at the lower rate of three-and-a-half-years' purchase: Tooke, the auditor, was to have 3,000 *l.*, Hanchett 3,500 *l.*, and Wilkinson, the messenger, 1,200 *l.* One or two other names appear, probably those of the Court's common attorneys,[7] who were not properly ancient officers at all; some of them sought, or obtained, other governmental positions.[8] Audley, the clerk, is not mentioned, perhaps because he was out of favour at the time—the attorney-general exhibited an information in the Exchequer against him and Tooke in Hilary 1649,[9] and already the year previous his lands had been sequestered for delinquency;[10] but in any case no sum would have been an adequate recompense for Audley's losses. Not that appearance in the list proved much advantage anyhow, for whatever happened about the principal officers' pensions, these other officials certainly received no payment, since, in spite of all the

---

[1] *H.C.J.*, 9 Jan. 1646-7.
[2] *T.N.T.*, p. 103.
[3] *H.C.J.*, 16 April 1662. *Memoirs of Danzil Lord Holles*, 1649, p. 136, put the figure at 3,000 *l.*
[4] H.M.C., *Report*, vol. VI, p. 218; *Report*, vol. XIII, App. I, p. 512.
[5] *A Brief of the Case of the Officers etc.*, 1654.   [6] *Ibid.*
[7] Roland Wilson is definitely stated to be one of the attorneys—H.M.C., *Report*, vol. VI, p. 215.
[8] H.M.C., *Report*, vol. VI, p. 208; *Committee for Advance of Money*, p. 60.
[9] P.R.O. Wards 14/7/15, papers concerning the Court's records under the Commonwealth etc.   [10] *Cal. of Committee for Compounding*, p. 91.

162 COURT OF WARDS AND LIVERIES [CHAP. VIII

committee's endeavours, the 'emergent occasions of the Parliament' prevented the report being considered at least up to 1654,[1] and the evidence from the Restoration period implies that this neglect was not remedied in the last six years of the Protectorate. On the whole, the Court's officers were hardly done by; but when the considerable profits that they had enjoyed in the past are re-membered, too much sympathy will not be lavished over their fate.

Although the Court had ceased to exist for fifteen years, and the original ordinance abolishing it had been confirmed under the Protectorate,[2] its re-erection was a possibility when once the restoration of the monarchy had become practical politics. Indeed long before that time, in 1651,[3] Sir John Berkeley had pressed the exiled king to make him master of the wards, basing his claim on the fact that Charles I had promised him the position. Hyde had opposed such an appointment for fear of offending the nobility and gentry with whom the Court had been so unpopular, but Berkeley later asserted that he held the king's warrant for the office.[4] It was perhaps not by chance, moreover, that Sir James Ley's *Reports* were posthumously published in 1659; the booksellers who spon-sored the edition may have anticipated the restoration of both monarchy and Court.

Nor was it immediately obvious that, if right about the former, they were wrong about the latter, for at the Restoration itself the revival of the Court was canvassed. Its chief apologist, and the defender of the whole system of feudal tenures, was Fabian Philipps, who tirelessly developed his theme in a series of pamphlets, of which the most important was *Tenenda non Tollenda*, published in 1660. Philipps brought to his task a wealth of antiquarian know-ledge, and some of his debating points did not lack shrewdness, but he was essentially a *laudator temporis acti* and very much a man of one idea. His literary style is characterized by an exaggeration that is the reflection of his whole attitude towards the Court of Wards and the old system of land-holding. 'The Court', he asserted, 'is

---

[1] *A Brief of the Case of the Officers etc.*, 1654.

[2] *Acts and Ordinances of the Interregnum*, vol. II, p. 1043.

[3] Or possibly 1650, Berkeley's date.

[4] Clarendon, *History of the Rebellion*, ed. Macray, vol. v, pp. 227-8; *H.C.J.*, 16 April 1662. It must be added that the claim was weak enough, if his only evidence was, as Clarendon says, an intercepted letter from Charles I to the queen, in which the sentence occurred—'As for Jack Barclay, I do not remember that I gaue thee any hope of making fo him Master of the Wards.'

CHAP. VIII]   FINAL DAYS OF THE COURT   163

such a flower of the Crown, as the power of an Act of Parliament, and consent of the King and his Nobility, and people cannot take away'.[1] Or again, although professedly writing on another topic, he breaks out enthusiastically 'the Tenures *in Capite*, and by Knight-service, those stronger Towers and Forts of our David, those Horsemen and Charriots of our Israel; and alwayes ready Garrisons composed of the best and worthiest men of our Nation; not hirelings taken out of the Vulgus, nor unlettered, unskilfull, and uncivilized, nor rude or debauched part of the people; but of those who would fight *tanquam pro aris & focis*.'[2] Whatever else, the Court's last champion did not lack vigour.

Along with the petitions of John and Robert Heath for pensions there are various papers outlining the case for the Court's continuance. One of these,[3] a prosy and tedious letter, interspersed with Latin platitudes, was addressed to a member of the House of Commons, and in 1661 was printed over the initials R. H.,[4] so that it is pretty clearly the work of Robert Heath himself. It traces the history of knight service to well before the Norman Conquest, but has little understanding of the contemporary situation. Another consists of thirteen reasons why the Court should not be abolished, among them the fact that the old sum of 100,000 *l.* yearly, which was again being offered as compensation, was insufficient, and that 2,000,000 *l.* was owing for wardships since 1642.[5]

In actual fact, the last point proved the great stumbling-block to reviving the Court: the simple fact was that such a revival was quite impracticable. Consequently a bill was introduced for the abolition of wardship and livery, retrospective as from 24 February 1645, the date of the Parliament's ordinance. A slight hitch occurred over the means by which the monarch's annual compensation was to be raised, at first a general rate being intended, abandoned later for a yearly grant from the excise revenue of beer, ale, cider, perry and strong water. Compensation from the excise was opposed by Philipps—first because it would hit the poor, and secondly because it would not be 'for the honour of England . . .

---

[1] *T.N.T.*, epistle dedicatory to Hyde.
[2] Fabian Philipps, *The Mistaken Recompense*, 1664, p. 64.
[3] B.M. Egerton MS. 2979, f. 41.
[4] *A Letter Written to a Friend, A Member in the House of Commons . . . concerning the Court of Wards*, 1661.
[5] B.M. Egerton MS. 2979, f. 45; see also P.R.O. Wards 14/3/20, reasons why the Court of Wards should continue.

164   COURT OF WARDS AND LIVERIES [CHAP. VIII

to have their provisions of War and Defence arise out of so low a businesse as Ale and Beer', though it might do very well for the Dutch![1] In the meantime, while the bill was in process of being passed, Charles was moved to suspend sittings of the Court.[2] In due course it became law, repealing the acts on which the Court had based its jurisdiction, turning tenures by knight service into socage, and abolishing the feudal incidents of tenure.[3] Presenting the bill of abolition, the Speaker of the House of Commons used language almost as extravagant, though in the opposite direction, as Philipps' phrases. 'Royal sir,' he told the king, 'your tenures *in capite* are not only turned into a tenure in socage . . . but they are likewise turned into a tenure *in corde*. What your majesty had before in your court of wards you will be sure to find it hereafter in the exchequer of your people's hearts.'[4]

Inevitably there were some outstanding questions. After a long struggle the crown had abandoned its profitable rights of livery and wardship; but what of the other side, its duties and responsibilities towards minor heirs? There had been a proposal under the Protectorate, never put into effect, for orphans to be placed in the care of their next of kin;[5] Charles II's act had granted fathers the free disposal of the custody of their children during minority, and allowed to guardians so named the right of action for ravishment of ward against anyone who took the child away from them. There was thus a lack of control of the guardian, and the protective function of the Court of Wards might have been missed, had there not developed the equitable jurisdiction of the Chancery over infant and guardian alike.[6] Similarly, idiots and lunatics were committed to the chancellor's care—even before the act abolishing the Court of Wards had passed through Parliament;[7] the chancellor issued writs to inquire into insanity, and it was natural that he should be granted the wider jurisdiction, formerly exercised by the Court. These were important developments subsequent to the abolition.

There followed, too, the tiresome business of assessing pensions —this time, of course, mainly for the officials who had supported the king and followed him to Oxford. The Commons committee

---

[1] *T.N.T.*, pp. 229-30.   [2] *H.C.J.*, 7 Sept. 1660.   [3] 12 Charles II c. 24.
[4] Blackstone, *Commentaries*, edn. of 1826, vol. II, p. 77 *note*.
[5] B.M Add MS. 32093, f. 395.
[6] Holdsworth, vol. VI, p. 648.   [7] *C.S.P. Dom. 1660-1*, p. 328.

CHAP. VIII]   FINAL DAYS OF THE COURT   165

in charge of the bill for the Court's abolition showed a proper appreciation of the difficulty of fixing compensation, and appointed a special sub-committee to receive petitions from the former officers.[1] Subsequently, on 11 December 1660, the House made this sub-committee a full committee to state the case of the petitioners and report on how they might be satisfied.[2] Ten days later a very comprehensive list of proposed pensions was submitted by the newly-formed committee: it apparently admitted Berkeley's claim to the mastership, and suggested 5,000 *l.* recompense for him; the clerk of the liveries, Cooke, was to have 2,000 *l.*, and Fleetwood the same sum, since his brother had already had 2,000 *l.*; Chamberlain's compensation was fixed at 1,500 *l.*, and it is odd to find both usher and messenger mentioned in the list, though both were probably of the Parliament party; except for the two chief auditors, who were omitted for a reason which will appear later, every conceivable official had some notice taken of his claim, and many who held in reversion only; a table of yearly values of feodaryships was even included, to be made the basis on which their recompense could be calculated, in the unlikely event of the Commons wishing to pension them. So far from that, the House shelved the whole question, declining consideration of the report.[3] Nor was anything done until the following summer, when a committee was again named to consider the matter,[4] and, after some interval, a new report made and submitted in April 1662. This reiterated the claims of Berkeley, Cooke and Wilkinson, the messenger, and proposed the same recompense for them as had been suggested earlier; Fleetwood's compensation was raised to 4,000 *l.*, since he had had no part of his brother's 2,000 *l.*, and the sum proposed for the usher was also increased; on this occasion the auditors were included, and 4,000 *l.* put forward, as a suitable amount for the two of them to receive; the committee advised against giving anything to the feodaries. Of this list, the Commons agreed to the amounts set down for Fleetwood and the auditors, they rejected (probably rightly) Berkeley's compensation; and then, characteristically, laid the whole matter on one side.[5] No evidence appears to show that anything further was done, or that most of the officers, who had been loyal to Charles I, fared any better than

[1] *C.S.P. Dom. 1660-1*, p. 110.
[2] *H.C.J.*, 11 Dec. 1660.
[3] *H.C.J.*, 21 Dec. 1660.
[4] *H.C.J.*, 14 June 1661.
[5] *H.C.J.*, 16 April 1662.

166   COURT OF WARDS AND LIVERIES   [CHAP. VIII

had those who adhered to the Parliament; neither side proved enthusiastic, or even strictly honourable, when it came to paying out pensions.

Charles II's position was not easy—1660 was a very qualified triumph; all the same, certain aspects of the pension problem suggest that the monarchy was guilty of black ingratitude to those who had supported it through the dark days of the Civil War. John and Robert Heath, who were appointed auditors in Oxford when Tooke and Maynard failed to attend there, were hardly treated. At the Restoration, when claims for compensation came up, their case would appear to have been strong; but though Tooke was dead, they had a hard struggle against Maynard, and in the midst of it John Heath wrote to the lord chancellor with some pathos—'Haueing receiued no fresh markes of his Majesty's favour since his retorne into England, I finde the world lookes on mee at my retourne to my profession, as one sett aside, or not so much valewd by the king as was expected. . . .'[1] Nor is the tragi-comedy of Richard Chamberlain very creditable to the government. He had served the Court faithfully for half a century before the transference to Oxford, and had followed the king there, losing—as his son claimed later—30,000 *l.* by his loyalty.[2] After the Court's dissolution, and Charles I's death, he had remained true to both; and in this late period of his life the strong opinions of the old clerk, and the picturesque language in which he advanced them, are extremely amusing.[3] What is not amusing is the fact that he was allowed to live the last years of his extraordinarily long life in want, waiting payment for the 1,500 *l.* compensation voted him by the first Commons' pension committee. Chamberlain's last petition, addressed directly to the king, is a document of real pathos;[4] but it was completely disregarded.[5] Charles I had found few servants more loyal than he, and Charles II's failure to grant him some reward seems inexcusable.

[1] B.M. Egerton MS. 2979, ff. 32-3.
[2] *C.S.P. Dom. 1661-2*, p. 30.
[3] See below, pp. 178-80.
[4] P.R.O. S.P. 29/20, no. 6, petition of Richard Chamberlain, 1660.
[5] *C.S.P. Dom. 1661-2*, p. 30.

CHAPTER IX

THE SITE AND BUILDINGS OF THE COURT

The Court was located, naturally enough, among the common law and prerogative courts in Westminster Palace. According to Stow, it was in the White Hall, that is, a little to the south of Westminster Hall itself, in the building which in 1801 became the House of Lords. 'Then at the vpper end of the great hall by the Kings bench', he says, 'is a going vp to a great Chamber, called the White hall, wherein is now kept the court of Wards & Liueries: and adioyning thereunto is the Court of Requests'.[1] Sandford's plan, made in 1687, however, shows that, as it stands, Stow's statement is misleading.[2] The Court of Requests, and not the Court of Wards, was in the White Hall; nor were Westminster Hall and the White Hall quite adjacent. Lying transversely between them was another, and smaller, building, its northern wall running some two-thirds of the breadth of Westminster Hall and projecting beyond it towards the Abbey, its southern wall standing clear for the most part but joining on to the north-west corner of the White Hall. It was this building that the Court of Wards occupied, and from it there was access to Westminster Hall on the one hand and to the White Hall on the other. Any doubt as to the correctness of Sandford's plan is removed by Robinson's description a hundred years earlier. 'This Courte', he says, 'is kept up the Stayres on ye right hand in Westminster Hall at ye nether end of the Court of Requests upon the left hand'—a succinct account of exactly what Sandford later on drew.[3]

Stow's 'going up' was thus a stone staircase that gave entry to the Court. This stair was re-built by the controller of the queen's works in 1574,[4] and from an indictment of some twenty years later

[1] *Survey of London*, ed. Kingsford, vol. II, p. 120.
[2] In *History of the Coronation of James II*; the plan is reproduced in Ivy M. Cooper, 'Westminster Hall', in *Journal of the British Archaeological Association*, 1937. I am greatly indebted to Miss Cooper for advice regarding the topography of Westminster Hall.
[3] New College MS. no. cccxxv, *Briefe Collection of the . . . Courts*. This valuable reference I owe to my colleague, Mr R. L. Rickard.
[4] P.R.O. Wards 9/380, f. 291.

167

168   COURT OF WARDS AND LIVERIES   [CHAP. IX

we know that it was called 'Courte of Wardes & Courte of requestes stayers'.[1] In Charles I's reign the remainder of the dividing wall was extensively glassed.[2] In the south-east corner of the Court there was a door leading to the White Hall. When the young Prince Henry was created Prince of Wales in 1610, the ceremony took place in the White Hall, and a contemporary account explains that 'the Prince came forth of the Cort of Wards, where he and the Knights of the Bathe, being 24, did attyre themselves'.[3] Since the Court had thus doors leading into both Westminster Hall and the White Hall, the normal passage between the two no doubt ran through it; this is the basis of Stow's remark, which is, strictly speaking, inaccurate.

The building was not large—about seventy feet long and thirty to forty feet broad; but it was divided into several rooms, the distinction constantly being made between the outer and the inner Court. The outer Court, where under the master's presidency judicial business was transacted, was constantly referred to as the great chamber. Yet a picture dating from Elizabeth's reign shows it as a not very large room, plentifully wainscoted and with Gothic windows. In the centre, and occupying most of the available space, is a large table, around which the officers are sitting; the master has his back to the chimneypiece, and on the three remaining sides a wooden partition runs at which counsel is shown pleading.[4] Of the inner rooms the most important was perhaps the so-called council chamber. In 1543 the receiver-general's account included a payment 'pro nova factura cuiusdam camere ibidem vocate le Counselles chamber',[5] and it was in this room that the officers met for private conferences, and for the conduct of some administrative matters such as the negotiation of sales of wardship; here too, and not in open court, they sat during the absence of a master after Burghley's death.[6] The room had a balcony, and over it there was domestic accommodation, perhaps for the usher.[7] Probably distinct again was the treasury, where the Court's records were kept,[8] perhaps the room that is described on occasion as an 'inner room

[1] P.R.O. K.B. 9/688, m. 40, indictment of Charles Topclyffe.
[2] P.R.O. in Wards 10/45, vouchers of r.g.a., various dates.
[3] *P.D. 1610*, p. 48.
[4] *Vetusta Monumenta*, 1747, vol. I, last plate.   [5] P.R.O. Wards 8/109.
[6] P.R.O. Wards 14/3/20, papers of Edward Latimer.
[7] P.R.O. in Wards 10/46, vouchers of r.g.a., 1635.
[8] P.R.O. in Wards 10/1, Chamberlain correspondence.

CHAP. IX]   SITE AND BUILDINGS OF COURT   169

where the officers bookes and gownes lye'.[1] The outer Court and these two principal inner chambers were almost certainly first-floor rooms, with vaults beneath.[2] In addition to them there are mentioned at various times a private withdrawing-room for the master,[3] a bedroom,[4] stables and privies.[5] Of course the possibility must be borne in mind that some of these domestic offices may have been outside the bounds of the building shown by Sandford, ephemeral erections that perished before his time.

The principal entrance to the Court is not known: there were doors at the north-west and south-west corners of the building, as well as those already indicated into Westminster Hall and the White Hall. It seems likely that there was direct access to the Court from outside the Palace—perhaps from St Margaret's Lane —for in Charles I's time a terminal payment of 2s. 6d. was made 'for the poore man that looketh to the gate.'[6] Like the officers themselves, this doorkeeper probably enjoyed his main income from what he received from suitors and others who had business in the Court; amongst the accounts of the Earl of Bedford for 1642 there is a note of a payment of 2s. to him.[7]

The main evidence for the history of the fabric of the Court comes from the ushers' accounts, which the receiver-general filed amongst the vouchers of his own account,[8] and, more accessibly, though in less detail, from the summarized versions under the heading Expenses and Repairs in the receiver-general's accounts. In 1549, for instance, there were relatively heavy payments—50 l. and 150 l.—for work on the roofs, repairs and new building;[9] in 1597, 13s. 4d. was paid to a mason 'for a New Mantell tre of frestone',[10] and in 1638 repairs costing 35 l. 3s. were made, Inigo Jones signing the bill, having done the work no doubt in connexion with his appointment as the king's surveyor.[11] Payments for brick-laying, glazing, plastering and tiling in various parts of the building

[1] P.R.O. in Wards 10/45, vouchers of r.g.a., various dates.
[2] P.R.O. Wards 9/413, f. 317.
[3] P.R.O. in Wards 10/46, vouchers of r.g.a., 1635.
[4] P.R.O. in Wards 10/46, vouchers of r.g.a., 1639.
[5] P.R.O. in Wards 10/78, vouchers of r.g.a., 1597.
[6] P.R.O. in Wards 10/46, vouchers of r.g.a., 1639.
[7] G. Scott Thomson, *Life in a Noble Household*, p. 60.
[8] See above, p. 46, note 2.
[9] P.R.O. Wards 9/365, f. 155.
[10] P.R.O. in Wards 10/78, vouchers of r.g.a., 1597.
[11] P.R.O. in Wards 10/46, vouchers of r.g.a., 1639.

M

170   COURT OF WARDS AND LIVERIES   [CHAP. IX

turn up repeatedly. The same sources also provide interesting details of the furnishings of the Court. The receiver-general's accounts in Edward VI's reign contain a note of payments for the making of chests for the records and accounts,[1] or again the vouchers for 1631 include the item 'for x cushions with the kinges armes 17 *l.* 10*s.*;'[2] Burghley had been more sparing in this particular when he was master, for although admitting 'greate wante of Quisshons bothe to serve the Officers . . . and suche personagies of nobillitie as hath occasion to repaire to the same Courte and that suche as are alredie theare are vearie olde and decaied', he had only warranted the expenditure of 5 *l.* 2*s.* upon new ones.[3] Even the smallest domestic purchases, down to the brooms used for sweeping out the building, appear in the ushers' accounts; and a regular item of expense was upon ink and pens, and the perfumed herbs that were provided to keep the plague and other sickness at bay. On one occasion, in 1571, structural work was necessary 'for the avoydinge of evill smelles'.[4]

Something of the life within the Court also emerges. There are detailed accounts of the dinners that it was the usher's duty to provide for the rest of the officers, and a note in 1582 of the provision of white wine and sugar as a mid-morning drink.[5] There were gardens around the Court in which the officers might walk in the intervals of business.[6]

Even while the Court was still in existence, the building was used for meetings of parliamentary committees.[7] There Arabella Stuart was summoned in 1610 to appear before the Lords,[8] and there, by a peculiar irony, the Commons committee on Cranfield met.[9] When wardship and livery had been abolished, and the Court no longer existed, it might have been expected to pass into parliamentary control. Certainly the old treasury was used, as will be seen in the next chapter, to house the Parliament's records; committees were still held in the Court—'to London about our Mint Commission, and sat in the Inner Court of Wards', noted Evelyn;[10]

[1] P.R.O. Wards 9/365, ff. 296 and 415.
[2] P.R.O. in Wards 10/46, vouchers of r.g.a., various dates.
[3] P.R.O. in Wards 10/78, vouchers of r.g.a., 1585.
[4] P.R.O. Wards 9/380, f. 68.
[5] P.R.O. in Wards 10/18, vouchers of r.g.a., 1582.   [6] *Ibid.*
[7] Many examples in *H.C.J.*, e.g. 12 Feb. 1620, 28 Feb. 1620, 19 May 1624.
[8] H.M.C., *Rutland*, vol. I, p. 427.
[9] *H.C.J.*, 28 May 1624.
[10] *Diary*, 24 April 1666

CHAP. IX]   SITE AND BUILDINGS OF COURT   171

as late as 1690 the Commons were sworn in the Court of Wards by the lord high steward.[1] But portions were no longer in official hands: in 1682 information was laid that a disaffected man, named Kiftell, held a part of the building, in which he held a coffee-house during term-time, where persons of like principles foregathered,[2] and seven years later the serjeant at arms was ordered to inquire why the rooms were no longer reserved to Parliament's service.[3] Their later history is a part of the complicated story of the Palace in the eighteenth century. In the first quarter of the century a coffee room and an auction room, where pictures were sold, occupied part of the Court, but in 1729 these were to be made convenient for footmen in attendance on members of the Commons.[4] The date at which the old building was demolished must remain uncertain: it is specifically described on William Capon's plan, made between 1793 and 1823, as 'now destroyed',[5] and nearly half a century before, in 1747, it was said to be divided into several parts,[6] one of which may have been the lord treasurer's room, which was on the site of the Court and in existence in 1795.[7] The clerk of the journals and papers of the House of Commons told the record commissioners a little later that Alice's Coffee-House stood where the Court had formerly been.[8]

It would be a mistake to overestimate the degree to which the Court's business was centralized. Even the most important legal arguments were heard, on occasion, not at Westminster but at Serjeants' Inn,[9] and one case was discussed for four-and-a-half hours at Burghley's house near the Savoy.[10] Petitions for wardships seem sometimes to have been considered in the same way, in the master's house,[11] though the *Instructions* of 1618 and 1622 forbade sales made elsewhere than in the council chamber.[12] On the administrative side, moreover, there was a striking decentralization:

[1] *C.S.P. Dom. 1689-90*, p. 517.
[2] *C.S.P. Dom. 1682*, p. 544.   [3] *C.S.P. Dom. 1689-90*, p. 41.
[4] *Cal. of Treasury Books and Papers 1729-30*, pp. 104, 502.
[5] Ivy M. Cooper, 'Westminster Hall', in *Journal of the British Archaeological Association*, 1937, plate iv.
[6] *Vetusta Monumenta*, vol. I, notes on print of Court.
[7] Plan by Soane, re-drawn by T. Chawner in *Report of Select Committee on Westminster Hall Restoration*, 1885.
[8] *Reports from Select Committee appointed to inquire into the State of the Public Records*, 1800 etc., p. 67.
[9] Dyer, *A.N.C.*, f. 286; Ley, *Reports*, p. 12.   [10] Dyer, *A.N.C.*, f. 286.
[11] P.R.O. in Wards 10/27, petitions.
[12] See above, p. 58.

172 COURT OF WARDS AND LIVERIES [CHAP. IX

there were, indeed, offices all over London, where the individual officers transacted much of their business.

The most important of these was the clerk's office in the Inner Temple, which was established by Hare in 1590. In that year he obtained leave to pull down the chambers in Fine Office Court, which he held with a certain Edward Carill, and to build at his own cost a room for the wards' business and others for his own accommodation, paying a yearly rent of 13s. 4d.[1] Thus, in the first instance, the situation of the clerk's office in the Inner Temple was determined simply by the chance that the clerk was a member of that inn. Upon Hare's death in 1613, it appears that a prolonged controversy broke out between his widow and one of his successors as clerk, Richard Chamberlain. In 1619 the matter was referred to the bench table,[2] and Chamberlain and his colleague, Audley, were ordered to leave Hare's office, removing all writings of the Court with them.[3] Later, however, it was decided to treat with Chamberlain as to his continuing within the Inner Temple, and to approach Mrs Hare with a view to buying her out.[4] This must have been brought about, for letters continued to be addressed to Chamberlain in the Temple almost up to the time when he went with Charles to Oxford. Early in the 'thirties there was mention of Audley's new buildings,[5] and in 1636 a certain John Finch, a boy of 16, was persuaded by a bricklayer named Evans to accompany him to the Temple, 'where Evans in the day time took money out of the chamber of Mr Audley of the Court of Wards'.[6] Audley remained in London at the time of the Civil War, and the address on a letter to him from Chamberlain gives in some detail the position of his room—'to the worshipfull Hugh Audely esqr. in his Chamber in Hares Courte over the Late Courte of Wardes Office nigh the Inner Temple Church-Door'.[7]

For the rest, it is clear that the other officials had their own offices—very often, no doubt, where they resided. After the death of William Dansell, for instance, his executors were ordered to make a declaration of the queen's treasure and bonds at his house and to remove it to Westminster;[8] Goring, a later receiver-general,

[1] *Inner Temple Records*, vol. I, p. 366.
[2] *Inner Temple Records*, vol. II, pp. 114-15.
[3] *Ibid*. vol. II, p. 115.   [4] *Ibid*. vol. II, p. 118.
[5] *C.S.P. Dom. 1633-4*, p. 428.   [6] *C.S.P. Dom. 1636-7*, pp. 29-30.
[7] P.R.O. in Wards 10/1, Chamberlain correspondence.
[8] H.M.C., *Salisbury*, vol. II, p. 506.

CHAP. IX] SITE AND BUILDINGS OF COURT 173

had a house at Chelsea.[1] One of the auditors in Charles I's reign had his office 'in Holborne over against Grayse Inne gate',[2] while the other was in Aldersgate street 'neere the signe of the Mayden head'.[3] When it is remembered that the suing out of a livery or the obtaining of a ward involved much coming and going from one officer to another, the inconvenience to the public resulting from this separation of offices is apparent. A suitor must have found himself running backwards and forwards over half of London—indeed a glimpse of one such may be gained from the Earl of Bedford's accounts for 1641, which include a note of the sum of 6d. paid for going by water from the Temple—no doubt the clerk's office—to show his bill at Westminster to the attorney and Maynard, the auditor.[4] Another interesting point is the private character of these offices—they were the responsibility of the individual officer, and he, not the Court, rented them. The whole suggests an administrative system that was incompletely formalized.

Against one kind of interruption to business, the outbreak of bubonic plague, no organization could fully provide. A serious epidemic meant one of two things—either the Court must abandon term altogether, with the resultant delay of causes pending and the possible loss to the crown of revenue that it could ill spare, or business must be adjourned to a safer place than Westminster. The latter expedient was adopted in 1563, 1581, and 1592, when the Court moved to Hertford—the first two evacuations being known because, in connexion with them, either the auditor or the usher received allowances for the cost of transferring the records,[5] the third because on that occasion a general proclamation ordered the removal of all the courts.[6] In 1603 the Court was adjourned because of plague, and also so as not to interfere with the coronation of James I[7]—an order that surely explains the very interesting account that Walter Tooke rendered of the cost of carriage of the records from Hatfield to Winchester, which seems to imply a double move;[8] later he was paid for bringing them back to Westminster.[9] In 1636 there was an interesting compromise arrangement. A

[1] H.M.C., *Salisbury*, vol. v, p. 278. [2] P.R.O. in Wards 10/50, affidavits, 1635.
[3] P.R.O. in Wards 10/51, correspondence.
[4] G. Scott Thomson, *Life in a Noble Household*, p. 56.
[5] P.R.O. Wards 9/369, f. 330; Wards 9/385, f. 97. [6] Steele, no. 855.
[7] P.R.O. Wards 9/527, orders of 1 Jas. I.
[8] P.R.O. in Wards 10/24, vouchers of r.g.a., 1603.
[9] P.R.O. Wards 9/400, f. 79.

174 COURT OF WARDS AND LIVERIES [CHAP. IX

proclamation of 27 May closed the Trinity term so far as judicial proceedings were concerned, and yet provided that accountants should continue to attend the Court, leaving them to take their chance of catching the infection.[1] The plague still not having abated by Michaelmas, however, a further proclamation transferred the Court to Acton.[2] In that financial year the usher included in his bill items of 7 *l*. 10*s*. 'for sevene greate trunkese with Cordese for the carrage of ye officerse writingese,' 5 *l*. 'for Cartese to Carrie and recarrie', and 22 *l*. 10*s*. for the Court of Wards house in Acton.[3] These chance examples, which should not be taken as necessarily representing the only adjournments of the Court,[4] suffice to show that the routine of Westminster Palace or of the Temple was liable to violent interruption, and that officials had to be prepared to adapt themselves to new surroundings and no doubt to face particular difficulties in the execution of their work, whenever the emergency arose.

[1] Rushworth, *Historical Collections*, edn. of 1721, vol. III, App. pp. 281-2.
[2] T. Birch, *Court and Times of Charles I*, vol. II, p. 253.
[3] P.R.O. in Wards 10/64, vouchers of r.g.a., 1637.
[4] There were, for instance, adjournments of part of the term in Mich. 1578 (P.R.O. Ind. 10219, f. 38) and Trin. 1625 (B.M. Lansdowne MS. 608, f. 49).

CHAPTER X

THE RECORDS OF THE COURT AFTER ITS ABOLITION

THE fate of the records of the Court was largely determined by the great unpopularity of its later days. Parliament was hardly likely to take much interest in the records of a jurisdiction which it had regarded as hateful and oppressive and which it had earnestly, and successfully, sought to abolish. Thus, after the Court's dissolution, its records as a whole were allowed to sink into confusion and decay, and only those classes that still possessed business significance were excepted from the general neglect.

The bringing in of arrears, and the conclusion of matters still pending at the date of abolition, could not be completed within a few weeks, or even within a few months.[1] To some extent, work of this kind implied a continued use of the records, and for some ten years the responsibility for producing such documents as were needed lay rather doubtfully between Hugh Audley, the former clerk of the wards, and Thomas Fabian, who acted as his assistant. In fact the two were not notable for their co-operation, nor do the authorities appear to have found it easy to decide which of them to approach on any particular occasion. Soon after the Court's dissolution, for instance, on 17 July 1646, the Revenue Committee, ordering Audley to lay certain bonds before them, found it necessary to add the rider—'In case the bondes be in Mr Fabian his Boxe Mr Awdeley ys required to breake open the boxe and bringe the bondes to this Committee as aforesaid'; and despite this instruction, six days later they had to issue a separate order to Fabian.[2] Bonds seem to have been requisitioned from Audley or Fabian in this way for one of two reasons—so that, on the one hand, if a debt were still outstanding, the Exchequer might put them into process; or, on the other, if the covenants had been performed, that they might be returned to the persons who had entered into them. In Michaelmas term 1649, the Revenue Committee ordered Audley to deliver to the chief remembrancer of the Exchequer all bonds

---

[1] See above, pp. 159-66. [2] P.R.O. Wards 9/557, last ff. of volume.

175

176   COURT OF WARDS AND LIVERIES   [CHAP. X

and indentures that remained in his custody, but it seems clear that transfers continued to be piecemeal: an entry book recording them has, indeed, survived.[1] Sometimes legal, as well as financial, papers were required. As late as 1654 Fabian brought into the Exchequer, on Audley's behalf, pleadings in a suit in the Court,[2] and the same year Audley was instructed to transcribe a decree of 1644 for the commissioners of the Treasury.[3]

These duties must, over the years, have involved Audley, and more particularly Fabian, in a good deal of work, and there is some evidence that theirs was a thankless task. After he had been engaged in it for some three years, Fabian petitioned the Revenue Committee for recompense in such terms as to make it clear that up to that date he had received no payment.[4] There were, moreover, efforts from time to time to hold one or other responsible for missing documents,[5] and it is difficult not to sympathize with Fabian's retort to one such—'And concerneinge what leases and bondes remaine yet in Courte are enumerable And wch of them are usefull for the seruice ys not knowne positiuely to any'.[6] On the other hand, it would be quite out of character for Hugh Audley to have undertaken any business that was unprofitable, and there is indeed evidence that he had somehow contrived to obtain, and hold, money on the Court's account.[7]

Another problem of the times concerned what were not really records of the Court itself at all—namely, the deeds deposited as evidence and exhibits in suits pending there. Throughout its existence the Court had frequently accompanied its privy seal directing appearance with a *ducens secum*, ordering the bringing in of muniments; on occasion, too, the feodary had been instructed to secure and deliver this kind of documentary evidence.[8] Since such deeds had often remained in court for many years at a time, it had been the custom to catalogue them, often with a note in the margin of the date of their withdrawal; an examination of the catalogues of deposits for 1621-45 gives some idea of the mass of

---

[1] P.R.O. Wards 14/3/20, entry book of bonds from the Court delivered to the Exchequer, 1649-56.   [2] *Ibid.*

[3] P.R.O. Wards 14/7/15, papers concerning the Court's records under the Commonwealth etc.   [4] *Ibid.*

[5] P.R.O. in Wards 10/59, papers relating to arrears and outstanding bonds, 1650; another possible reference in P.R.O. Wards 14/7/15.

[6] P.R.O. in Wards 10/59, file relating to arrears and outstanding bonds, 1650.

[7] *Cal. of Committee for Compounding*, p. 3118.

[8] P.R.O. Wards 2/153/10, commission to feodary of Lancaster.

CHAP. X]   RECORDS OF THE COURT   177

material of this sort remaining amongst the records of the Court at the time of its abolition.[1] There was some truth in Fabian Philipps' boast that the Court preserved 'many a Deed and Evidence which would otherwise have been lost, or not easie to be found'.[2]

In this connexion alone the problem of disposal was of some magnitude, and it was only dealt with in a spasmodic and piecemeal fashion. In 1646 the Revenue Committee issued instructions for the return of various sets of evidences to their rightful owners,[3] and during the next decade exhibits of the same sort were delivered out of the Court's records with some frequency.[4] Even as late as 1658 Audley and Peter Fabian, Thomas' son, received an order to bring evidences into the Exchequer.[5] But return of evidences on a large scale, such as was contemplated in the terms of reference of the House of Commons committee of 1649,[6] was never accomplished. It is amusing to find the Record Commissioners reporting in 1800 'If the owners of these estates could now be ascertained, it might perhaps be desirable to return to each such as relate to his Property.'[7] After a century and a half, the ideal had not been abandoned. The greater part of the deeds and evidences, however, remained among the public records, and some 4,698 of them were listed by Frederick Devon in the nineteenth century.[8] This list, however, covers only a portion of the existing class of these documents; moreover, it was the opinion of the late Mr S. C. Ratcliff, who worked extensively on the problem, that the Public Record Office class Ancient Deeds A included groups originally wards' deeds and evidences.

Bonds and exhibits apart, a third category of records remained potentially useful even after the Court's dissolution. The records of the king's Court of Wards at Oxford might have been expected to provide valuable evidence in connexion with delinquency proceedings, and in 1651 the Committee for Compounding ordered

[1] P.R.O. Wards 9/182 and 183; Ind. 10217 (2).
[2] *The Mistaken Recompense*, 1664, p. 65.
[3] P.R.O. Wards 9/557, last ff. of volume.
[4] P.R.O. Wards 14/7/15, papers concerning the Court's records under the Commonwealth etc.
[5] P.R.O. in Wards 10/70, order of Exchequer with writ of Richard Lord Protector attached, 1658.   [6] *H.C.J.*, 26 May 1649.
[7] *Reports from the Select Committee appointed to inquire into the State of the Public Records*, 1800 etc., p. 39.
[8] They now form P.R.O. Wards 2.

178   COURT OF WARDS AND LIVERIES   [CHAP. X

Chamberlain, the former clerk, to give an account of what compositions for wardship had been made at Oxford, and deliver up the contracts, writings etc. of the three years administration in that place.[1] But it is not likely that the order was effective. Most probably, in the stress of the past years, there had been a return to the old practice which Sir Thomas Wilson had fought so hard as keeper of the state papers—at the termination of their appointments officials carried away documents which they had held in an official capacity; some few records of the Court at Oxford survived in this way in private collections.[2] In any case, the old clerk, Chamberlain, was a law unto himself; so far from surrendering documents, a year previous to the order of the Committee for Compounding he had written to Westminster for certain of the records there to be sent to him at Oxford—'if you will send by George the stationer to my friend Mr Turnor at his lodging in the Outer Court of the Inner Temple church, he will come to you presently, and will buy either a trunk or a basket (as you shall direct) and will send therin by our carryer those Black Sheriffs' Books to me hither.'[3] When the sheriffs' books were returned from Oxford, if indeed they were ever sent there, is not known.

Such was the limited, and ineffective, interest in the Court's records during the period after its abolition. This interest was concerned, it is scarcely necessary to add, with the merest fraction of the great body of archive material that the Court had built up during its hundred years' existence. For the rest, neglect was so complete that the fate of the records as a whole cannot be reconstructed from official sources; it is only through the chance survival of a vivacious series of letters from Chamberlain to Fabian that their history is known.[4]

After the collapse of the king's cause, the old clerk, Richard Chamberlain, lived on in retirement at Oxford, and it was from Kettle Hall, in the Broad there, that in 1650 he addressed his forthright letters to Fabian. It was typical of Chamberlain that, although Fabian had been employed by Parliament to work in the Court's records, the old man persisted in regarding him as his own deputy. In fact, of course, Chamberlain had no *locus standi*. The House of

---

[1] *Cal. of Committee for Compounding*, p. 465.
[2] P.R.O. P.R.O. 30/26/91; B.M. Egerton MS. 2978.
[3] P.R.O. in Wards 10/1, Chamberlain correspondence.
[4] P.R.O. in Wards 10/1, Chamberlain correspondence. The late Mr S. C. Ratcliff, who discovered these letters, made available to me his transcripts of them.

CHAP. X]   RECORDS OF THE COURT   179

Commons had sequestered him of his office of clerk in December 1643;[1] but this fact, and even the abolition of the Court, did not prevent him from considering the records as still within his custody. 'If the courte be put down', he demanded, 'how can I then execute my office? And why should I suffer anybody to take anything out of the same without my consent and warrant?' With a good deal of pomp and circumstance, he appointed Fabian, 'a very honest and old experienced man' in both the Court of Wards and the Exchequer, to act for him at Westminster, informing him at that time that John Taylor, his previous agent, had gone to live in the country and would never visit London again—'Therefore I do hereby give to you full power and authority to execute his place under me and to keep everything safe in your own custody for me.' Only Chamberlain's side of the correspondence has survived, but he had an odd trick of summarizing the contents of Fabian's last letter at the beginning of his own, so that, in effect, we have the substance of the letters of both parties.

The story that unfolds itself is a sad one, and is the explanation of the decayed condition of many of the Court's records. Some members of the Long Parliament became nervous of the great weight of records of the two Houses, deposited in the Parliament House; a committee, appointed to inquire into the matter, found that the records totalled nearly 300 hundredweight, and recommended their removal into the treasury of the old Court of Wards. This meant the turning out of the wards' records, and the plan was to place these in an upper room in Westminster Hall, formerly used by the king's fishmonger. This was bad enough, but worse was to befall during the period when this room was being prepared —'The fishloft being not fit to keep the records, they placed the Court of Wards records in the cellar under the fishloft which was the place where the salt was placed, there to abide until the fishloft or fish-storehouse should be made fit, which is now near finishing, only a little plastering, glazing and presses wanting, and when finished will be convenient.'

Chamberlain's anger at these proceedings may be imagined. He refused to believe that there could be 5 hundredweight, let alone 300 hundredweight, of parliamentary records 'as they call them'; he took exception to an order being executed that was not entered in the Parliament book; most of all, he felt as insult added to injury

[1] See above, p. 152.

180   COURT OF WARDS AND LIVERIES   [CHAP. X

the fact that such action had been taken without his being informed. He was anxious to know who was responsible for the deed—'I desire to know the names of every of those that caused you and who else to remove the records, evidences and writings out of the treasury into the hell-like fish-cellar, and what was the true cause why they were so removed.' It is clear that he suspected principally Hugh Audley, but even Fabian does not quite escape his censure as an accessory—'It seems to me that Mr Awdely having agreed with those two Committee men (did) lock up their order in his desk and left you behind him to hold the candle and to look on as those did who stood by and saw the hangman cut off our . . . king's head at his own Court gate.' The old clerk found small consolation in the preparations that were being made in the fish-loft; in his opinion, there was one place, and one alone, where it was fitting for the records to be, and that was in their old home in the treasury of the Court.

But Chamberlain, for all his rage, was powerless, and meantime neglect continued uninterrupted. It is true that a committee of the House of Commons was set up in 1649 to consider the disposal of the wards' records,[1] and that the year following Parliament resolved that they should be transferred to the Exchequer. But although various Exchequer orders were made to implement this, and though the name of Salway, chief remembrancer of the Exchequer, was now bracketed with Audley's in the custodianship of the records,[2] it seems that in fact little change was made. Audley simply ignored these instructions, and nobody appears to have been interested enough to enforce them. It is apparent from an order of 22 June 1658 that the Exchequer had not then received any of the records except for those bonds and evidences that had been separately, and individually, requisitioned. Once again it was ordered that Audley should bring in all the records in his care for delivery to the lord protector's remembrancer, but there is absolutely no evidence that this instruction proved any more effective than those that had preceded it, although this time the order was accompanied by a threat of attachment.[3]

After the Restoration, the yeoman of the king's store of fish and salt petitioned the Privy Council that the rooms in Westminster

---

[1] *H.C.J.*, 26 May 1649.
[2] P.R.O. Wards 14/7/15, papers concerning the Court's records under the Commonwealth etc.   [3] P.R.O in Wards 1/119.

CHAP. X]　　　RECORDS OF THE COURT　　　181

Hall were still occupied by the wards' records, to which, to increase the confusion, records of the King's Bench and Common Pleas had been added. The petition was referred to the lord chief justice, who was to report to the lord chancellor.[1] Seven years later, in December 1669, the Privy Council ordered the chief justices of King's Bench and Common Pleas to report on the best place to keep the records, but the matter was held up by the absence of Peter Fabian—the son of honest Tom, by that time dead some ten years—who had the key to the room where the documents were said to be. Consequently arrangements were made to break open the doors, but once again there is no evidence that any action was taken—in any case, the only plan the judges appear to have had in mind was removal to another room, adjacent to the one in which the records lay. By this time, the inconvenience caused to 'the officers of his Majestie's Aquatery' was the point at issue, much more than the safety of the records.

Certainly the next opportunity that offers of learning how the records progressed provides a gloomy picture. By 1687 Peter Fabian was dead, and William Grymes, who succeeded to his office, presented a report on what he found in the room in Fish Yard. It is a classic account of the factors that can operate towards the destruction and dispersion of records. First and foremost, it details physical conditions calculated to produce the maximum of decay. The room where the records lay was much out of repair, it had a flat roof from which much of the lead was gone, and a great deal of rain came in. Nor was that all. However it may have been with his father, who had, after all, served the Court when it was a going concern and had perhaps a proper respect for its records, Peter Fabian had clearly not been a very conscientious custodian. Indeed, if Grymes' allegation is correct, he had been an absentee archivist, residing in the country 'except sometimes in an Issuable term'. The most serious feature of this dereliction of duty had been that it gave the king's fishmonger, always a rival for the premises, a free run of them. This official had somehow or other got control of the key, so that, on the one hand, Fabian had only been able to enter with his permission and, on the other, all sorts of unauthorized persons seem to have got in, notwithstanding that 'not knowing how to search or use records they do manifest damage every time they go to search'. In the whole report there is no encouraging

[1] P.R.O. P.C. 2/56, p. 138

182 COURT OF WARDS AND LIVERIES [CHAP. X

feature: appended to it, however, is a short list, headed *An account of the Records now (1687) remaining in the Treasury of the late Court of Wards*. This is very interesting indeed, for it is the sole indication so far noted that not all the wards' records were moved from the treasury to the 'hell-like fish-cellar'. Perhaps it is not a coincidence that amongst the items on this list are some of the record series that are today least broken and decayed.[1]

More than twenty years later, when Grymes' son, Charles, appeared before the House of Lords committee on the records of public offices, these same allegations were renewed—very often in almost the same words. Tuckwell, the royal fishmonger, on the other hand, stoutly denied that he ever even saw the door to the room open.[2] In the face of a flat contradiction of this sort, it is difficult to apportion responsibility. It is in favour of William and Charles Grymes that they both told the same story—the one in 1687 and the other in 1708, but in fact neither was quite above suspicion. William was certainly energetic and did a great deal of work (for which he was never paid) in calendaring and indexing the records, both on his own account and by means of his sons and of other clerks;[3] Charles Grymes also claimed that his father had discovered, and brought back, a great number of records from the house of 'one Garret of Paternoster Row in Spitalfields'.[4] But the committee was informed that Grymes had removed records to his own house and, being called to account, Charles admitted that some feodaries' certificates had been moved to the Chapel of the Rolls,[5] and as late as 1732 eleven bags of these were still in his own possession.[6] He was also asked by the 1708 committee 'why the door of the office in the Fish Yard was left open last week',[7] and it is clear that he got across them, for they removed the records from out of his care.[8]

Whoever was to blame—and at the root of the matter there was governmental negligence—by 1708 the records of the Court of Wards were in a wretched condition. The committee itself visited the room in Fish Yard, over which the controversy between Grymes and Tuckwell had raged, 'where they found a great

---

[1] P.R.O. T.1/157 (4); but *H.L.J.*, 20 April 1709, makes it doubtful whether the distinction between 'Treasury' and 'Fish Cellar' is a real one.
[2] H.M.C., *House of Lords*, N.S. vol. VIII, p. 27. [3] *R.C.C.*, 1732, pp. 140-1.
[4] *Cal. of Treasury Papers 1708-14*, pp. 452-3.
[5] H.M.C., *House of Lords*, N.S. vol. VIII, p. 28. [6] *R.C.C.*, 1732, p. 6.
[7] H.M.C., *House of Lords*, N.S. vol. VIII, p. 28. [8] *R.C.C.*, 1732, p. 140.

CHAP. X] RECORDS OF THE COURT 183

Number of Books and Papers lying upon the Floor in the greatest Confusion and Disorder . . . the Lead being stolen from the Top of the Roof, and the Windows broken, the Rain has corrupted and destroyed many of these Papers';[1] the place was frequented, as might be imagined, by vermin.[2] Charles Grymes advised quite shamelessly that 'the old rotten stuff might be thrown in some odd Hole, or else flung out of Doors'.[3] One fact was obvious: the records, if they were to be preserved, must be moved into a more suitable place.

As early as March 1708-9 the earl marshal offered to receive them in the Heralds' Office,[4] and the offer was repeated in 1711.[5] For some reason, however, it was not immediately accepted; and in both 1712 and 1714 John Anstis, garter king, again offered the heralds' services.[6] He was prepared to take the wards' records into his charge, and had even a scheme ready for dealing with them. He proposed that calendars should be made, and possibly printed, with indexes of surnames, lands and matters under each county, three clerks, with salaries and sworn not to embezzle or alter the records, being employed on them. The loose papers, 'whereof there are an immense quantity', were to be bound into volumes. Anstis himself was willing to supervise the work without payment, though he suggested that expenses for binding and paper should be from time to time repaid.[7] By February 1718-19 the records were indeed in his custody, but the more ambitious plan for their arrangement had not been carried out.[8] They had, however, been transferred from the office in Fish Yard to a room over the Prince's chamber, and thence moved again to a room over the Black Rod's room, in which latter place the records of the Court of Requests were also stored[9]—a fact which explains the confusion of the records of the two courts, which is not altogether eliminated at the present time.[10]

[1] *H.L.J.*, 20 April 1709.   [2] *Ibid.*   [3] *Ibid*
[4] H.M.C., *House of Lords*, N.S. vol. VIII, p. 28.
[5] H.M.C., *Portland*, vol. V, pp. 102-3.
[6] P.R.O. T. 1/152 (24), letter of 24 Sept. 1712; H.M.C., *Portland*, vol. V, pp. 419-20.   [7] *Ibid.*   [8] *Ibid.* pp. 577-8.
[9] P.R.O. T.1/220 (45), report of Lords' committee, 16 April 1719.
[10] Court of Requests records still turn up in several classes of the P.R.O. Wards' miscellanea. The class known as Wards 16, Unopened Documents, consists of two large boxes of records, very many of which are of the Court of Requests. These records are interesting in another way, for they consist of returns to commissions etc., still unopened (and usually sealed) in just the form in which they were delivered into one or other of the two courts. How they came to be left unopened and disregarded it is impossible to say.

184   COURT OF WARDS AND LIVERIES   [CHAP. X

Neither of these transfers was more than a temporary expedient. In 1728 the House of Lords ordered that the records of both Wards and Requests should be sent to the Chapter House,[1] and this was reinforced by the recommendation of the Commons' committee of 1732.[2] Accordingly a warrant was issued for delivery of the records to the Chapter House, and in due course the keeper there acknowledged their receipt.[3] At length, after a chequered history, the wards' records were housed in a recognized repository, where something might be done to repair the ravages of the unhappy century after the Court's dissolution: many volumes were bound, and two clerks were employed to methodize the records.[4]

Behind the gradually increasing demand for the effective preservation of the records of the Court was a realization of their genealogical, and later, in a wider sense, of their historical, importance. It was not by chance that the movement was, roughly speaking, contemporary with the publication of works like Rymer's *Foedera* or Madox's researches into the history of the Exchequer— indeed in 1711-12 Madox himself petitioned the lord treasurer that, as a 'poor sufferer in the cause of history', he might be employed as keeper and digester of the wards' records.[5] The significance of these records as a *corpus* of genealogical material had been stressed by Chamberlain, when Fabian was indiscreet enough to state that the evidences of the Court concerned 'above 600 persons and families besides records'.—'I desire to know what you do mean hereby', retorted the former clerk, '600 persons and families besides records! I undertake there are above six hundred thousands families and records and as many thousands more as I told King Charles publicly *alta voce* in Oxford'.[6] The usefulness of inquisitions as preserving pedigrees had been seriously put forward at the Restoration as a reason for continuing the Court.[7] Kindred notions had inspired Grymes in his researches, and were no doubt in the earl marshal's mind when he offered to take the records into the Heralds' Office. When it was realized that, family history apart,

[1] P.R.O. T. 1/165 (47a), order of 25 May 1728.   [2] *R.C.C.*, 1732, p. 6.
[3] *Cal. of Treasury Books and Papers 1731-4*, pp. 266-7.
[4] *Cal. of Treasury Books and Papers 1731-4*, pp. 540, 558; also *Cal. of Treasury Books and Papers 1739-41*, pp. 252, 272.
[5] H.M.C., *Portland*, vol. v, p. 153.
[6] P.R.O. Wards 10/1, Chamberlain correspondence. As early as Burghley's time there had been a project for enrolling the pedigrees of all who sued liveries —B.M. Harleian MS. 293, no. 112.
[7] B.M. Egerton MS. 2979, f. 58. *T.N.T.*, p. 163, makes the same point.

CHAP. X]   RECORDS OF THE COURT   185

the records had a general historical significance, their preservation became a certainty.

Even so, there was much ground to be made up. Many series were hopelessly broken, and of those that had survived large portions had become fragmentary and decayed. Nor should the extent of the work done at the Chapter House, prior to the Public Record Office Act of 1838, be exaggerated. On the physical side, it seems that little was done for the vast mass of wards' miscellanea: the official calendar of the contents of the Chapter House in 1807-8 described these documents, packed on the sides of the grand entrance from the cloisters, as being covered with dirt and in great confusion.[1] Nor, after the initial effort, is it likely that a great deal was done in the way of listing and indexing—though the Record Commissioners reported in 1819 that the calendar of the books of surveys was under way.[2]

The work done subsequent to the 1838 act can be traced in successive Deputy Keeper's reports. A first step was taken in 1839, when the records, previously stored without any covering material, were disposed in eight chests and seventy sacks,[3] and ten years later a drive was made to clean them.[4] Meantime, Frederick Devon and others were labouring on lists of the miscellaneous books,[5] deeds and evidences,[6] and inquisitions post mortem,[7] and above all on the Herculean task of sorting the miscellanea and removing extraneous documents. In 1859-60 the records of the Court were moved from the Chapter House to the Public Record Office,[8] and there still another class was brought under arrangement—the important series of pleadings in the Court.[9]

The sad history of the Court's records has a double significance, technical and general. From the archivist's point of view, it is an object lesson illustrative of almost all the dangers that may threaten records—damp, dirt and vermin; ill-considered and hasty transfers, and intermingling with the archives of other institutions; careless

[1] Quoted in *Deputy Keeper's Report*, no. XII, p. 6.
[2] *Reports from Commissioners, 1800-19*, p. 329.
[3] *Deputy Keeper's Report*, no. I, p. 16.   [4] *Ibid.* no. XII, p. 6.
[5] *Ibid.* no. IV, Appendix II; vol. VIII, Appendix IX.
[6] *Ibid.* no. VI, Appendix II.
[7] *Ibid.* no. IX, p. 2; no. XXI, p. xiv.
[8] *Ibid.* no. XXI, Appendix, pp. 21-4.
[9] *Ibid.* no. XXVIII, p. xix.

N

186 COURT OF WARDS AND LIVERIES [CHAP. X

use, and even embezzlement, by the searcher. On more general grounds the fate of the records has its importance too. As they have come down to us, the wards' records are not easy to use and, indeed, are repellent to the user. Their physical condition is unequal—some of the entry books of the Court are in fair enough shape, but series are frequently broken, so that often a vital link in the chain of evidence is missing; and, beyond the territory of the entry books, there is the vast mass of original proceedings, judicial and administrative, embarrassing alike in its bulk and lack of order. These facts, it would seem, have discouraged historians from making use of the first-rate material that the records contain for the social history of Tudor and Stuart England; they also account for the absence of any full-scale, modern study of the Court of Wards and Liveries.

APPENDIX I

A MEMORANDUM RELATING TO WARDSHIP IN
HENRY VIII'S REIGN

P.R.O.: S.P. 1/159, f. 47; see above, pp. 6, 9-10.

Hereafter ensueth A Remembrauns for a good Ordre to be takyn for the king our souerain lordes wardes by reason wherof our seid souerain lord may dewly and truely be ansuerd from yere to yere of the Revenues issues and profightes of the same by wey of accompt in eschewing such Inconuenyences losses And damages as haue ensued and yet likely to ensue onles some resonable reformacion in this behalf may be provyded Wherfore it is to be remembred that in the tyme of our late souerain lord king Henry the VIIth whoes Sowle god pardon dyuerse offycers wer appoynted for the dew orderyng of the said wardes that is to sey A master A generall Receyuour an Auditour and particuler Receyuours in euery Shyre And the seid master for the tyme beyng didde delyuer euery terme to the said auditour a bill of all suche names as werre the kinges wardes and a tytleyng of euery office by reason wherof the particuler Receyuours had knowlege of the same whiche answerd the issues and profightes of their landes euery yere by wey of accompt as by a boke therof made for oon hole yere endyng at Michelmas in the xxiiijti yere of the Reigne of our said souerain lord king Henry the vijth playnly it may Appere And syth that tyme hetherto ther hath no like ordre be takyn nor no like boke hath been made / For lak wherof it is supposed ther hath ensued not only gret losse and damage to our souerain lord the king that now is / but also ther is likely to ensue gretter losse hereafter euery yere more And more / Onles some other lawfull order in this behalf may be provyded and executed / For the Remedy wherof

Fyrst it is thought expedyent that like officers may be newly auctorised now / as wer in the tyme of our souerain lord king Henry the vijth. Provyded alwey that no man entermytte or medyll with eny wardes landes but upon good and sufficyent mater of Recorde founde for the king And that some able person of the Chauncery or of the eschequor may be auctorysed with a Conuenyent Fee to enter euery terme from hensforth in a boke engroced the Copy of euery office found for the king concernyng eny of his Wardes And also to make and delyuer otherlyke bokes of all suche offyces as be past eny tyme sith the begynnyng of the king our souerain lordes Reigne hetherto And that the said Copyes may remayne there Where as the seid officers may resorte un to them at all tymes for the kinges auauntage

187

COURT OF WARDS AND LIVERIES

Item that A generall commaundement may be yeven to the Master of the kinges wardes for the tyme beyng to make no Sale of no wardes londes but oonely of the body / nor to let no wardes londes to Ferme in a some ingrose / For by reason of the sale the kinges grace lesyth commynly half in half / And by reason of letyng any wardes landes to ferme his seid grace lesith the libertie of all commodites belongyng to the same as Baylywykkes parkershippes and other plesures and auauntages with the whiche his grace might rewarde his owne seruauntes which sue un to his seid grace for other Recompences and rewardes in consideracion of their good seruice / And also it cawsith the particuler Receyuours and other officers of the said wardes to be lothe to medle in the mater bycawse they see no landes likely to remayne in the kinges handes but Rates Reseruacions and Reuercions whiche be but tryfulles in effect in comparison to them that be sold and letyn to ferme / And little profight or noon comyng of them nowther to the kinges grace nor to them that schall medle with them / And whan men haue taken peyne to see the kinges title truely found / and the londes to be vewid and accompted / and the money therof comyng to be receyvid and paid / whiche is most peynefull to euery man in the begynnyng / And then schortly after to be dischargid by reson of sale or lettyng the same londes to Ferme / For he that takith them to ferme dischargith the kinges officers by and by / and puttith in other at his plesur / yt geueth men small corage to take peyne or to medle in yt / Wherefor whoso cowde fynde the meanes that the kinges grace And his honorable counsell myght be utterly determyned to kepe the landes of al his wardes in his owne handes tyl euery heire had sued his lyuerye / and to be Answerd of the yssues and profightes of the same euery yere by wey of Accompt / yt is thought yt wold proue within few yeres to be oone of the goodlyest commodites of a casualtie / that his grace schuld haue within this his Realme / And noone like it / And in case that the kinges grace and his honorable counsell at eny tyme hereafter woll nedes make sale of any wardes landes or let them to ferme yf it might be so ordred that ther shuld no patent be sealid tyll suche tyme as the kinges generall Surveyours the generall Receyuour of the wardes And oone of thauditours of the kynges wardes for the tyme beyng had sette their handes to the bill / to thentent yt myght be knowen what euery of them cowde sey for the kinges profight and Auauntage therin / And also till suche tyme as he or they whiche schuld take suche landes to ferme haue covenauntid suerly with the kinges grace and his counsell that all the kinges officers of the seid landes be (*sic*) patent schuld enioye their offices duryng the nonage in as large and like maner And fourme as they did for the kinges grace duryng his enterest / yt is thought it schuld be much mor benyficiall for the king than it hath been / And

APPENDIX I 189

also it schuld cawse euery man that schuld medle in yt to be the better—
Willyng to take peyne to see his seid grace truely serued And Answerd /
But onles yt may plese your grace to be at some comynycation in yt
yourself And to haue certen articles drawen and subscrybed for the
spedynes of the same yt is supposed it wulbe long or this mater woll
forward or come to eny good purpose/
Endorsed—
  a bille concernyng thorder of and for the Kinges Wardes.

APPENDIX II

DESCRIPTION OF THE RECEIVER-GENERAL'S ACCOUNTS AND
ABSTRACTS OF REVENUES IN SELECTED YEARS

The act founding the Court of Wards imposed on the receiver-general
the obligation of accounting annually before the attorney and the
auditor, and on the auditor the duty of engrossing the account in
parchment.[1] This provision resulted in there being three series of
receiver-general's accounts:

(i) *Original accounts in English*.[2] These are in book form and virtually
complete from 1547 to 1641. They bear traces throughout of auditing.
Individual items have a note, *Examinatur*, against them in the righthand margin. Against some the letters *a.p.* were added at audit, and
from Elizabeth's reign many items in certain sections of the accounts
were marked *R*. On occasion under Elizabeth the auditor appended his
signature to the year's account, and from 1625 they were signed by the
master, surveyor, attorney and auditor.

(ii) *Paper drafts of formal accounts in Latin*[3] and (iii) *Parchment engrossments of formal accounts in Latin*.[4] The accounts in these two series are
bulky files with very full supporting documentation (patents, decrees
etc. set out at length.) Neither series approaches completeness, and
accounts in both are completely lacking for the period 1579-99. Moreover, even where an account in either of these series is listed in P.R.O.
Wards Guide, it not infrequently proves on examination to be damaged
and lacking essential figures. Again, physical decay apart, especially in
the latter half of the Court's existence totals were not always entered in
the parchment engrossments.

All three series agree as to the heads under which they set out the
receiver-general's *charge*. There were six principal heads—arrearages,
issues of wards' lands, sales of wardships and marriages, mean rates
(the profits of heirs' lands during the period prior to the suing out of
livery), fines for liveries, and fines for leases. Minor sources of revenue
set out under separate heads were fines for contempts and widows' fines
for licences to re-marry; latterly fines for concealments and other heads
of revenue were added, and primer seisins were separated from fines
for liveries and formed a separate item.

---

[1] 32 Henry VIII c. 46 (xix).   [2] P.R.O. *Wards Guide* calls these Series C.
[3] Series A in P.R.O. *Wards Guide*.   [4] Series B in P.R.O. *Wards Guide*.

190

APPENDIX II 191

Nevertheless, despite the similarity of form, the relationship of (i) the original accounts with (ii) and (iii) the formal accounts is at first sight puzzling, for their totals under individual heads, and grand totals too, are widely divergent. This divergence reflects a basic difference in purpose. The original accounts were concerned with sums actually received during the current year. As a rule, amounts falling due, but not paid, had no place in them; nor had accumulated arrearages, the entry under the head of arrearages simply including the receiver-general's own debt for the year previous, i.e. his cash in hand when the financial year started, plus such old debts as were actually paid during the year. In the formal accounts, on the other hand, the receiver-general was charged with all debts as they became due—these also being entered, if unpaid, in the *Supers*, or arrearages, which were listed at the foot of the account. This had the effect of producing higher totals under certain heads of revenue—notably mean rates and liveries—than appeared in the original accounts. It meant too, that, in order to keep the series in line with each other, sums noted as received in the original accounts were on occasion omitted in the formal accounts, since they formed part of a larger sum with which the receiver-general had already been charged. It was items of this character that were marked at the audit *a.p.*—letters which stand for *arrearagia pendentia*. Moreover— and this it was which produced the greatest divergence in grand totals— the formal accounts endeavoured to give a complete view of the finances of the Court, and included all arrearages back to its earliest days.[1]

The essential point in this detail is that it is the original accounts that give the best view of the income of particular years; the formal accounts, with their long lists of uncollected arrearages, have little save academic interest. It is fortunate that the original accounts are the best preserved of the three series, and fortunate too that conservatism as to their form makes comparison over the century relatively easy.

The original accounts give a total gross revenue which is the sum of the separate heads of income already noted. From this total certain deductions have to be made in order to reach the nett revenue. First it is necessary to deduct the Court's expenditures, itemised in the accounts as fees and diets of the officers, annuities, jointures and exhibitions,

---

[1] The conclusions in this paragraph were originally based on a comparative study of the accounts of Series A-B and C. They are borne out, however, by P.R.O. Wards 9/387, ff. 314-18, a most interesting set of memoranda of the business at the audit and declaration of account in 36 Eliz. This contains the following passage:

'Md. that Mr. Auditor did wryte in the book of accompt dd. to him att the end of euerie some confessed (ex^r.) and in the first margent of some (a.p.) that is Arr. penden, and is where the monie was due before the tyme of this yeeres accompte, and of others which were due but in the said tyme this lre (r) which stands for respondet and ys wher the monie is paid as yt growes (?) due.'

192 COURT OF WARDS AND LIVERIES

miscellaneous payments by decree, and the costs of upkeep and repairs; on occasion too it seems reasonable to deduct certain payments made by royal warrant or bill, where these were clearly for services rendered to the Court or can for any other reason be included amongst its legitimate overhead charges. Then there is the question of arrearages. As Mr J. Hurstfield has pointed out, so far as these consisted of payments made in the current year, which had not appeared in previous years' totals, they must be counted as part of the nett income, while that portion of them that represented the receiver-general's indebtedness on the previous year, since it had already been included in the total for that year, does not form part of the nett revenue and, like the expenditures, must be deducted from the gross revenue before the Court's nett income is reached. The same goes for such debts of the receiver-general as were collected after he had ceased to hold office.[1]

Table A below, based on the original accounts, shows heads of revenue and expenditure, and nett income figures for selected years.

Table B gives an abstract for a smaller number of selected years of the receiver-general's charge and discharge as these appear in the formal accounts. With the exception of 1542, an interesting year for which no original account is available, the years illustrated have been chosen so as to coincide with dates covered by Table A, thus making possible a comparison between figures in the original and the formal accounts.

Table C, taken from a recently discovered paper, is a view of accounts of the Westminster Court in the years 1642-5. For this period both original and formal accounts are lacking. The document on which Table C is based appears to stand midway between the two types of account. It shows accumulated arrearages after the style of the formal accounts; on the other hand, under the principal heads of revenue as set out in Table C the document itself lists further figures against the letters *a.p.*, *R.* and *Or.*, which suggests an association with the original accounts. In view of this uncertainty it has not been thought proper to use the view to calculate the annual nett revenue of the Westminster Court.

Figures in the Tables are to the nearest £ only.

---

[1] *T.R.H.S.*, 4th Series, xxxi, 102, note 5.

Table A, Table B and Table C are available for download from www.cambridge.org/9780521200288

APPENDIX III

Fees Paid to Officers of the Court, 1623

Bodleian MS. Tanner 287, *Returns made to the Commissioners for inquiring into the oppression of exacted fees in civil and ecclesiastical courts and offices in the year 1623*, ff. 11-26; see above, p. 36.

A Certificate of all fees due to the Surveyor of his Majesties Court of Wardes and Liveryes in Anno 30 nuper Elizabethae and before.

For a spetiall livery with pardone which the Clerke of the liveryes Receyveth of him	xxiij*s*.	iiij*d*.
To his owne Clerke	o	o
For a generall livery where the landes exceed 5 *li*. per annum which the Clerke of the liveryes also Receiveth for him	xxs.	
To his owne Clerke		
For liveryes under the value of 5 *li*. per annum beinge tow (*sic*) partes of three which passe his hand noe Fee at all.		
For every tender and euery Continuance of a Livery	vj*s*.	viij*d*.
To his Clerke	iij*s*.	iiij*d*.
For an Estallment of the Fine of a livery or Meane Rates if the partye desier it which happen Seldome there havinge but tow passed this last Terme.	xx*s*.	
To his Clerke	iij*s*.	iiij*d*.
For every order with his hand	x*s*.	
To his Clerke for writinge and enteringe	iij*s*.	iiij*d*.

Memorandum that the Surveyor Confines his Fees to liveryes only and takes none at all uppon any Wardshipe.

The Certificate of the kinges Majesties Atturney of the Court of Wardes and Liveryes of all his Fees due in his office in Anno XXX° nuper Elizabethae Regine and before.

1 Inprimis for penninge and signinge of every decree	xx*s*.	Mr Morice had but x*s*.
To his Clerke	ij*s*.	
2 For signinge of euery case and attending the Judges therewith	xx*s*.	
To his Clarke	ij*s*.	

193

194 COURT OF WARDS AND LIVERIES

3 For signinge of euery Schedule
lease Informacion Replicacion License
to alien the Wardshipe Licence to
allien leases Biles of Cost and for
such orders as are signed by him   x*s.*

> Mr Morice
> had nothing
> for he signed
> none. But
> Sir Thomas
> Hesket
> succeeding
> him did signe
> them and
> tooke x*s.*

To his Clerke   ij*s.*
4 For signinge of every Lyverye
aboue the value of V *li.*   iij*s.* iiij*d.*
5 For euery warrant for Writtes   iij*d.*
6 Since the kinges Majesties
instructions for Composicions for
Wardships which was in February 1610
there is due to him for his greate
labor in Consideringe of the Schedule
and abstracte made by the sayd Clerke
of the said Courte and setlinge downe
the estate and what is Come to his
Majestie   x*s.*

> Not taken
> before his
> Majesties
> Instructions
> for Compo-
> sition of
> Wardships
> Reg. nor the
> ij*s.* for his
> Clarke.

To his Clerke   ij*s.*

Mr Receyuer.

A note of such fees as haue beene taken for the Receiver generall of his Majesties Court of Wardes and Liveuery beinge incident to his said office uppon Recipts and paymentes and other services thereto belonginge.

1 For Acquittances uppon Fines of
Liveryes and Meane Rates of full age   xvj*d.*
2 For Feodaries Acquittances   xvj*d.*
3 For Arrerages in proces Wardships
fines leases for leases (*sic*) licence
of Marriage Rentes and Meane Rates
and Sheriffe fines every Acquitance   ij*s.*

> All Acquittances
> longe since 30
> Elizabethae were
> but xvj*d.* a peice.

4 For enteringe the Receipt uppon
payment of bondes and the
discharge thereof   ij*s.* x*d.*
5 For indorcement of payment uppon
euery bond and Constat for the same   xvj*d.*

APPENDIX III

6 For enteringe a decree only for
mony that is payd out of the Receipt   vj*s*.   viij*d*.
7 For enteringe a debentur for
payment of mony oute of the Receipt   iij*s*.   iiij*d*.
8 For enteringe a privy Seale for
payment of mony out of the Receipt   vj*s*.   viij*d*.
9 For enteringe of warrantes to pay
oute mony   ij*s*.
10 Euery noble man giveth doble
fees in the Cases aforesade
11 For Portage mony of pencioners
and extraordinary paymentes out
of the Receipt upon Patentes and
Pryvy Seales *pro qualibet libra*   vj*d*.
12 For Portage of Exhibicions
and mony repaid by decrees
or Warrant *pro qualibet libra*   iiij*d*.
13 Note that there is about xvij (*sic*)
payd by setled assignacions
yearely to the kinges household
Officers and Judges fees for
which there is noe Portage mony
allowed.   nil.

Fees Received by the Receivor generall his Clarke belonginge to himself.

1 The Receivor generall his Clarke
entereth into a booke all Schedules
particulers or other estallmentes
upon the First Ratinge and before
bondes taken for such monyes assessed
Whereby is knowen what the seuerall
fines and debtes are by whome to bee
payd and at what feastes and tearmes
the paymentes are to bee made which
doth greately expedite his Majesties
service and giveth dispatch to the
subiecte   xij*d*.
2 Also for writinge pencioners
acquittances uppon the Receipt of
theire Annuities oute of this Courte
the forme of which acquittances and
discharge beinge very large   ij*s*.

196 COURT OF WARDS AND LIVERIES

3 For enteringe A lettres Patentes
or a Privy Seale   ij*s*.

4 For enteringe a decree for payment
of mony out of the Receipt   xij*d*.

5 For enteringe of euery debentur   vj*d*.

6 For every Onus   vj*d*.

Fees in the Auditors office of his Majesties Court of Wardes and Lyveryes.

	Thauditors	Clerkes
1 For a perticuler wheruppon to passe a lease	xx*s*.	x*s*. and more according to the length.
2 For drawinge downe each seuerall Accompte of the wardes landes accordinge to the Inquisicion Survey and Composicion		vj*s*. viij*d*.
3 For Entery of the Survey uppon the Schedule of the wardshipe if it bee a Concealement	iij*s*. iiij*d*.	nil.
4 For inrollinge the Schedule of the landes the heire beeinge within age for every sheete at 3*s*. 4*d*. the sheete.		
5 For inrollinge of an Order made at the Composicion for direcion for the Auditors for abatement of Rent which the office doth not warrant	iij*s*. iiij*d*.	xij*d*.
6 For a Quietus est for payment of in euery County for every yeare	ij*s*.	xvj*d*.
7 For an Onus what Rent is to bee payd to the Receivor in euery County	ij*s*.	xvj*d*.
8 For inrollinge of Patentes decrees leases and Assignmentes for every of them	x*s*.	xiij*s*. iiij*d*.
9 For a debentur for Exhibicion and other payment to bee made out of the Receipt	v*s*.	iij*s*. iiij*d*.
10 For a particuler for dower where the third parte of the value is C *s*. per annum	xiij*s*. iiij*d*. yf under C *s*. vj*s*. 8*d*.	x*s*.

APPENDIX III

11 For Inrollment of the Assignement of dower — vjs. viijd. | xiijs. iiijd.

12 For inrollment of a divicion for particion of Wardes landes — xs. | xiijs. iiijd.

13 For settinge out and making eleccion of the kinges parte upon the divicion by Commission — xs. | nil.

14 For Castinge the Rates of a Spetiall livery — xvs. | xjs. viijd.

15 For Castinge the Rates of a generall livery — xjs. | vjs. iiijd.

16 For inrollement of a Spetiall lyvery — xs. | xxs.

17 For Inrollement of a general lyvery aboue value — vjs. viijd. | xiijs. iiijd.

18 For a Lyvery under value — iijs. iiijd. | xiijs. iiijd.

19 For Inrollinge of a Travers or Pardon — xxs. | xxs.

20 For a Coppy of a Survey — iiijs. | iiijs.

21 For signinge of the warrant of the generall lyvery for searches if the Fyne of the marriage Rents within age and Rates of full age bee payd or secured. } xijd. and for a spetiall lyvery ijs.

22 For a Certificate for the delyveringe of a bond upon Inrollment of the lyvery — xijd.

23 For a docquet for discharge of Proces for Arrerages if the some bee xli. or aboue — xs. }
24 Yf under xli. and aboue C s. — vs. } ijs.

25 Yf under C s. — ijs. vjd. | ijs.

26 For a Coppy of a Charge — xijd. yf it bee under the Auditors handes vs.

27 For the Coppye of decrees Indenters and Inquisicions by the sheete — iiijd. | iiijd.

28 For the officers hand — ijs. | nil.

29 For abatement of the Rates upon the Schedule of the lyvery by decree or other warrant — xjs. | ijs. vjd.

198   COURT OF WARDS AND LIVERIES

30 For the declaracion of
lunatiques and Ideotes Accompts   iiij*s.*   x*s.* and more
accordinge to
ye length

31 For Ingrossements according
to the Resurvacion uppon
thaccompte   nil.

32 For a Constat for discharginge
Respect of homage or that landes
are in Ward by the minorytye of
any heire   v*s.*   v*s.*

33 For a Constat or Certificate
to declare the kinges title what
hath beene answered uppon a
Charge Reserued   x*s.*   ij*s.*   vj*d.*

34 For Accompt betweene partye
and partie accordinge as the Case
Requiers   [no figure entered]

35 For takinge a yearely Accompt
of the Feodary for the Revenue
within that County   xl*s.*

36 For searchinge and settinge
forth what benefit is answered to
his Majestie uppon Rulinge of
Feodaries peticions   xx*s.* per annum and if it be a
smale shire x*s.* per annum.

37 For ingrossinge of Accompts
of Wardes landes allowed by his
Majestie duringe the minority   ij*s.* per annum And after
full age by the heire
untill Livery or other
discharge bee brought in
to discharge Thaccompt.

38 The possession of noble men payes doble fees

39 These Fees have beene by the Relacion of Auncyent Clerks before anno XXX^mo domine Elizabethae nuper Regine which was longe before eyther of the sayd Auditors were Officers savinge the fee for inrollinge of Orders uppon Composicions and for discharginge of Rates of full age uppon the Schedule of the livery which hath growne since his Majesties newe instructions and thereby haue inforced new labors and much increased the Charge of ingrossinge the bookes of the sayd officers.

APPENDIX III

199

The Certificate of the Clarke of his Majesties Court of Wardes and Liveryes of all fees due in his office in Anno XXX° nuper Elizabethae Regine and before

1 Inprimis for every warrant for writte
or Commission to fynd offices and for
Entery of the same   ij*s.*

2 The bond for Returninge the office   xij*d.*

3 For drawinge of every Schedule
uppon the office to passe the wardshipe x*s.* wherof to his under Clarke
iij*s.* iiij*d.*

              x*s.* But when the office
              if of large Content ye
              under Clarke taketh
              more as the partie is
              willinge to give.

4 For grants of wardshipe of an heire
male to the Clarke xxxv*s.* viij*d.* and
to his under Clerke for ingrossinge
the Indentures and Schedules xiij*s.*
iiij*d.*

              xlix*s.* When ye schedules
              are of great length
              the under Clerke
              taketh more as the
              partie is willinge to giue.

5 If it bee an heire Female the Clerke
hath doble fees and doble fees also if
the ward bee a noble man

6 For every lease to the Clarke xiiij*s.*
to his under Clarke for drawinge the lease
in paper iij*s.* iiij*d.* and for ingrossinge
it in parchment xiij*s.* iiij*d.*   xxx*s.* viij*d.*

7 For every obligacion for payment of
mony and upon spetiall Orders ij*s.* whereof
to his under Clarke vj*d.*   ij*s.*

8 For every Escheators bond for executinge
his office vj*s.* viij*d.* whereof to the
Clerke iij*s.* iiij*d.* and to his under Clerke   vj*s.* viij*d.*

9 For every Privy seale ij*s.* vj*d.* whereof
to the Clerke xviij*d.* and to his under
Clerke xij*d.*   ij*s.* vj*d.*

10 For every Inunction (*sic*) and for the
draught and entery of it into a booke to
the Clarke ij*s.* vj*d.* and to his under
Clarke ij*s.*   iiij*s.* vj*d.*

11 For the enteringe every aparance with
the Privy Seall enioyninge   ij*s.* iiij*d.*

12 For every generall Commission and
dedimus potestatem Attachment proces of
Contempt and supersedeas betweene partie
and partie to the Clarke ij*s.* vj*d.* and
to his under Clarke ij*s.*   iiij*s.* vj*d.*

200 COURT OF WARDS AND LIVERIES

13 For every speciall Commission uppon
decree or Order and writt of Assistance for
drawinge and enteringe it in a booke and
ingrossinge it to the Clarke v*s*. and to
his under Clarke ij*s*.   vij*s*.

14 For Coppyinge any pleadinge or other
Record (except Orders) for every sheete
viij*d*. wherof to his under Clarke ij*d*.
and for engrossinge any Bill for dedimus
potestatem for every sheete x*d*. whereof
to his under Clarke iiij*d*.   viiij*d*.

15 For every Super in proces when it is
paid or discharged beinge xx*l*. or aboue
to the Clarke x*s*. to his under Clarke ij*s*.   xij*s*.

16 For every Super under xx*li*. to the
Clarke v*s*. to the under Clarke   vj*s*.

17 Of Every sherefe upon Returne of his
general proces for entery thereof and of
ye Returns etc. to the Clarke vj*s*. viij*d*.
and to his under Clarke iij*s*. iiij*d*.   x*s*.

18 For each some levyed by seuerall proces
of levari of the debtors landes seised and
for all enteries apperteyninge thereunto
to the Clarke ij*s*. and to his under Clarke ij*s*.   iiij*s*.

19 For Rulinge the bookes uppon any staye
of proces by Order to the Clarke ij*s*. and to
his under Clarke xij*d*.   iij*s*.

20 For discharge of every seisure of landes
for any debt and all thinges thereunto
apperteyninge to the under Clarke   ij*s*.

21 For Copeinge any Charge of Arrerages
to the under Clarke   xij*d*.

22 For Cancelinge and deliuery of any
Conditionall bond not beinge for payment
of mony   ij*s*.

23 For drawinge enteringe examininge and
signinge of every order and affidavit to
the Clarke ij*s*. and to his under Clarke xij*d*.   iij*s*.
and for Orders of dismission vj*s*. whereof
to his under Clarke ij*s*.

APPENDIX III

24 For euerye decree and assignement
of dower enteringe it in a booke and
ingrossinge it in parchment examininge
and signinge it to the Clarke xs. and
to his under Clarke vjs. viijd.

xvjs. viijd. When
ye decree is longe then
ye under Clerk taketh
more as the partie is
willinge to give.

25 To the Clarke that Readeth in
Court at the dayes of hearinge of each
Cause of the parties plaintiff or
defendant and for Receipt wherof there
is an order in Courte

iijs.   iiijd.

26 For Copyinge any Case Certificate
Iniunction or other proces writinge
examininge and signing of it to the
Clarke ijs. and to his under Clarke
xijd.

iijs.

27 For every search to the Clarke
xviijd. to his under Clarke vjd.

ijs.

28 For every presentacion to a benefice
drawinge enteringe and ingrossinge it
to the Clark xxs. and to his under
Clarke xs.

xxxs.

29 For euery Exemplification under
seale after the Rate of xxvjs. viijd.
for euery skine and so proportionablely
for that which is lesse

xxvjs.   viijd.

30 For examinacion of euery witnes and
defendant taken in Court to the Clarke
ijs. and to his under Clarke xijd.

iijs.

31 For all Evidences brought into Court
to the under Clarke for enteringe them
in a booke and orderly placynge them in
the Treasurie

ijs.

32 For deliuerye forth of Evidences from
the Treasurye by order and discharginge
the booke to the Clarke vjs. viijd. and
to his under Clarke ijs.

viijs.   viijd.

33 For a Feodaryes pattent enteringe
drawing and ingrossinge to the Clarke
xxs. to his under Clarke vjs. viijd.

xxvjs.   viijd.

34 For every feodaryes bond to the
Clarke vjs. viijd. and to his under
Clarke iijs. iiijd.

xs.

o

COURT OF WARDS AND LIVERIES

35 For a lettre in the nature of a
proces for apperance of a noble man .... iiij*s*.   vj*d*.
36 For enteringe the oath of every
witnes sworne to be examined in Courte .... iiij*d*.
37 For drawinge enteringe and Copyinge
of every Contynuance of lyvery iij*s*.
and if it bee exprired (*sic*) vj*s*. .... iij*s*.
38 For searchinge amonge all the Recordes
of the Court for the tenures of any lands .... vj*s*.   viij*d*.
39 For enteringe and indorsinge of every
licence of Assignment of wardship or lease .... x*s*.
40 For enteringe of deeds for assignement
of any debtt to his Majestie and other
deedes of deputacion to the Clark x*s*. to
the under clarke vj*s*. 8*d*. .... xvj*s*.   viij*d*.
41 For Receivinge and delivery forth of any
mony deposited in Court for ever (*sic*) pound .... ij*d*.
42 For surrender Cancelinge and deliuery
forth of the Counter parte of every Indenture .... vj*s*.   viij*d*.
43 For euery Constat of any Inquisicion
Wardship or lease to the Clarke iij*s*.
iiij*d*. to his under Clerke 3*s*. 4*d*. .... vj*s*.   viij*d*.
44 To the under Clerke for ingrossinge
euery Bill to bee signed by his Majestie
vj*s*. viij*d*. if it bee with grant of
exhibicion but if without v*s*. .... vj*s*.   viij*d*.
45 For deliuery to the parties of euery
of those bylls signed by his Majestie
iiij*s*, wherof to the Clarke ij*s*. to the
under Clarke ij*s*. .... iiij*s*.
46 For drawinge ingrossinge and
enteringe of a spetiall extent uppon
an Assignement of a debt to his Majestie
wherof to the Clarke ij*s*. vj*d*. to his
under Clerke iiij*s*. .... vj*s*.   vj*d*.

The labors
hereof is
very great
as is well
knowne to the
officers and to
the Suitors
also. Richard
Chamberlen.

47 Since the kinges Majesties instrucions
for Compoissions (*sic*) of wardships etc.
there is allowed to the Clarke for
drawinge enteringe and Copyinge euery
Rule .... ij*s*.
48 Also there is allowed to the Clarke
for all enteries and Certificates of euery
grant Compounded for .... xij*s*.   iiij*d*.

APPENDIX III

A note of all such Fees which haue beene usually taken and Received by the Clarke of the Liveryes upon the prosecution and passinge of Liveryes within thoffice of the said Clarke of the Liveries as followeth.

The officers of ye Court their fees for spetiall and generall Liveryes.
1 The fees due to the officers of Court
upon every spetiall Livery viz. To the
Master of the Wards and Liveryes xxiijs.
iiijd. to Mr. Surveyer of the Liveryes
xxiijs. iiijd. To Mr. Atturney of ye
Court iijs. iiijd. to the Clarke of ye
liverys iij li. xs.

In all   vjl.

2 The officers fees upon a generall livery
aboue value viz. To the Master of the
Wardes and Liveryes xxs. To Mr. Surveyor
xxs. To Mr Atturney iijs. iiijd. To
the Clerke of the Liveryes xxxvijs. viijd.   iiijl.   xijd.

3 The Fee due to the Clarke of the
Liveryes uppon euery generall livery under
value is   xxvjs.   viijd.

The Clarke of the office their fees for a spetiall livery
4 For drawinge and enteringe uppon Record
of euery Schedule beinge a spetiall livery
viz. for ye first sheete   xiijs.   iiijd.
For euery other sheete   vjs.   viijd.

5 For ingrossinge of a paire of Indentures
tow (*sic*) bondes and towe (*sic*) Schedules
beeinge but one sheete   xxiiijs.

6 For euery other sheete beinge twice
ingrossed   ijs.

7 For the warrant ingrossed and made
Readye for the Seale   xs.

8 For a spetiall warrant for the seale
upon the livery of Coheires   xxs.

For a generall Lyverye aboue value.
9 The drawinge enteringe upon Record of
euery Schedule uppon a generall livery
aboue value viz. for the first sheet   xs.
10 For every other sheet   vs.
11 For ingrossinge tow (*sic*) payre of
Indentures tow Schedules beinge but one
sheet and tow bonds upon the same livery   xviijs.

COURT OF WARDS AND LIVERIES

12 For euery other sheete twice ingrossed   ij*s*.
13 For the warrant ingrossed and made
Readye for the Seale   vj*s*.   viij*d*.

For a generall Lyverye under value.
14 The drawinge and enteringe upon Record
of every Schedule upon a generall livery
under value beinge but one sheete   x*s*.
15 And for euery other sheete   v*s*.
16 For ingrossinge of a payre of Indentures
and tow Schedules beinge but one sheete
and towe bonds   xiiij*s*.
17 For every other sheete twice ingrossed
for the warrant made Ready for the seale   iij*s*.   iiij*d*.

Fees due to the Clarke of the Liveryes and his under Clarks.
18 For enteringe euery decree Concerninge
lyvery   xiij*s*.   iiij*d*.
19 For enteringe and Filinge of every
Caveat for stay of livery   xiii*s*.   iiij*d*.
20 For enteringe and filinge euery Survey   iij*s*.   iiij*d*.
21 For entringe and filinge euery oder (*sic*)
for liuerye   iij*s*.   iiij*d*.
22 For entringe and filinge euery tender
and Continuance of livery   xij*d*.
23 For every Certificate to the Auditors
of fine and meane Rates of full age payd
to Mr. Receivor   xij*d*.
24 For every bond for the Fine or meane
Rates of livery enstawled   ij*s*.
25 For the Enteringe of every Comission
taken oute for the sealinge of Indentures   xij*d*.
26 For enteringe the Returne therof and
filinge the Comission   ij*s*.
27 For procuringe euery warrant of liverye
to bee signed by the officers of the Court   xviij*d*.
28 For every search made in the said office   xviij*d*.
29 For every Copye of a Schedule of
livery for euery sheete after the Rate of   iiij*s*.
30 For the hand of the Master of the
office to the same   ij*s*.

APPENDIX III

205

Spetiall fees of Barons and Coheires.

31 Every Coheire but one upon spetiall
livery payeth to the Clarke of the liveryes
over and aboue the fee aforesaid of iij *li*. x*s*.   xlij*s*.

32 And upon euery generall lyverie aboue
value ouer and aboue thabouesaid fee of
xxvij*s*. viij*d*.   xxij*s*.

33 And upon every generall livery under
value over and aboue the foresaid fee of
xxvj*s*. viij*d*.   xiij*s*.   iiij*d*.

34 And for the drawinge and enteringe of
the Schedule ingrossinge the same with
thindentures and bondes and warrant for
the seale. The Coheires doe pay the
same Fees and no more then is before set
downe

35 But in all the Rest of the Fees they
doe answere them doble.

36 Every Barron upon the livery of a
Barrony desended payeth doble Fees

37 The Clarke of the liveryes hath no fee From his Majestie nor any
allowance for the makinge upp and keepinge of the livery booke of
Record Nor for the Indentures Schedules and bondes sealed by ye
subiecte kallendred upp and kept upon Record by the Clarke of the
Liveries Nor any allowance for and towardes the Rent of his office
maynetenance of his Clarkes nor any other necessary Charges whatsoeuer.

Fees due and belonginge to the toow (*sic*) Atturnies of the Courte of
Wardes and Liveryes from Anno 30 Elizabethae Regine and before.

1 For a note or warrant to the Clarke
of the Court for proces to bee made against
defendants befor the bill be brought into Court   iij*s*.   iiij*d*.

2 Of every plaintiff and defendant for
every tearme attendinge their Causes
daylie in Court   iij*s*.   iiij*d*.

3 For every mocion they make for their
Clientes Causes in Courte   v*s*.

4 For drawinge such affidavites as come to them   xij*d*.

5 For drawinge of every bill of Costs   iij*s*.   iiij*d*.

These fees the tow Atturnies of the said Court doe usually Receive
except it bee of such Clientes as bee admitted to sue *in forma pauperis*.

INDEX

Descriptions of those holding offices connected with wardship and livery prior to the establishment of the Court of Wards and Liveries are given in full; those holding office under the Court are, however, described in shortened form ('master' for master of the wards, 'clerk' for clerk of the wards, etc.). The letter w. after a name indicates that the person mentioned was a royal ward.

Abbot, George, Bishop of London, later Archbishop of Canterbury, 125
Acton, Middlesex, Court of Wards temporarily at, 174
age, proof of, 83-4
Aile . . . , John, clerk of the wards, 12 note
Anderson, Sir Edmund, 89
Anstis, John, garter king of arms, 183
Anton, Thomas, clerk, 26
Archer, Sir Simon, 43
Arundel, Lord, see Howard, Thomas, Earl of Arundel
Assize, Justices of, 42
attorney-general, 18, 44, 98, 161
Audley, Hugh, clerk, 28, 29, 32, 35, 38, 40, 70, 152, 155, 159, 161, 172, 175-7, 180
Auger, John, 43, 54
Augmentations, Court of, 14, 23

Bacon, Francis, Baron Verulam and Viscount St Albans, 8, 20, 41-2, 49, 52, 65, 103, 116, 133, 143
Bacon, Sir Nicholas, attorney, 22 note, 23, 67, 117 note, 120-1
Banister, Sir Robert, 118
Banks, John, w., 152 note
Barbaro, Daniel, Venetian envoy, 127, 134
Barraclough, Toby, 157
Bath, Somerset, 18
Battisforde, John, receiver-general, 25
Beaumont, Sir John, receiver-general, 25, 37
Bedford, co., feodary of, 55 note
Bedford, fifth Earl, later Duke of, see Russell, William

Bedford, second Earl of, see Russell, Francis
Belknap, Sir Edward, master of the wards, 10, 11
Berkeley, Sir John, pretended master, 162, 165
Berkley, Sir Maurice, 138
Berwick, 46
Bossevile, Henry, clerk, 26, 34
Bossevile, Ralph, clerk, 26, 34, 102
Boteler, Sir Oliver, w., 153 note
Bray, Sir Reginald, 5, 6
Bridgeman, Sir Orlando, attorney, 151
Brinklow, Henry, 126
Bristol, Earl of, see Digby, John
Brooke, Francis Lord, see Greville, Francis
Brooke, Sir Robert, 67
Broughton, Richard, 55 note
Buckingham, Duke of, see Villiers, George
Burghley, Lord, see Cecil, William
Bussey, Francis, 97

Caesar, Sir Julius, 49
Calthorpe, Sir Henry, attorney, 22 note, 23 note
Cambridge, recorder of, see Hynde, John
Capon, William, 171
Carew, Sir George, master, 19, 20, 22, 45 note, 62, 72, 103, 112, 119, 133
Carill, Edward, 172
Carleton, Sir Dudley, later Viscount Dorchester, 20
Carlisle, Bishop of, see Sever, William
Carmarthen, co., feodary of, 55 note
Carter, Henry, 101
Cary, Walter, 95

206

INDEX

207

Cavendish, William, Earl, later Duke, of Newcastle, 156

Cecil, Robert, Earl of Salisbury, master, 18-19, 20, 24, 28, 33, 48-9, 58, 59, 65, 98, 114, 115, 116-17, 119, 124, 125, 136-7, 139-45, 147

Cecil, Thomas, Earl of Exeter, second Baron Burghley, 124 *note*

Cecil, William, Baron Burghley, master, 17-18, 20, 26, 27, 33, 34-5, 38, 48-9, 50, 52, 53, 55, 57, 58, 59, 93, 99, 110, 116, 120, 124, 129 *note*, 137, 168, 170, 171

Chamberlain, John, 20

Chamberlain, Richard, clerk, 28-9, 31, 32, 34, 35, 37, 38, 136, 151, 152, 153, 160, 165-6, 172, 178-80, 184, 203

chancellor, 102, 128, 132, 135, 147, 164, 181

Chancery, 2, 4, 70, 71, 75, 85, 87, 91, 95, 110, 135, 136, 164, 187. *See also* Petty Bag

Charles I, 65, 147, 150·1, 162

Charles II, 162, 164

Chelsea, Middlesex, 173

Chester and Flint, cos., feodary of, 41

Chester, co., feodary of, 55 *note*

Chester, Exchequer at, 50

Cholmeley, Harry, 97

Cholmeley, Robert, 97

Chomley, ——, feodary of co. Lincoln, 40, 44

Clarendon, Earl of, *see* Hyde, Edward

Clifford, George, Earl of Cumberland, w., 124 *note.*

Coke, Sir Edward, 8, 22, 36, 40, 49, 67, 69, 76, 77, 78, 89, 90 *note*, 145, 146, 147

Cole, Thomas, 90, 108, 110

Coles, John, 43

Colles, Humphrey, feodary of co. Warwick, 40, 43

Colvill, John, 56 *note*

Common Law, Courts of, 5, 23, 109-10

Common Pleas, Chief Justice of, 23, 28, 98, 102, 147, 181

Common Pleas, Court of, 135

Commons, House of, 32, 135, 138-43, 145, 146, 147, 148, 151, 152, 158, 159, 160, 164, 165, 166, 170, 171, 177, 179

Compounding, Committee for, 177

Compton, Spencer, second Earl of Northampton, 125

Compton, William, Lord Compton, first Earl of Northampton, 125

concealments, 3, 48, 50-2, 70, 104, 197

Constable, Robert, 67, 69

Cooke, family of, clerks of liveries, 30, 33

Cooke, William, clerk of liveries, 165

Cope, Sir Walker, master, 19, 45, 48

Copley, Anne, w., 118

Copley, Mary, w., 118

Corbett, Miles, clerk, 29, 152

Cornwall, feodary of, 137

Corry, Richard, 97

Cottington, Francis, Baron Cottington, master, 19, 34, 148, 151

Council Learned in the Law, 4, 5, 10, 12

Counter prison, 101

Coventry and Lichfield, Bishop of, *see* Moreton, Thomas

Crane, Sir Robert, 156

Cranfield, Lionel, Earl of Middlesex, master, 19, 32, 36, 38, 51, 60, 61, 65, 97, 110, 137, 146, 147, 170

Cresswell, John, w., 82

Croke, Sir George, 89

Crompton, Richard, 109

Cromwell, Sir Henry, 106-7

Cromwell, Oliver, 106-7

Cromwell, Robert, 106-7

Cromwell, Thomas, Earl of Essex, 13

Cumberland, Earl of, *see* Clifford, George

Cumberland, feodary of, 157

Cumberland, receivers-general of, 5

Curle, Edward 25

Curle, Francis, auditor, 25

Curle, William, auditor, 16, 25

Dacre, George, Lord Dacre, w., 124 *note*

Dansell, Sir William, receiver-general, 25, 34, 172

Daunce, Sir John, receiver-general of wards' lands, 9, 10

Delaval, Sir Ralph, deputy lieutenant of Northumberland and special commissioner for matters concerning the Border, 93

208 INDEX

Denham, Sir J., 13
de Vere, Edward, Earl of Oxford, w., 124
Devereux, Robert, Earl of Essex, 17, 48
Devon, feodary of, 39
Devon, Frederick, 177, 185
Dewes, Henry, 41
Dietz, Professor F. C., 3
Digby, John, Earl of Bristol, 47
Doylie, Marie, 100
Draper, Thomas, w., 156
Drope, Edward, 118
Dudley, Anne, Countess of Warwick, 93
Dudley, Edmund, 7, 8, 76
Dugdale, Sir William, 43
Dunbar, Earl of, see Home, Sir George
Dyer, Sir James, 85, 89, 99

Edmondes, Sir Thomas, 47, 140
Edward VI, 83
Elizabeth, 23, 46, 82-3, 122
Elliot, John, 101
Ellis, Thomas, 70
Empson, Sir Richard, 7, 8, 76
Englefield, Sir Francis, master, 11 note, 16, 82, 129 note
Englefield, Thomas, see Inglefield, Thomas
escheators, 2, 8, 10, 14, 39, 41-3, 53, 54, 69, 70, 71, 72, 73, 74, 75, 78, 84, 85, 128, 145, 148, 157, 200
Essendon, co. Hertford, 24
Essex, Earl of, see Devereux, Robert
Essex, feodary of, 38
Evelyn, John, 170
Exchequer:
9, 14, 15, 42, 46, 62, 72, 79, 104, 159-61, 175-7, 179, 180, 187
at Chester, 50
Exchequer Chamber, 5, 136

Fabian, Peter, 177, 181
Fabian, Thomas, 175-81, 184
feodaries, see Wards and Liveries, Court of, officers
feodaries' surveys, 40, 54-7, 59, 61, 74, 81, 107, 182, 197, 198
Fiennes, James, 156
Fiennes, William, Viscount Saye and Sele, master, 19, 148, 150, 151, 152, 161

Fitzherbert, Sir Anthony, 67, 71
Fitzherbert, William, w., 156
Fleet prison, 92, 101
Fleetwood, Charles, receiver-general, 25, 152, 161, 165
Fleetwood, Elizabeth, 38
Fleetwood, family of, 33
Fleetwood, Sir Miles, receiver-general, 25, 34, 37, 132
Fleetwood, Sir William, receiver-general, 1594-1609, 17, 25, 31, 37, 48
Fleetwood, Sir William, receiver-general from 1640, 25, 151, 152, 160, 165
Forster, George, 110
Fortescue, Sir John, 2, 119
Fortescue, Sir Thomas, 18
Fowler, Mr R. C. 84
Frederick Henry, Prince of Orange, 135
Fuller, Nicholas, 146

Garret, ——, 182
general surveyors, 9
Gerard, Gilbert, Baron Gerard, 118
Gifford, William, 128 note
Gilbert, Sir Humphrey, 121, 123
Giustinian, Sebastian, Venetian envoy, 10
Glamorgan, feodary of, 157
Glascocke, Philip, junior, feodary of Essex, 38
Gloucester, co., feodary of, 55
Godolphyn, Sir Francys, 92 note
Goodhand, John, feodary of West Riding of co. York, 44
Goodrich, Richard, attorney, 22 note, 23
Goodwin's case, 138
Goring, George, receiver-general, 25, 37, 38, 46, 172
Grand Remonstrance, 148, 149
great contract, 19, 139-45
Gresham, Sir Thomas, 43
Grevill, Sir Edward, 93
Greville, Francis, Baron Brooke, w., 152 note
Grymes, Charles, 182, 183
Grymes, William, 181, 182, 184

Haddington, John Viscount, see Ramsay, John

INDEX

209

Hakewill, William, 49

Halifax, co. York, Scottish troops at, 157

Hanchett, Edward, usher, 38, 161

Hare, Hugh, clerk, 26

Hare, John, clerk, 26-8, 29, 33, 49, 59 *note*, 64-5, 82, 138, 145, 172; common attorney, 26, 31, 33, 90, 97, 109

Hare, Mrs., widow of John Hare, 172

Hare, Nicholas, clerk, 26, 28

Hawkins, John, 56 *note*

Heath, Sir Edward, 153

Heath, John, auditor, 151, 163, 166

Heath, Robert, auditor, 151, 163, 166

Heath, Sir Robert, lord chief justice, 151

Henningam, Walter, w., 125

Henry VII, 2-8

Henry VIII, 8-15

Henry, Prince of Wales, 144, 168

Herbert, Philip, Earl of Montgomery and fourth Earl of Pembroke, 47

Herbert, William, w., 152 *note*

Herbert, William, third Earl of Pembroke, 22, 130

Herman, Nicholas, secretary, 32 *note*

Herris, Christopher, 56 *note*

Hertford, co., deputy feodary of, 39

Hertford, co., feodary of, 39

Hertford, Court of Wards temporarily at, 173

Hertford, Earl of, *see* Seymour, Edward

Hesketh, Sir Thomas, attorney, 22 *note*, 23, 37, 113, 195

Hickman, 'my Lady Dixie', 38

Hickman, Walter, 38

Hickman, William, 38

Hille, Richard, 131

Hitchcock, ——, 135

Hobart, Sir Henry, attorney, 22 *note*, 89, 99

Holdsworth, Sir W. S., 1

Holles, Gervase, 123

Hollowes, Nathaniel, 156

Holmes, Robert, 96

Home, Sir George, Earl of Dunbar, 143

Household, royal, 46

Howard, Thomas, fourth Duke of Norfolk, 124 *note*

Howard, Thomas, Earl of Arundel, 130

Humfrey, Michael, clerk remembrancer, 31

Huntingdon, Augustinian friary in, 106

Hurstfield, Mr J., 34, 35, 48, 124, 192

Hussey, Sir John, overseer of royal wardships, master of the wards, 6-9

Hyde, Edward, Earl of Clarendon, 148, 162

Hynde, John, recorder of Cambridge, overseer of liveries, 13; surveyor, 20

Hyrst, Godfrey, under-clerk, 28

idiots and lunatics, 4, 6, 16, 102, 109, 128-32, 164, 199

Inglefield, Thomas, master of the wards, 10-11, 12; overseer of liveries, 13

Inns of Court:

Court of Wards officers members of, 20, 21, 22, 26, 29, 102

readings at, 5, 67

See also London: places in or near

inquisitions post mortem, 2, 3, 8, 13, 14, 27, 40, 41, 42-3, 53-4, 55, 57, 69-76, 77, 78, 79, 80, 81, 82, 84-5, 105-6, 115, 146, 148, 155, 157, 184, 185, 187, 200

Ireland, 46

Ireland, solicitor-general of, 21

James I, 20, 83, 124, 125, 138-47, 173

Jones, Inigo, 169

Jonson, Ben, 22

judges assistant, *see under* Wards and Liveries, Court of: officers

Keilwey (Keilway), Robert, surveyor, 21, 35, 99

Kent, feodary of, 157

Kent, under-sheriff of, 157

Kiftell, ——, 171

Kinge, William, 92

King's Bench, chief justice of, 18, 98, 102, 147, 151, 181

King's Bench, Court of, 135

King's Chamber, 6, 7, 11, 46

Kingsmill, Richard, attorney, 22 *note*, 33, 91; surveyor, 21, 33, 62

Knollys, William, Viscount Wallingford, master, 19, 35, 83

210 INDEX

Lake, Sir Thomas, 141, 144
Lamb, Ann, 153
Lancaster, Duchy of, 11, 23, 46, 62, 91, 110, 136
Latimer, Edward, clerk to Sir William Fleetwood, 17, 31, 48, 51, 52, 58
Latimer, Hugh, 120
leases, fines for, 60, 195
Leicester, Adam, 56 *note*
Leicester, co., feodary of, 40
Lenox, Duchess of, *see* Stuart, Catherine
Lewknor, Sir Edward, 138
Ley, Sir James, later Earl of Marlborough, attorney, 22 *note*, 23-4, 65, 68, 69, 84, 89, 90, 98, 102, 113, 162
Lincoln, co., feodary of, 40, 44
Lincoln, co., under-sheriff, 157
Lingen, Edward, 131
Littleton, Sir Thomas, 67
livery, 27-8, 51, 60-2, 76-9, 83, 104, 105, 108, 146, 147, 194-5, 198-9, 203-6
    See also Wards and Liveries, Court of, wardship and livery
London and Middlesex, feodary of, 25
London:
    city of: chamberlain of, 110
        escheator of, 73
        feodary of, 157; *see also* London and Middlesex
        Orphans, Court of, 110
        recorder of, 23, 110
    places in or near: Aldersgate, auditor's office in, 173
        Holborn, auditor's office in, 173
        Inner Temple, office of clerk of wards in, 29, 172-3
        Rolls, Chapel of the, 182
        Savoy, Burghley's house in the, 99, 171
        Serjeants' Inn, cases argued at, 99, 171
        Tower, 23
        See also Counter prison, Fleet prison, Inns of Court, Westminster
lord keeper, 18, 23
lord treasurer, 18, 23, 171, 184
Lords, House of, 111, 135, 138-42, 150, 151 *note*, 152, 159, 160, 182, 184

Lovell, Sir Thomas, master of the wards, 9, 10
lunatics, *see* idiots and lunatics
Lychefelde, William, receiver-general of wards' lands, 6-7, 11

Madox, Thomas, 184
Magnus, Thomas, receiver-general of wards' lands, 10
Maitland, F. W., 4
Mallett, John, w., 152 *note*
Manners, Edward, Earl of Rutland, 96
Manners, Elizabeth, Countess of Rutland, 93
Marches, Council of the, 131
Markham, Thomas, w., 152 *note*
marriage, 1, 3, 57, 80, 104-5, 113, 123, 125-7, 195
Marshalsea, Court of the, 110
Mary, 82-3, 111
master of the rolls, 62-3
May, Sir Humphrey, surveyor, 21
Maynard, Charles, auditor, 25, 151, 166, 173
Maynard, Sir John, 159
mean rates, 51, 53, 60, 77, 84, 194, 195, 205
Melior, Thomas, 92
mesne lords, 1, 79, 127, 139, 144-5
Middlesex, Earl of, *see* Cranfield, Lionel
Middlesex, feodary of, 55 *note*
Molineux, Bridgett, w., 117
Montgomery, Earl of, *see* Herbert, Philip
Moore, Sir Francis, 89
Mordant, Henry, 157
Mordant, Lord, *see* Mordaunt, John, Lord Mordaunt
Mordaunt, John, Lord Mordaunt, w., 125
Moreton, Thomas, Bishop of Coventry and Lichfield, 125
Morice, *see* Morris, James
Morris, James, attorney, 22 *note*, 23

Naunton, Sir Robert, master, 19, 40, 97, 136; surveyor, 21
Nevell, Sir Thomas, overseer of liveries, 12
Newcastle, Lord, *see* Cavendish, William

INDEX

211

Newcastle-upon-Tyne, 93

Newre, Thomas, deputy feodary of co. Hertford, 39

Nicholas, Sir Edward, secretary of state, 153

Norfolk, Duke of, see Howard, Thomas

Norfolk, feodary of, 157

Norroy, king of arms, 113

Northampton, co., feodary of, 157

Northampton, Earl of, see Compton, Spencer, Lord Compton

Northumberland, receivers-general of, 5

Norwych, Robert, overseer of liveries, 12-13

Nowell, Alexander, 23

Nowell, Lawrence, 23

Nowell, Robert, attorney, 22 *note*, 23

office, see inquisitions post mortem

Onslow, Richard, attorney, 22 *note*, 23

Orange, Prince of, see Frederick Henry

ouster le maine, 84-5, 128

Owen, Thomas, justice of the Common Pleas, 17

Oxenbregge, William, 96

Oxford, co., feodary of, 41, 157

Oxford, Earl of, see de Vere, Edward

Oxford, Kettle (Kettell) Hall, Broad Street, 178

Oxford, royalist Court of Wards at, see *under* Wards and Liveries, Court of

Paris, Philip, receiver-general, 25

Parliament, privilege of, 111, 147

Parry, Sir Thomas, master, 17

Paulet, George, clerk of liveries, 30

Paulet, William, Marquis of Winchester, master of the wards, 10-13; surveyor of the king's widows and governor of idiots and naturals, 16; master, 16, 17, 33

Pembroke, Earl of, see Herbert, William, third Earl of Pembroke

Pepper, Sir Cuthbert, surveyor, 21

Perceval, Richard, clerk remembrancer, 31, 98

Perks, Thomas, 56 *note*

Peryent, Sir John, auditor of wards' lands, 10; auditor, 24

Petre, Sir William, 117 *note*

Petre, William, Baron Petre, w., 125

Petty Bag, 75, 146

Philipps, Fabian, 124, 134, 146, 162, 177

Pickarell, John, common attorney, 97

Pickeringe, see Pickarell, John

Pilgrimage of Grace, 14

plague, 121, 173-4

Player, William, 56 *note*

Plowden, Edmund, 89

Pole, Reginald, Cardinal, 120

Polsted, Thomas, attorney, 22 *note*

Popham, Sir John, chief justice of the King's Bench, 137

Porteman, William, attorney of the wards, 12 *note*

Powell, Thomas, author of *The Attourney's Academy*, 35, 81, 130, 131

Prerogativa Regis, 5, 67, 128

Prideaux, ——, w., 82

Privy Council, 111, 180, 181

Purdye, John, 135

Purley, Leonard, 110

Pye, Sir Walter, attorney,), 22 *note*, 37, 136

Quarles, Hester, w., 157

Quarles, James, 56 *note*

Radcliff, William, clerk remembrancer, 31

Ramsay, John, Viscount Haddington, 46

Rastell, William, 68

Ratcliff, Mr S. C., 177, 178 *note*

Rawson, Robert, clerk of the wards, 12 *note*

Raynsforde, Paul, 51

Record Commission, 177

Requests, Court of, 91, 135, 136, 167, 183-4

requests, master of, 21

retrenchment, commissioners for, 47

revenue, commissioners for, 62

Revenue, Committee of, 152, 159, 175, 176, 177

Richardson, Richard, teller, 31

Riche, Sir Richard, overseer of liveries, 13

Robertes, Thomas, auditor of wards' lands, 9, 10

Roberts, John, 93

Robinson, Richard, 167

212 INDEX

Rogers, Bartholomew, usher, 35
Rogers, Richard, w., 118
Rudyerd, Sir Benjamin, surveyor, 19, 21-2, 132, 152
Russell, Francis, second Earl of Bedford, 124 *note*
Russell, William, fifth Earl, later Duke, of Bedford, 169, 173
Rutland, Earl of, *see* Manners, Edward
Rutland, Elizabeth, Countess of, *see* Manners, Elizabeth
Ryce, Richard, 82
Rymer, Thomas, 184

St John, Oliver, 159
Salisbury, Earl of, *see* Cecil, Robert
Salop and Montgomery, feodary of, 44 *note*
Salway, Humphrey, chief remembrancer of the Exchequer, 180
Sandford, F., 167, 169
Saunders, Sir Edward, 99
Saye and Sele, Viscount, *see* Fiennes, William
Schaftow, William de, 83
Scroope, Emanuel, 70
Seckford, Thomas, surveyor, 21, 35
See, Henry, attorney of the wards, 12 *note*
Selden, John, 159
Servant, Marmaduke, usher, 35
Sever, William, Bishop of Carlisle, 5
Sewster, John, attorney, 22 *note*
Seymour, Edward, Earl of Hertford, 74
Sheffiield, Edmund, third Baron Sheffield, 37, 114
Sherfield, Henry, 102
Shirburn, co. Oxford, 29
Skynner, Robert, clerk of the wards, 12 *note*
Slaning, Nicholas, w., 152 *note*
Smith, Sir Thomas, 123, 127, 134
Smyth, Hugh, w., 153 *note*
Solemn League and Covenant, 152
solicitor-general, 23, 98
Somerset, deputy feodary of, 131
Spelman, Sir Henry, 14, 117, 148
Spenser, Edmund, 23
Stafford, Alexander, clerk remembrancer, 31
Stafford, Sir Edward, 115
Stafford, Sir Reade, 115
Stanhope, Sir John, 39

Star Chamber, 44, 91, 94, 95, 102
Starkey, Thomas, 120
statutes:
 12 Charles II c. 24 (abolition of Court of Wards and Liveries and of feudal tenures), 164
 6 Edward I c. 5 (stat. of Gloucester), 133 *note*
 28 Edward I c. 18 (*Articuli super Cartas*), 133 *note*
 31 Edward III, 128
 34 Edward III c. 14, 76
 2 Edward VI c. 8, 71, 76
 13 Elizabeth c. 5, 52 *note*
 27 Elizabeth c. 4, 52 *note*
 31 Elizabeth c. 16, 51-2
 4 Henry VII c. 17, 4
 1 Henry VIII c. 8, 8
 1 Henry VIII c. 12, 8
 14 and 15 Henry VIII c. 14, 158
 26 Henry VIII c. 13, 13
 27 Henry VIII c. 10 (stat. of Uses), 13, 106
 27 Henry VIII c. 27, 14
 32 Henry VIII c. 1 (stat. of Wills), 14, 106-7
 32 Henry VIII c. 46 (foundation of Court of Wards), 14, 16, 190
 33 Henry VIII c. 22 (annexation of Liveries to Court of Wards), 14-15, 16
 34 Henry VIII c. 5 (stat. of Wills), 14, 106-7
 35 Henry VIII c. 14, 14
 21 James I c. 35, 52
Staunford, Sir William, 23, 67, 68, 85, 86
Stewkeley, Hugh, w., 152 *note*
Stoke Edith, co. Hereford, 131
Stow, John, 167, 168
Stradling, Sir Edward, 152 *note*
Straunge, Robert, 55
Stuart, Lady Arabella, 170
Stuart, Catherine, Duchess of Lenox, 47
Stukeley, Thomas, 82
Suffolk, feodary of, 43, 54
Surrey, escheator of, 44 *note*
Surrey, feodary of, 44 *note*
Sussex, escheator of, 44 *note*

Taverner, R., 144
Taylor, John, 179

INDEX

213

Thorne, Professor S. E., 4, 5, 67
Thurbarne, John, 97
Thynne, Sir John, 74
Toms, John, 56 *note*
Tooke, family of, 33
Tooke, James, auditor, and feodary of London and Middlesex, 25, 151, 157, 159, 160, 161, 166
Tooke, John, auditor, 24-5
Tooke, Thomas, auditor, 25
Tooke, Walter, auditor, 24, 25, 35, 39, 173
Tooke, William, auditor, 24, 35
Tooke, William, junior, 35
Tothill, Katheryne, 132
traverse, 8, 76, 106, 146, 198
Treasury, commissioners of, 176
Trelawney, ——, w., 134
Trevor, Edward, w., 153 *note*
Tuckwell, Francis, royal fishmonger, 182
Turnor, ——, 178

uses, feoffments to, 3-4, 13-14, 106-7

Ven, John, 56 *note*
Verge, Court of the, 110
Villiers, Sir Edward, 47
Villiers, George, Duke of Buckingham, 38, 65, 110

Walderne, John, 56 *note*
Wallingford, Viscount, *see* Knollys, William
Wandesford, Sir Rowland, attorney, 22 *note*, 161
Warburton, Peter, w., 55 *note*
Wardrobe, 46
wards:
  education of, 119-25
  exhibitions of, 57-8, 81, 122, 196, 197
  issues of lands of, 6-7, 11, 59-60
  sales of, 5, 6, 7, 10, 11, 12, 34-5, 40, 57-9, 80-3, 114-19, 122, 136-7, 152-3, 156-7, 160, 168, 188, 195, 197, 199, 200
  See also Wards and Liveries, Court of, wardship and livery
Wards and Liveries, Court of:
  abolition of, 158-9, 162, 163-4
  accounts of receivers-general of, 6, 10, 11, 47, 169-70, 190-2

arrears of, granted, 65
buildings of, 167-74
complaints against, 133-6, 146-9
erection of, 13-15
officers of:
  their fees, 30, 32, 33, 34, 36, 40, 44, 61-2, 79, 81, 98, 146, 193-205
  pensions proposed for them, 145, 160-2, 164-6
  specific:
  attorney, 18, 19, 21, 22-4, 37, 39, 58, 61, 62, 67, 68, 70, 88, 89, 91, 92, 98, 99, 100, 112-13, 136, 151, 161, 173
  auditors, 18, 23-5, 33, 35, 36, 38, 39, 58, 61, 64, 78, 81, 100, 104, 107, 130, 151, 159, 161, 166, 173, 197-9
  clerk of liveries, 27-8, 29-30, 61, 78, 105, 165, 204-6
  clerk of wards, 18, 26-9, 34, 35, 36, 37, 38, 61, 62, 63, 64, 80, 81, 87, 88, 100, 130, 136, 151, 152, 159, 161, 165-6, 172, 175, 178, 200-3
  common attorneys, 30-1, 34, 90, 97, 103, 161, 206
  feodaries, 9, 12, 34, 38-45, 50, 53, 54, 60, 64, 70, 71, 73, 74 *note*, 82, 133, 137, 145, 148, 157, 165, 195, 199, 202
  judges assistant, 52, 98-100, 104, 109, 151
  master, 16-20, 28, 32-3, 34, 38, 48, 51, 58, 61, 69, 70, 74, 80, 83, 98, 99, 121, 135, 136, 139, 144, 151, 152, 161, 162, 165, 168
  messenger, 30, 38, 64, 151, 161, 165
  minor officers, 31-2, 35,
  pursuivants, 30 *note*
  receiver-general, 17, 25, 31, 33, 34, 35, 37, 38, 46, 61, 70, 100, 132, 151, 152, 159, 161, 165, 169, 172, 190, 195-7
  secretary, 32, 36, 41, 147
  surveyor-general, 18, 19, 20-2, 28, 35, 36, 61, 70, 78, 100, 132, 151, 161, 194-5
  usher, 30, 35, 38, 68, 110, 151, 161, 165, 168, 169, 170

214 INDEX

Wards and Liveries, Court of:—*cont.*
Oxford, royalist Court of Wards at,
16, 19, 150-9, 164, 177-8
procedure of, legal:
answers, 30, 92-4
bills, 30, 91-2, 94, 113
costs, 100-1, 195
counsel, 100, 102-3
debt, process for, 104, 198, 201
demurrers, 94, 109
evidences, 96, 176-7, 185, 202
hearing, 97-8
informations, 91-2, 94, 113, 195
injunctions, 96-7, 110, 200, 201
interrogatories, 94, 95-6
penal powers, 101-2
pleadings, 30-1, 87-8, 185, 200
records of, 27, 88-9, 154 *note*, 168,
175-86
relations of, with other courts,
109-10
revenues of:
collection of, 62, 157
level of, 47-50, 57-62
seal of, 14, 112, 150, 151, 152, 159
wardship and livery:
administration prior to foundation
of Court of Wards and Liveries:
general, 1-13, 187-9
officers, 5-6, 8-13, 187
records, 2, 11 *note*
legal cases concerning:
Bailie, 105
Blewit, 132
Browne and Coke, 108
Buckingham, Duchess of, 78
Constable, 80 *note*
Cotton, 52
Cromwell, 106
Dakin, 105
Digby, 108
Drury, 80 *note*
Duncombe v. Pattenham, 99, 111
Earle, 80 *note*
Frances, 129
Fuller v. Hall, 110, 135
Gonson, coheirs of, 100
Gray, 107
Hale, 108
Harcourt v. Roberts, 136
Hollyday v. Ferrers *et al.*, 100
Jon, 105
Lutterell, 99

Menfield, 107
Mody, 107
Parker, 107
Pickering, 80 *note*, 99
Price, 107
Probert, 99
Radclife, 80 *note*
Raysing, 105
Thornton, 107
Tourson, 109
Tyrrel, 106
Wellar v. Carrill, 100
Wroughton, 99
tracts on:
Additions of Instructions, 1617,
53, 69 *note*
Apology for the late Lord Treasurer
(Cope), 19
*Articles devised for the bringing
up in vertue and lerninge of
the Queenes Majesties wardes*
(Nicholas Bacon), 23-4, 120-1
*Collections for the King's Majesties
service,* 51, 53, 70, 83
Decrees (Hare), 90, 109
*Directions for the master of the
wards* (Francis Bacon), 20, 49
Diverse Cases for Liveries (Rastell),
68
*Exposicion of the Kinges Prero-
gative* (Staunford), 23, 67
Instructions, 1610, 49, 51, 52, 58,
60, 69 *note*, 115, 117, 126, 130,
134 *note*, 137, 147, 195
Instructions, 1618, 51, 58, 65-6,
69 *note*, 117, 130, 137
Instructions, 1622, 41, 58, 60, 61,
69 *note*, 82, 117, 130, 137, 147,
199
Judgments (Cole), 90
*Learned Treatise Concerning Wards
and Liveries* (Ley), 68, 75 *note*,
89, 102
Liber president' special', 68
*Manner of obtayninge A grant of
A Ward,* 68
Queen Elizabethes Achademy (Gil-
bert), 121-2
*Reports of Divers Resolutions in
Law Arising upon Cases in the
Court of Wards etc.* (Ley), 68,
89, 162
Rules for Liveries, 68, 72, 76

INDEX

wardship and livery: tracts on:—*cont.*
   Tenenda non Tollenda (Philipps),
    162-3
   Tertia Lectura (Constable), 67
   See also livery, wards
   Wards and Liveries, Court of
Warwick, Anne, Countess of, *see*
   Dudley, Anne
Warwick, co., feodary of, 40, 43, 157
waste, 133-4
Weare, Humfrey, feodary of Devon, 39
Welby, co. Lincoln, manor of, 110
Wenyeve, Edward, feodary of Suffolk,
   43, 54
West, William, author of *Symboleo-*
   graphy, 52, 90, 91, 130
Westminster:
   St Margaret's Lane, 169
   Chapter House, 184, 185
   Westminster Hall, 12, 167-9, 179
   White Hall, 167-9
Westmorland, feodary of, 157
Westmorland, receivers-general of, 5
Weston, Sir Richard, master of the
   wards, 10, 11
Whitelock, Bulstrode, 148, 159
Whitelock, Sir James, 22
widows, 4, 60, 85
Wigston, Roger, receiver-general of
   wards' lands, 10
Wilbraham, Ralph, feodary of cos.
   Chester and Flint, 41

Wilbraham, Sir Roger, surveyor, 21
Wilbraham, Thomas, attorney, 22
   note, 23 *note*
Wilkinson, Edward, messenger, 161,
   165
Wilson, Richard, 92 *note*
Wilson, Roland, common attorney,
   161 *note*
Wilson, Sir Thomas, 49, 178
Wiltshire, escheator of, 73
Winchcombe, Henry, w., 152 *note*,
   156
Winthrop, John, common attorney, 31
Wolsey, Thomas, Cardinal, 124
Wood, Thomas, 51
Wray, Sir Christopher, 158
Wroth, Sir Robert, 138
Wyderington, John, son of Roger de,
   83
Wyderington, Roger de, 83

Yonge, Walter, 139, 144
York, co., receivers-general of, 5
York, co., sheriff of, 13
York, co., West Riding, feodary of,
   44, 70
York, minster of, 113

Zouch, Lord, *see* Zouche, Edward La
Zouche, Edward La, Baron Zouche of
   Harringworth, w., 124 *note*

For EU product safety concerns, contact us at Calle de José Abascal, 56–1°,
28003 Madrid, Spain or eugpsr@cambridge.org.

www.ingramcontent.com/pod-product-compliance
Ingram Content Group UK Ltd.
Pitfield, Milton Keynes, MK11 3LW, UK
UKHW010850060825
461487UK00012B/1027